# LITERARY ANNUALS AND GIFT BOOKS

FREDERICK W. FAXON

# Literary Annuals and Gift Books

A BIBLIOGRAPHY

1823–1903

Reprinted with
supplementary essays by

ELEANORE JAMIESON
& IAIN BAIN

PRIVATE LIBRARIES
ASSOCIATION
1973

Reprinted by photolitho from the
original edition of 1912
Published by the
Private Libraries Association
Ravelston, Southview Road
Pinner, Middlesex


1750 copies printed
of which 750 are for sale

ISBN 900002 62 X

Printed in Great Britain
at The Gresham Press by
Unwin Brothers Limited
Old Woking, Surrey

# PREFATORY NOTE

Although at the beginning of this century there was clearly a strong enough interest in the Annuals to warrant the publication of Faxon's work, the interest waned and for many years the material available to the collector was both cheap and abundant, and it was possible to put together a substantial collection for very little money. But within the last few years the situation has very much changed and it is the growing interest in the 19th-century book that has prompted the decision to reissue this little known but extensive bibliography. Because many of Faxon's entries are relatively brief and may well need correction, the main text has been printed with facing blanks to aid the addition of new matter. Twenty-five pages of illustrations have been added together with two brief essays on the bindings and illustrations of the Annuals. As the page numbering of the original has been retained, that of the new material has been displayed in square brackets.

Despite the fact that the engraved plates were very often the sole reason for an Annual's existence, there were nevertheless a considerable number of interesting contributions from the leading writers of the day: the late Andrew Boyle's *An Index to the Annuals, 1820–1850*, 1967, is therefore an essential companion to this book. The following may also be found to be helpful sources of further information on the Annuals and their social background:


Alaric Watts: various introductions to his editions of *The Literary Souvenir*, 1825–35.

William Jerdan, *Autobiography*, 1852.

R. R. Madden, ed., *The Literary Life and Correspondence of the Countess of Blessington*, 1855.

'The Annuals of Former Days', *The Boookseller*, 29 November 1858.

David Hogg, *The Life of Allan Cunningham*, 1875.
S. C. Hall, *Retrospect of a Long Life*, 1883.
A. A. Watts, *Alaric Watts, a Narrative of his Life*, 1884.
Michael Sadleir, *Bulwer and his Wife: a Panorama, 1803–1836*, 1933; *Blessington d'Orsay: a Masquerade*, 1947.
Ian Jack, *English Literature, 1815–1832*, 1963.
Anne Renier, *Friendship's Offering, an Essay on the Annuals and Gift Books of the Nineteenth Century*, 1964.

# THE BINDING STYLES OF THE GIFT BOOKS AND ANNUALS

ELEANORE JAMIESON

The origin of the annual is well documented. C. H. Timperley in his *Dictionary of Printers and Printing* (1839)[1] says that:

> Mr. Ackermann was the father and originator in England of those elegant *bijouteries* of the festive season, *the Annuals*, which was a spirited attempt to rival the numerous publications issued in France and Germany. It is well known that his successful attempt to furnish in the *Forget Me Not*, a worthy offering to an object of kindness and affection, has generated in this country a new class of elegant works.

The *Forget Me Not; a Christmas and New Year's Present for 1823* was published in November 1822, bound after its German model, the *Taschenbuch*, with glazed paper boards and a cloth spine, the covers printed with a decorative title and in a slip-case bearing the same design. Its success was such, particularly amongst the Ladies, who were anxious to receive such 'worthy' offerings, that other publications were soon to be issued in similar format.

Two years later *The Literary Souvenir; or Cabinet of Poetry and Romance, for 1825* edited by Alaric A. Watts was published by Hurst, Robinson & Co. 'handsomely boarded, in ornamental Covers'[2] and late in 1826 the second volume of *The Amulet; or Christian and Literary Remembrance for the year 1827* was issued 'elegantly bound in an engraved Cover, with Gilt Edges; and the utmost care has been taken to have this Portion of the Work executed by the most skilful and experienced Hands.[3]

*Friendship's Offering*, the second, and one of the most long-lived of the annuals, was first published as 'a Christmas Present or New Year's Gift for 1824' 'most tastefully fitted up in an Embossed Case, with an external Emblazoned Title Page.'[4] The Bodleian have a copy of *Friendship's Offering* for 1827[5] which is also bound with white board sides engraved with an oval border of leaves and lilies encircling a lady holding an open book, and the volume itself, like the one for 1824, is enclosed in a slip-case embossed with the same design. However, *The Pledge of Friendship* for 1826[6] was actually bound with embossed paper covers, although it was not until two years later, at least in the case of the annuals, that the idea of embossing onto paper was transferred and applied to leather.

In the meanwhile, the more recent volumes of the annuals were being published in silk bindings, this conveying a greater sense of luxury than mere engraved or embossed paper covers. In 1827, *The Mirror* actually complained about the new binding for *The Amulet* as 'somewhat gay for so grave a title being crimson silk'.[7] In October 1828, an advertisement in *The Lady's Magazine* announced that *The Literary Souvenir* was 'elegantly bound in rich Crimson Silk, price 12s.', although a few larger sets were issued in white ribbed silk cloth. In the same year *The Athenaeum* carried announcements for *The Bijou*,[8] *The Gem*[9] and *The Keepsake*[10] all bound in crimson silk. Indeed as *The Mirror* commented: 'seven out of nine of these elegant little books are in watered silk bindings'.[11] Yet it was not until 1832 that Ackermann decided that it was necessary to change the style of binding for the *Forget Me Not*, for by that time its success had inspired a number of competitors who

> may be said to have surpassed in beauty their accomplished prototype . . . while they were richly apparelled in all the gay colours of silk or gold, or splendid embossments, the humble paste-board cover, however prettily coloured, could no longer be considered worthy of this great age of improvement. The proprietor has therefore remodelled the external appearance of his offspring, and clothed it in the splendid but durable attire of crimson silk, which supersedes the necessity of a pasteboard case, as heretofore, to protect it from the soil of a dusty table.[12]

In the Prologue to the 1830 volume of *Friendship's Offering*, the following lines appear;

> That the meek prudish AMULET
> With bitter jealousy will fret;
> That KEEPSAKE, GEM, FORGET-ME-NOT,
> And some whose names I have forgot,
> Who dress themselves in silk attire,
> For very envy will expire.

Possible envy might have been caused by the appearance of *Friendship's Offering* at the end of 1827 in an embossed leather binding. In the Preface to this volume, attention is drawn to the unusual binding: '. . . the Proprietors, regardless of expense, determined to adopt such a mode of binding as would unite beauty with durability, in a way never before attempted'.[13] The uniqueness of the binding is noted in a review of *Friendship's Offering* in a Supplementary number on the annuals in *The Mirror* for December 1827:

> 'To begin with the exterior, which is somewhat novel in taste, the proprietors seem to have invited the *utile cum dulci*, by substituting for the usual paper covering, an elegantly embossed leather binding. This is altogether an improvement . . . since slight coverings of silk or paper are scarcely safe out of the drawing room or boudoir.'[14]

*Friendship's Offering* had been taken over from the publishers, Lupton Relfe by Smith, Elder & Co. late in the year of 1827. Possibly the publishers and the temporary editor, Charles Knight, felt that an unusual binding might disguise the hastiness of assembly within. Although *Friendship's Offering* was probably not the first book to have an embossed leather binding, it was the first of the annuals and as such was an immediate success. The following year *The Mirror* again commented that 'the elegant embossed binding is similar to that of last year which we mentioned to our readers and which we think an improvement on silken array'[15] and by 1829, its success was such that an advertisement in *The Athenaeum* 21 October 1829 announced that: 'A few sets of "Friendship's Offering", from its commencement in 1824, have just been completed, price 3*l*.12*s* per set of Six Vols. uniformly done up in the improved binding.'[16]

*Friendship's Offering* for 1829 is the first volume at the British Museum in an embossed leather binding (although it has recently been rebacked).[17] The book is bound in dark blue leather and in a similar manner to the following in the series is embossed in blind except for a Greek lyre which is blocked in gold in the centre of each cover. The lyre is set in a small rectangle with quadrant corner panels with shell inserts. Arabesque ornament surrounds the rectangle and is contained by a narrow frame also with quarter-circle corner panels. In the frame at the top is embossed: FRIENDSHIP'S OFFERING, and in the frame at the foot: SMITH, ELDER & CO., CORNHILL, LONDON. A floral border around the edge of the covers is missing in the 1829 and 1830 volumes but it is signed at the left foot: BAIN BROAD COURT. Later volumes (but not those for 1832 and 1836 at the British Museum) are signed at the centre foot: A. BAIN F. Alexander Bain, who called himself a toolcutter as well as a binder in *Pigot's London Directory* for 1838, was presumably responsible for the binding of *Friendship's Offering* but may also have cut the die used for embossing the design.

'The very beautiful and unrivalled binding which has given so much satisfaction'[18] was not to remain without competition for long. By November 1830 *The Juvenile Forget Me Not* was published in an embossed binding 'the latter being both more elegant and more durable than the delicate paper hitherto used'[19] and *The Comic Offering* (1831–1835) was published from the start 'elegantly whole bound in Morocco, and richly embossed in a style of art and oddity quite unrivalled'.[20] Sometimes annuals were offered with alternative bindings to suit an individual purse: 'On the 31st December, 1831, will be published, price 10*s*. 6*d*. in cloth, or 14*s*. handsomely bound in embossed morocco, demy 12mo., THE YOUNG GENTLEMAN'S BOOK',[21] and in 1830 *The Gem* could still be had 'price 12*s*. in rich silk, or splendidly bound in Morocco, without any extra charge'.[22] *The Remembrance*, first published in 1830 for the Christmas and New Year season of 1830/1831 was 'bound in arabesque morocco, of an appropriate design, price 10*s*. 6*d*. A few copies are taken off in crown 8vo. same size as the "Keepsake" and "Landscape Annual", . . . neatly half-bound in morocco, uncut edges, price 1*l*.1*s*,'[23]

Embossed bindings were usually executed in one of three styles – cathedral, arabesque or engine-turned. Cathedral designs were mostly used for Bibles or collections of prayers and hymns, although occasionally they were applied to a quite incongruous work). At first, the annual or giftbook was usually covered with a floral or pictorial design as being more appropriately lighthearted. I have used the term arabesque to describe these designs as the term is used by John Andrews Arnett in his *Bibliopegia* (1835):[24]

'The arabesque, a description of binding common in earlier times, was revived in France, and introduced into this country in the year 1829, by Messrs. Remnant and Edmonds. . . . It was first only adopted in the binding of Bibles and Prayers, but soon carried to great extent in many other bindings, particularly of albums and books of illustration.'

I have seen no advertisements or other references which confirm that the term 'arabesque' was actually used to describe bindings embossed with a 'cathedral' design, although Arnett implies that this was so. The term was certainly in current usage. *The Juvenile Forget Me Not* for 1831 was 'beautifully bound in Arabesque morocco',[25] and *The Boy's Own Book* for the same year was 'handsomely bound in Arabesque Embossed Morocco'.[26] Both the bindings on *The Juvenile Forget Me Not* and *The Boy's Own Book*, and many other bindings embossed with arabesque design, have a central lozenge panel or circular medallion which is either left plain or contains line ornament or a picture. Often these pictures, particularly on bindings signed by Remnant & Edmonds and De La Rue, are separately signed, usually with a French or German name which suggests that the design came from or was copied from continental sources.

In 1837 *The Remembrance*[27] was issued in covers embossed with engine-turned ornament, although this same annual had been published in 1831 with two alternative arabesque bindings.[28] The very fine lines were produced from dies engine-turned upon the Rose Engine. The Rose Engine, which originated in Germany, was first used in England by Sir William Congreve in conjunction with the Donkin Pantograph Engraving Machine for compound plate printing in an attempt to produce bank notes that would avoid forgery.[29] In the mid 1830s the technique was applied to embossing dies as a cheaper and more convenient substitute for an elaborate cathedral or arabesque design which would have to be cut by hand. Usually bindings embossed with engine-turned ornament are unsigned since binders or die-cutters felt it was unnecessary to add their name to a design that was cut by machine.

Bindings embossed in the cathedral or arabesque manner were however frequently signed, and some of the finest were executed by Remnant & Edmonds and De La Rue.[30] Remnant and Edmonds were responsible for the different bindings on the larger and smaller edition of *The Remembrance* for 1831.[31] The binding on the larger edition is particularly splendid and the same embossing die, with minor variations, was used for a number of different publications. Thomas De La Rue, as a general stationer, embossed some very impressive bindings for albums and scrapbooks, but he also embossed the covers for *The Juvenile Forget Me Not . . . for 1831*,[32] *The Comic Offering* (1831–1835)[33] and an identical design for *The Missionary Annual for 1833*[34] and *The Iris* (1835).[35]

James Barritt, a die-sinker originally in the employ of a silversmith named Eley, was engaged by Remnant and Edmonds to cut their first embossing dies. The new style proved so immensely popular and profitable that Barritt, although fully occupied in cutting dies for Remnant, decided to invest his own savings in a press and emboss and sell covers privately to binders. When Remnant discovered this, he ceased to employ him further, so Barritt turned to general embossing for stationery, in the manner of Thomas De La Rue. It was not until 1831 when Eley joined him with some capital, that Barritt once again started to emboss leather bindings particularly for bibles and other religious works.[36] He did, however, cut an arabesque design for the second volume of *The Keepsake Français* for 1832.[37]

Other names which appear on embossed bindings include F. Westley, G. Rawley, I. Dobson, Bell & Co. and Rock. George Rowley embossed the covers of *The Literary Keepsake for 1834*[38] and perhaps other annuals, but as far as I know, the rest, with the exception of Westley, specialised in producing covers for albums and religious works. Francis Josiah Westley was a binder who embossed his own book covers as well as using covers embossed by De La Rue and others. (His binder's ticket occurs inside the British Museum copy of *The Juvenile Forget Me Not . . . for 1831*[39] and in a copy of *The Boy's Own Book* (1834) in the John Johnson Collection at the Bodleian.[40]) In 1830 he embossed the covers for *The Cameo*[41] with a floral design and he must have embossed the covers for *The Gem* (n.d.)[42] about the same time as it was discontinued in 1831. *The Gem* has a very plain design of double descending links and he embossed an even starker design of a Greek lyre on a strippled background for the 1836 volume of *The New Year's Gift and Juvenile Souvenir*[43] but a copy of *The Drawing Room Album*[44] has a much more exciting design of two herons and a winged dragon intertwined with foliage.

Many of the designs on embossed bindings were exceedingly attractive, yet produced by machine 'at a rate of economy considering the richness of the ornaments and perfection of execution almost incredible'.[45] The machine which made this type of covering possible was the fly-embossing-press probably introduced sometime in the mid 1820s. It was an enormous structure, but great strength was required in order to crush the leather or cloth between a finely engraved die and counter-die.[46] Often the same dies seem to have been used by different binders on differently sized books. Presumably a block might be cut for a quarto size and then the various books chosen for this design would be approximately centred. The covers were embossed wholly in blind otherwise the very fine impression would be lost and the gilt ornamentation – usually a one line gilt fillet round the edge of the covers – and the gold lettering on the spine were carried out after the books were bound, the lettering often being put on with a type-holder.

When the style first became fashionable, embossed books were usually bound in highly polished, straight-grained morocco of a dark colour, mostly maroon, but bottle green, black and dark blue leathers were also popular. However, in the mid 1830's roan (full thickness sheepskin) and skiver (half thickness sheepskin) were increasingly used for the cheaper type of gift book. Although some annuals and gift books such as *The Lady's Keepsake* (1837) continued to be 'elegantly bound in embossed Morocco',[47] numerous other books such as *The Historical Keepsake, for 1836*, were 'handsomely bound in embossed roan'.[48] About the same time bookcloth began to be used extensively as a cheaper alternative to leather. The Victoria & Albert Museum have a magnificent arabesque binding in leather of Fisher's *Drawing Room Scrapbook* for 1832 signed by Remnant and Edmonds,[49] but by 1835 the *Scrapbook* was being produced with a leather spine blocked in gold and cloth sides embossed in blind.[50] Although according to the account of Messrs. Westley's and Clark's bindery,[51] cloth could be embossed between the two revolving cylinders, often the same dies which were used on leather were also applied to cloth in the fly-embossing press. The 1837 volume of Fisher's *Drawing Room Scrap Book*[52] is embossed in green cloth with the same design embossed in leather on a copy of *The Waldenses* (1838) by William Beattie.[53]

In 1832, Cope and Sherwin brought out the Imperial Arming Press.[54] This larger, improved blocking-press probably accounts for the rapid refinement in blocking techniques, particularly in gold, onto cloth as well as leather. Embossed bindings required so sharp and detailed an impression over the whole cover that they were embossed before the material was placed on the boards, whereas blocked bindings were impressed after the boards were added, though usually before the book was inserted into the case. Gold and blind blocking, particularly of cloth book covers, eventually superseded embossing techniques as an equally attractive but less expensive process of decoration. The *Forget Me Not* for 1836 was issued in leather covers blocked in gold[55] but the volume for 1846 was 'elegantly bound in green [cloth], and richly gilt, price 12*s*.'.[56] The same year *The Recreation for 1846* was published in 'cloth gilt, price 5*s*.'[57] and two years later *Heath's Book of Beauty*[58] was blocked in gold with a very intricate design onto blue cloth. Alas, a photograph of the final volume of *Friendship's Offering* in *Victorian Book Design and Colour Printing* (2nd ed. 1972) by Ruari McLean illustrates how by 1844 the annual was no longer issued in embossed leather but in yellow cloth blocked in gold.[59]

English trade connections abroad introduced the concept of the annual and giftbook into India and North America and as in England they were issued in a variety of binding styles. The Bodleian has a copy of *The Bengal Annual* for 1834 in an embossed binding and there is a ticket inside stating that it was '*Bound by*/*R. MACCULLOCH*/No. 143 Mirzapore/*CALCUTTA*.[60] It was published by Samuel Smith & Co., Hare Street, Calcutta, perhaps connected with the firm Smith, Elder & Co. in London, who had an important book and stationery business, and very important commercial trade with East India. Nevertheless the embossing-die was probably cut in England because the same binding occurs on a copy of *Moderation: A Tale* by Mrs. Holland, published the same year, 1834, in London by A. K. Newman and Co.[61] From the beginning of the 1830s annuals and giftbooks enjoyed a tremendous vogue in America, most of them being published in the two great literary centres, Boston and Philadelphia. Soon after embossed binding became popular in England, Gaskill and Co., binders in Philadelphia, adopted the style with great success, and their name is to be found on numerous book covers of this period. At first many of their designs appear to be based on or copied from English sources, particularly bindings signed by Remnant & Edmonds. (*The Token*, which was published in Boston in 1832,[62] has embossed covers identical to the Bodleian copy of *The Remembrance* for 1831,[63] excepting that the central 'picture' is different. This is signed by the American engraver, Gobrecht.) Soon however they employed local engraving talent to cut new embossing dies for them. A. C. Morin 'D. & SCULP PHILA' embossed the covers of *The Religious Souvenir for 1840*[64] and the American version of *Friendship's Offering* for 1845.[65] Some of the American annuals even crossed the Atlantic to vie with England's own giftbook trade. In November 1835, the *Monthly Literary Advertiser* announced that *The Pearl, or Affection's Gift. A Christmas and New Year's Present for 1836* which was published in Philadelphia, was 'sold in London by Richard Groombridge, Paternoster Row . . . elegantly bound in embossed morocco, price 12*s*.[66]

From 1822 until the 1850's the annual and giftbook was issued in a variety of binding styles calculated to attract the eyes of a suitable clientele, particularly those of the ladies who for the first time were considered worthy of commercial attention. They were not intended for serious reading but for intermittent perusal, yet because the receiver wished to be seen engaged in literary or pious pursuits, the covers were particularly important. As *The Athenaeum* commented on the 22 October 1828:

> The binding of "The Winter's Wreath" excels that of any Annual which we have yet seen; and, considering that not the least honourable office of an Annual is to adorn the tables of drawing rooms, this is far from slight praise.[67]

Since the enormous demand for such books coincided with the introduction of new machine methods of binding, this meant that large sales could offset costly methods of production and materials. However, by the 1840s changes in public taste and new conceptions in binding styles signified that the day of the giftbook or keepsake in a semi-luxury binding was over.

## NOTES AND REFERENCES

1 p. 932
2 *Monthly Literary Advertiser*, 10 December 1824, p. 89
3 *Monthly Literary Advertiser*, November 1826, p. 84.
4 *Monthly Literary Advertiser*, 10 November 1823, p. 83.
5 Per.2705 f. 196.
6 Bodleian (John Johnson Collection).
7 Vol. X, p. 420.
8 *The Athenaeum*, 19 November 1828, p. 894.
9 *The Athenaeum*, 22 October 1828, p. 830.
10 *The Athenaeum*, 22 October 1828, p. 830.
11 Vol. XII, No. 340, p. 305.
12 *The Gentleman's Magazine* (July-Dec. 1831), vol. 101, p. 34.
13 p. vii.
14 p. 418.
15 *The Mirror*, Vol. XII, No. 344. Supplementary number on annuals.
16 p. 668.
17 B.M. PP. 6605
18 *Monthly Literary Advertiser*, September 1829, p. 70.
19 Preface to *The Juvenile Forget Me Not . . . for 1831.*
20 *The Athenaeum*, 30 October 1830, p. 687.
21 *The Athenaeum*, 17 December 1831, p. 824.
22 *The Athenaeum*, 27 November 1830, p. 751.
23 *The Athenaeum*, 30 October 1830, p. 688.
24 p. 126.
25 *Monthly Literary Advertiser*, November 1830, p. 84.
26 *The Athenaeum*, 13 November 1830, p. 719.
27 Bodleian (John Johnson Collection).
28 One copy is illustrated and described by H. M. Nixon, *Broxbourne Library* . . . (1956,) no. 105. The other copy is in the Bodleian (Per. 2705.f.210).
29 British Patent 4521. December 1820.
30 For further information about Remnant & Edmonds and Thomas De La Rue see *English Embossed Bindings 1825–1850* (1972) by Eleanore Jamieson, pp. 11–15.
31 The larger edition is illustrated and described by H. M. Nixon in the *Broxbourne Library*, no. 105. Perhaps this larger copy is a rebinding of a crown 8vo edition issued in half leather covers. A copy of the smaller edition is in the Bodleian Per.2705 f.210.
32 B.M. C.108. b.20.
33 B.M. PP. 6615.
34 Collection: Mrs. E. Jamieson.
35 Collection: Mr. D. Chambers.
36 Information from an obituary of James Littler Barritt (1801–1863) which appeared in *The Bookseller* for 31 August 1863.
37 V & A 29.M.83.

38 Collection: Mr. D. Chambers.

39 B.M. C.108 b.20.

40 Uncatalogued.

41 Bodleian (John Johnson Collection).

42 Bodleian (John Johnson Collection).

43 B.M. PP.6785.

44 Collection: Dr. A. N. L. Munby.

45 J. A. Arnett, *Bibliopegia* (1835), p. 126.

46 There are two detailed descriptions of embossing presses, one in an account of Messrs. Westley's and Clark's bindery which appears in the *Penny Magazine* Supplement for September 1842, pp. 383–384, and the other in an article on bookbinding practice at Messrs. Remnant, Edmonds & Remnant's in Tomlinson's *Cyclopaedia of Useful Arts* (1854), Vol. 1, p. 158.

47 Advertisement at the back of *The Remembrance* (1837).

48 *The Athenaeum*, 24 October 1835, p. 807.

49 V&A Drawer 74. 9.X.1868.

50 Collection: Mr. D. Chambers.

51 *Penny Magazine* Supplement, September 1842, p. 383.

52 Illustrated on p. 25 of Ruari McLean's *Victorian Book Design and Colour Printing* (2nd ed. 1972).

53 Formerly belonging to Francis Edwards Ltd.

54 Described by J. A. Arnett in his *Bibliopegia* (1835), pp. 170/171 and illustrated as a frontispiece to the book.

55 Anne Renier, *Friendship's Offering* (1964), p. 12.

56 *The Athenaeum*, 15 November 1845, p. 1110.

57 *The Athenaeum*, 8 November 1845, p. 1085.

58 Collection: Mr. D. Chambers.

59 p. 216.

60 Bodleian. Per2705.f.33.

61 Collection: Miss M. Pollard, Trinity College, Dublin.

62 Sotheby's *Catalogue of Children's Books and Juvenilia*, 24 February 1969. Lot 82.

63 Per.2705.f.210.

64 B.M. PP.6838.

65 Parke-Bernet Galleries Inc. *Fine Books and Manuscripts*, 13 October 1970. Lot 46 (Spine illustrated on Pl. 10).

66 p. 125.

67 p. 819.

# GIFT BOOK AND ANNUAL ILLUSTRATIONS

## some notes on their production

IAIN BAIN

Illustrations played such an important part in the spectacular popular success of the Annuals, that some notes on their means of production – so often ignored or misunderstood – may here be considered useful.

It was a happy chance for their publishers that in 1819, four years before the first of the Annuals appeared in England, an American, Jacob Perkins, had taken out a patent for the processing of steel printing plates that was to bring very great benefits to the trade.[1] The use of steel as an engraving medium was not new: the steel of such things as sword blades, punches, dies, and button moulds had long been worked in general engraving shops,[2] and by 1811 Abraham Raimbach had produced a steel plate for the Bank of England,[3] but until this time, for book illustration plates, copper had been used almost exclusively. Perkins was a bank note engraver seeking means to achieve the exact duplication of intricate security work. His new process involved the decarbonising of steel to make it soft enough to take impressions from cyclindrical transfer dies, and subsequent retempering to a hardness that gave it a printing life many times greater than copper. While the details of the discovery were not originally devised for the benefit of the engraver of book illustration, the patent awakened the trade to the economic potential of the long-life steel plate.[4] The abrasive action of the plate printers' wiping canvasses – not printing pressure as is sometimes assumed – could break down fine work on a copper plate within a hundred impressions, and during a long run the cost of rebiting and repairs could absorb almost as much as the expenditure on the original work.[5] So for the publishers of potentially popular works, the appearance of a hard plate that could print many thousands of impressions without any deterioration was an exciting event.

For the line engraver, the relative hardness or softness of the

Architect's drawing of the interior of W. B. McQueen's plate printing workshop, Tottenham Court Rd, London, 1832.

Magnification $\times 5$ of a section of the original steel plate engraved by Edward Finden after Turner's 'Bolton Abbey' for *The Literary Souvenir*, 1826, showing needle etching.

plate was not of particular consequence, for by far the greater part of his work was etched with acid rather than cut with the graver. In Fielding's *The Art of Engraving* we find the clearest confirmation of this in his chapter on Line Engraving: 'Formerly, however, it was the custom to begin and finish a plate with the graver only; but this method has long been laid aside, as the use of the etching needle gives so much greater freedom in the representation of almost every object.'[6] Prints of this class were employed almost exclusively in the Annuals and any one of them examined under a strong glass, displays an intricate freedom in the worm-like lines, particularly in foliage and landscape, that could only have been achieved with a needle working through an etching ground. And yet it has been remarked by more than one authority on book illustration, that the fineness and small scale of many steel engravings was a direct result of the difficulty of working on a very hard metal.[7] This is not to say that the graver was never used, but its use would have been confined to the finishing stages for slight areas of very light work and sometimes for getting more depth into the very strong lines of previously etched dark areas. No doubt the continued use of the word 'engraving' – possibly to make a distinction betweeen this kind of work and the loose treatment of the autographic painter-etcher – has confused us into thinking of the graver rather than the needle.

The engravers bought their plates from specialist copper-smiths who, in London, congregated in the Shoe Lane district off Fleet Street, and with the advent of steel they included the new material in the supplies they offered to the trade. The plates were prepared for etching by using a soft dabber to apply an acid resisting ground of asphaltum, burgundy pitch and white virgin wax. This was then blackened in the smoke of burning tapers. The original drawing or painting was copied either by the system of squaring or by using a camera lucida. Squaring involved stretching a grid of threads across the original and then copying everything in each square into its related square in a similar grid drawn on paper in an appropriately reduced scale. The camera lucida, patented by Woolaston in 1807, employed a small prism through which a reduced image of the original could be seen together with the copyist's pencil point which was then able to follow its outline and principal features onto paper. After damping, the copy drawing was applied face down onto the blackened surface of the prepared plate and passed through the rolling press. By this means the pencil lines were transferred and the result glittered with a clear silvery effect on the black ground. A variety of pointed needles were used to cut through the resist to bare the metal below; some of the needles had sliced points which with dexterous handling could produce lines that tapered in the manner of a graver stroke. The engraver's hands rested on a wooden bridge placed over the plate and he employed an extensive range and combination of lines to achieve the various effects of drapery, foliage, and masonry. Certain other effects such as skies and water were often laid in with the aid of a ruling machine on which was fixed a fine diamond point: besides being run along a straight edge this could be advanced by minute and precise steps and lines could thus be laid very regularly and very close together.[8]

With the needle work completed, a rim of bordering wax made from burgundy pitch, beeswax and oil was built up round the edge of the plate to form a shallow bath for the subsequent application of the acid. The depth to which the lines were bitten in depended on the length of time the acid remained on the metal. The fact that some lines had to be stronger and deeper than others, meant that the finer lines had to be 'stopped out' and protected from further action, and this was done with a solution of asphaltum and turpentine spirit. The biting agent for steel was a solution of equal parts of pyroligneous acid and nitric acid in six parts of water.[9]

It might be thought that etching made for speed, but in fact the delicacy of the work and the necessary variation in acid biting could take a considerable time: Charles Warren is known to have spent 'thirteen weeks of regular and incessant exertion' on a single small plate illustrating Scott's *The Lady of the Lake*. For this he was paid 50 guineas – at least £500 in today's value and a considerable expense to the publisher, but still a modest enough reward for the close and exacting labour of thirteen weeks.[10]

The printing of the plates was given to a small specialist group of men whose activities have been much neglected by historians of the trade. Few, if any, of the principal letterpress book printers had the rolling presses necessary for intaglio work, and it has too often been assumed that the printers whose names appeared in the books they printed had also been responsible for the illustrations The printing of an engraved plate was a relatively slow and laborious business: a single man at the press could take ten minutes or more to take off a single impression from a moderately sized book illustration. The plate had first to be charged with ink and the surface wiped clean with various grades of stiff gauze and muslin in such a way as to avoid dragging the ink from the engraved lines – a process that demanded much care and skill, particularly in fine work. After further wiping with the palm of the hand, the margins of the plate were cleaned down with chalk and fine muslin before it was placed on the bed of the press. Damp paper was laid over the plate, and plate and paper under three or four layers of blankets were passed through the very heavy pressure of the press rollers. The pressure forced the damp paper into the lines and thus it picked up the ink. In the larger printing houses the production rate was increased by working as many as four men to a press: one each for inking, wiping, paper handling and press operation.[11] Even so it was often necessary for the publishers to place the printing with several firms, and while the entire edition of the text was printed off at once, it was not unusual for the plates to be printed piecemeal according to the demands of the market.[12] The names of the plate printers are not frequently found on their work, though they occur more often on the Annual prints than elsewhere. The McQueen family, John Dixon, Gad & Keningale, and Lloyd & Jennings are among those recorded. There were not more than fifty firms working in London during the 1840s – compared with at least 400 letterpress printers[13] – and the greater number of these would have been concerned solely with jobbing work rather than book illustration and large prints.

A number of the Annuals were issued in both ordinary and special large paper format, and with the latter it was usual to issue plates taken on india paper which could also be bought separately in portfolios. The thin india paper produced a particularly fine and sweet result, achieved by placing it damp onto the plate having had the upper side dusted with a flour paste.

A stouter backing sheet, also damp, was in turn placed over the india paper. The subsequent printing pressure resulted in fixing the one to the other. (It has sometimes mistakenly been assumed that the india paper was glued to the backing sheet after printing.)

The progress of wood engraving was such that by the late 1820s the fineness of execution was beginning to rival that of the work on steel. But the economic advantage of working the wood block at the same time as the accompanying text began to be lost in the extra time and care the printer had to take to achieve a satisfactory result. Although lithography was well established by the 1830s, there does not appear to have been any attempt to transfer plate impressions to the lithographic stone to take advantage of the possibility of having multiples of the same image taken off in a single impression. In fact the taste for a high degree of detailed finish in the engraved plate continued strongly to the end of the main period of Annual publishing, but sadly the capacity of steel to hold very fine work eventually brought about a severely mechanical debasement of style. This last phase unfortunately jaundiced the view that was later taken of the entire output of the steel engravers and only in recent years have their works again been considered worthy of attention.

## NOTES AND REFERENCES

1 Printing Patent No. 4400, 11 October 1819.

2 Evidence from the Engraving Books of Ralph Beilby and Thomas Bewick, 1769–1815 (Laing Gallery, Newcastle upon Tyne and Victoria & Albert Museum, London).

3 Pye, *Patronage of British Art*, 1845, p. 372.

4 The earliest example of book illustration on steel that I have so far discovered is an edition of Thomas Campbell's *The Pleasures of Hope*, 1820, in which the plates carry the imprint 'Engraved on Steel by Charles Heath' and 'Perkins, Fairman & Heath'. In an edition of Campbell's *Gertrude of Wyoming*', 1822, the line 'Patent Hardened Steel

Plate' is added to the names 'Perkins & Heath'. A plate engraved by Charles Warren after Wilkie's 'The Broken China Jar' (painted in 1817) and with the publication date of 1 January 1822 appears in Peter Coxe's *The Social Day*, 1823: according to A. C. Coxhead in his life of Stothard (1906) this is 'said to have been' the earliest book illustration on steel. Coxe complained in his introduction that the work had been in Warren's hands for nearly five years.

5 Pye, *op. cit.* p. 375.

6 T. H. Fielding, *The Art of Engraving, with the various modes of operation*, 1844, pp. 31–2.

7 David Bland, *A History of Book Illustration*, 1958, p. 250.

8 The ruling machine was invented by Wilson Lowry in about 1790. See Redgrave, *A Dictionary of Artists of the English School*, 1873, and Pye, *op. cit.* p. 387. Some engravers were accustomed to send their plates to Lowry for ruling work: see the correspondence of Thomas Bewick and Robert Pollard in the Victoria & Albert Museum, London.

9 Fielding, *op. cit.* p. 23.

10 Pye, *op. cit.* p. 373.

11 Berthiaud, *Nouveau Manuel Complet de L'Imprimeur en Taille-Douce*, Paris, 1837.

12 The edition sizes of the Annuals have been recorded as running between 10,000 and 20,000 copies.

13 London Trade Directories, Guildhall Library, London.

# PLATES

1. Printed green paper boards binding for the *Forget Me Not*, 1830. Original size.

2. Embossed maroon binding
for *The Remembrance*, 1832. $6\frac{1}{2} \times 4\frac{1}{8}$ in.

3. Pink watered silk binding
for the *Forget Me Not*, 1834. Original size.

4. Embossed maroon binding
for *Friendship's Offering*, 1836. $6\frac{1}{4} \times 4$ in.

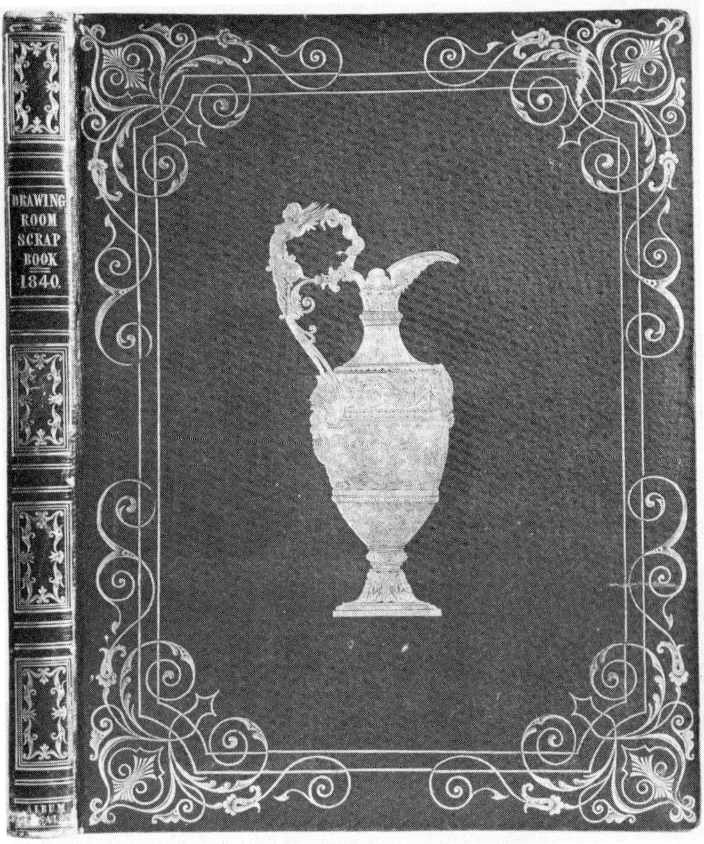


5. Gold-blocked blue cloth boards and leather spine for *Fisher's Drawing Room Scrap Book*, 1840. $11\frac{1}{8} \times 8\frac{3}{4}$ in.

6. Gold-blocked blue cloth binding
for *Heath's Book of Beauty*, 1848. $9\frac{1}{2} \times 6\frac{5}{8}$ in.

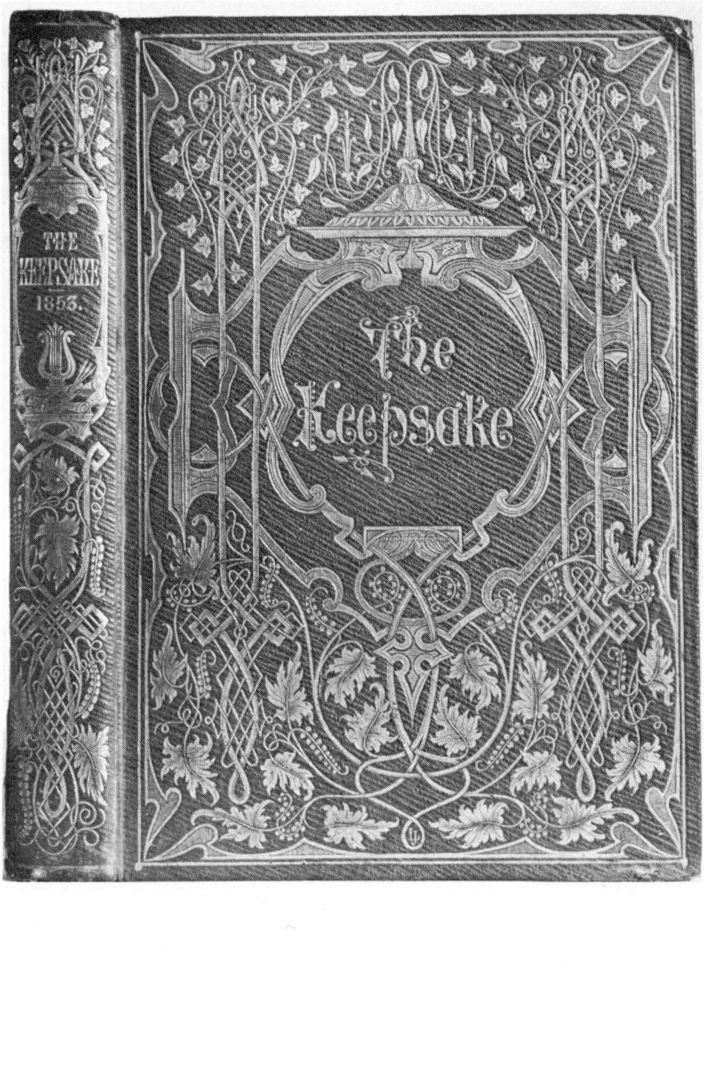


7. Gold-blocked red cloth binding for *The Keepsake*, 1853. $9\frac{5}{8} \times 6\frac{5}{8}$ in.

8. Hand-coloured engraved title-page for the first number of *Friendship's Offering*, 1824. Original size.

9. Engraved title-page on india paper for *The Literary Souvenir*, 1827. Engraving $4\frac{7}{8} \times 3$ in.

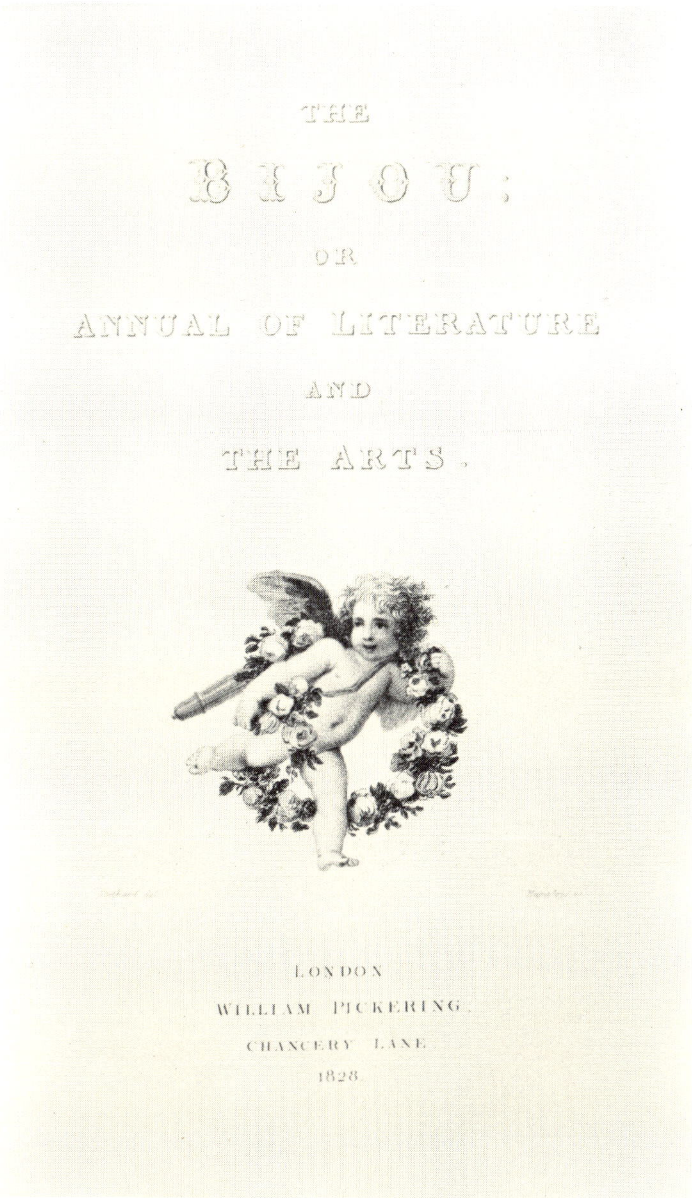
THE

BIJOU;

OR

ANNUAL OF LITERATURE

AND

THE ARTS.

LONDON

WILLIAM PICKERING,

CHANCERY LANE

1828.

10. Engraved title-page for *The Bijou*, 1828. $6\frac{1}{4} \times 4$ in.

THE

# JUVENILE FORGET ME NOT.

A

CHRISTMAS AND NEW YEAR'S GIFT, OR

BIRTHDAY PRESENT,

FOR THE YEAR 1829.

---

EDITED BY MRS. S. C. HALL.

LONDON:

N. HAILES, PICCADILLY;

FRED. WESTLEY AND A. H. DAVIS, STATIONERS' COURT;

AND R. JENNINGS, POULTRY.

11. Title-page with vignette wood-engraving for *The Juvenile Forget Me Not*, 1829. $6\frac{7}{8} \times 4$ in.

12. Engraved title-page
for *The English Keepsake*, 1831. $7\frac{1}{2} \times 4\frac{5}{8}$ in.

13. Engraved title-page for *The Remembrance*, 1832. $6\frac{1}{4} \times 4$ in.

14. Engraved title-page for *The Keepsake*, 1832. $7\frac{3}{8} \times 4\frac{3}{4}$ in.

15. Engraved title-page
for *The Landscape Annual*, 1833. $7\frac{5}{8} \times 4\frac{7}{8}$ in.

THE GIFT OF FRIENDSHIP;

A

PRESENT FOR ALL SEASONS.

LONDON:
I. J. CHIDLEY, 123, ALDERSGATE STREET.

16. Engraved title-page
for *The Gift of Friendship*, 1845. $6\frac{1}{4} \times 4$ in.

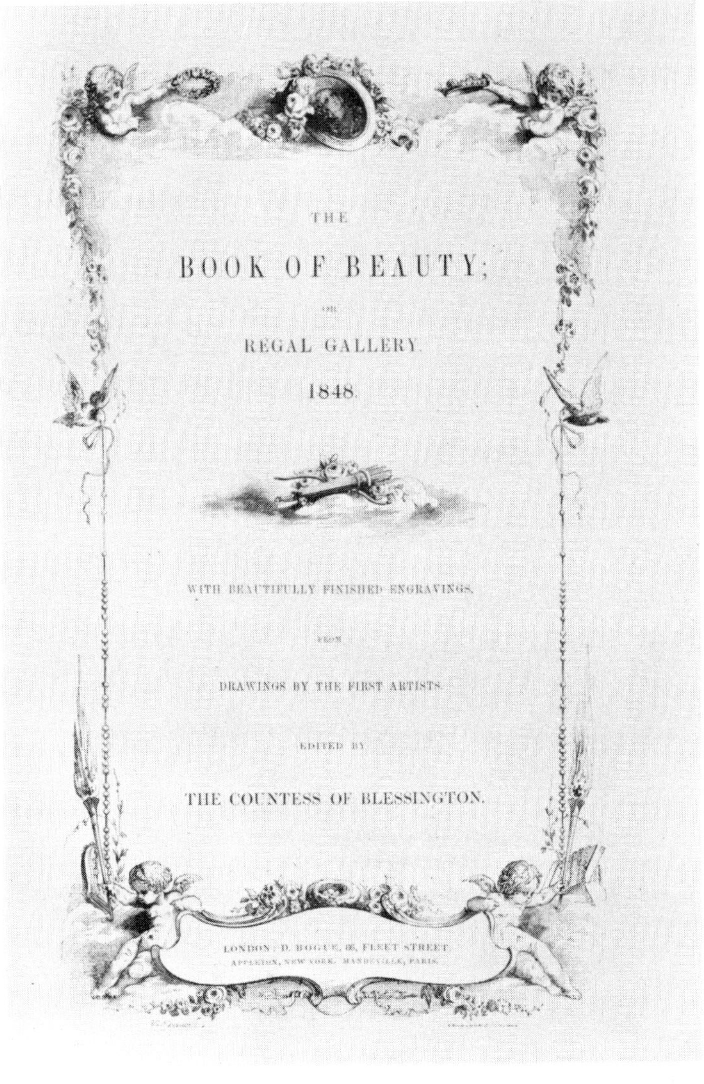
THE

BOOK OF BEAUTY;

OR

REGAL GALLERY.

1848.

WITH BEAUTIFULLY FINISHED ENGRAVINGS,

FROM

DRAWINGS BY THE FIRST ARTISTS.

EDITED BY

THE COUNTESS OF BLESSINGTON.

LONDON: D. BOGUE, 86, FLEET STREET.
APPLETON, NEW YORK. MANDEVILLE, PARIS.

17. Second wood-engraved title-page for *Heath's Book of Beauty*, 1848. $9\frac{1}{8} \times 6\frac{1}{2}$ in.

THE

KEEPSAKE

EDITED BY

MISS POWER

FOR 1853

LONDON:

DAVID BOGUE, [illegible] FLEET STREET;

18. Title-page with wood-engraved vignette for *The Keepsake*, 1853. $9\frac{1}{4} \times 6\frac{1}{2}$ in.

19. Wood-engraved presentation plate
for *The Anniversary*, 1829. Engraving $3\frac{1}{4}$ in. wide.

20. Engraved presentation plate
for the *Forget Me Not*, 1839. $6\frac{1}{4} \times 3\frac{7}{8}$ in.

21. Engraved plate for *The Keepsake*, 1828. Engraving $4\frac{1}{8} \times 3$ in.

22. Engraved plate for *The Keepsake*, 1828. Engraving $4 \times 3\frac{1}{8}$ in.

23. Engraved plate for *The Anniversary*, 1829. Engraving $4 \times 3\frac{1}{4}$ in.

24. Engraved plate for *Fisher's Drawing Room Scrap Book*, 1840. Engraving $7\frac{3}{4} \times 6$ in.

USEFUL REFERENCE SERIES NO. 6

# LITERARY ANNUALS AND GIFT BOOKS

# LITERARY ANNUALS AND GIFT-BOOKS

A Bibliography with a descriptive introduction

by

FREDERICK WINTHROP FAXON, A.B. (HARV.)

Former Secretary American Library Association

Member Bibliographical Society of America, American Library Association, Special Libraries Association, Massachusetts Library Club, etc., etc.

BOSTON, MASS.
THE BOSTON BOOK COMPANY
1912

Reprinted, with many changes and additions, from the Bulletin of Bibliography, 1908 to 1911. The introduction, addenda and chronological index now first published.

One hundred and fifty copies printed from type,

*The Riverdale Press, Brookline, Mass.*

# CONTENTS

Attention is called to the Addenda, pages 113–128.

# PREFACE

Some ten years ago my attention was first called to this interesting and well-nigh forgotten phase of printing, by the discovery of a few choice copies of literary annuals and gift-books in my father's library. Not being able to discover any even partially complete bibliography, I began listing every copy that came to my notice, as a revival of interest in these books was apparent among collectors owing to the fact that the first editions of articles by noted writers, and engravings by well-known artists, were often included.

The *Boston Public Library Bulletin* of October, 1893, contains a list of some one hundred and twenty-five titles, representing that library's collection at that time.

In the July, 1902, issue of the *Bulletin of the New York Public Library* is printed a list of that library's literary annuals, a large collection of these having been acquired by gift at about that time. This list contains one hundred and eighty-five titles, and over four hundred volumes. It makes note of the curious fact that certain American "gifts" had different titles, but the same contents. But the notes on this subject there printed are far from exhaustive, and as far as the writer knows, no study of these spurious and duplicate issues has hitherto been made. It is one of the most interesting phases of the subject in hand,

and while the notes made in this bibliography are probably not complete, they will save many a collector from needless duplication of matter, and they throw a strong light on this rather questionable practice of certain publishers. The English publications were known as "Drawing-room annuals," and the only printed list of them known to me is by Charles T. Tallent-Bateman of Manchester. It is in tabular form, contains one hundred and nine titles, and may be found in the *Papers of the Manchester Literary Club* for 1897. The assistance Mr. Tallent-Bateman has given me is acknowledged below.

There are included in my list several titles of magazines which, in order to share in the sale of annuals, were gotten out at the end of each year with slightly changed titles. A few entries, with proper notes, are made covering books with titles which make them appear to be "annuals" when they are really miscellanies not in true "gift-book" form.

In 1908 was commenced in the *Bulletin of Bibliography* the serial publication of my bibliography with a request for additions and corrections. Owing to the impracticability of holding the type indefinitely, the matter was rearranged in octavo form and shortly after each installment appeared was, with any additions available, printed off and the type distributed.

About the time this serial publication began, I determined to include in the list the little 32mo books of which "The Hare-bell," "The Golden Gift" and "The Flower Vase" are examples. These flourished in the forties, and while not "annuals," were "literary gift books." Some of them ran into ten, or even more, editions, each practically from the same type. In book-sale catalogues these are usually included with the "annuals," and, while most of them would more properly be classed under "selected poetry," they also claim a position in a list of "gift-books." This explains the rather long list in the Addenda, a large proportion of the added entries being these modest $4\frac{1}{2}$ x $2\frac{3}{4}$-inch gifts. Much as I deplore having to look in two places for what should be found in one alphabet, it seemed better to include all titles discovered up to the date of publication, as the list is thus rendered more nearly complete.

The chronological index to titles which has been added will be found useful as showing when the various gift-books started and the extent to which their publication was carried in certain years.

I wish to make especial mention here of the valuable assistance given me on Part II of this volume, The English Annuals, by a fellow enthusiast in Manchester, England, C. T. Tallent-Bateman, Esq., whose printed list of the English annuals has been referred to above. He has kindly consented to read the galley for this part of the bibliography, and has added over two hundred and fifty titles to the list, many of them not in the British Museum. It is only to be regretted that he has been unable to supply the full record of these new titles — size, pagination, etc., — in time for inclusion here. The initials T.-B. are added after the entries supplied by him, and none of these have been found by me in any of the American libraries I have checked.

I also wish here to record my grateful appreciation of the courtesies extended to me at the Library of

Congress, New York Public Library, Philadelphia Mercantile Library, Boston Public Library, Columbia University Library, Harvard University Library, and the Boston Athenæum, where every facility was afforded me for the study of their collections.

F. W. F.

WEST ROXBURY, MASS., January, 1912.

# LITERARY ANNUALS AND GIFT-BOOKS

## *INTRODUCTORY*

### I

### ORIGIN AND DURATION

As a mere list of these interesting books would mean but little to those not familiar with the volumes at first hand, and as the custom of collecting them is growing, I venture to introduce the list by a few explanatory pages, in the hope that many book-lovers and lovers of art may become interested.

"The Forget-me-not," published in England in 1823, was undoubtedly the first "literary annual." It was published by R. Ackermann, and edited by Frederic Shoberl, who noted the success of certain "Almanacs" and "Pocketbooks" which were then appearing in Germany. His surmise that an improved variety of these books would find support in England seems to have been correct. The results must have exceeded his fondest hopes, for the "gift-book" demand increased until it can only be called a fad or a craze. The lone Forget-me-not of 1823 was joined by two others in 1824, and nine came forth in 1825. In 1832 sixty-three different "gifts" under as many different titles claimed a share of the public's patronage.

The decline was as rapid as the rise, for in 1857, the year of the final or 30th annual issue of the

"Keepsake," this phase of book-making in England was practically over.

"The Forget-me-not" had appeared regularly for twenty-five years, "Friendship's Offering" had twenty-one volumes to its credit, "Heath's Book of Beauty" came forth seventeen times to adorn my lady's boudoir, or grace her drawing-room table. The best account of the English Annual "craze" will be found in *Papers of the Manchester Literary Club*, 1902, pp. 78–98, the article being entitled, "The Forget-me-not," and contributed by Mr. Tallent-Bateman.

In the United States, while publishers were a little slow in getting started, the fad developed into even greater proportions and lasted longer.

In 1826, three years after the English pioneer, the "Atlantic Souvenir" saw light in Philadelphia, compiled after the pattern of its English brethren, getting its pictures abroad, but employing American writers, as did most of the early American annuals. In 1832, when the English output was at high-water mark, America had but twelve or thirteen. It may be assumed that the British volumes sold in the American shops, thus dividing the demand. As the English "tokens" gradually disappeared, the American publishers issued an ever-increasing number, until from 1846 to 1852 an average of sixty appeared each year — sixty-six have been recorded for 1851, and there were probably others. By 1860 the American literary gift-book was practically a thing of the past, henceforth only to be found in attics, or second-hand stores.

"The Rose of Sharon" holds the American record for duration, with its eighteen volumes. "The

Token" was successful during fifteen years, while the "Odd Fellows Offering" gladdened the hearts and eyes of its patrons for twelve years.

Many lived for two or more years, but the great majority came only once, and, not being strong enough to hold their place, were soon forgotten.

Many there were which, in bidding for part of the public's favor, were not ashamed to take on the name of some famous issue, lately deceased; still others were these same well-known "back numbers" brought forth anew with different names and current dates, thus successfully passing as new "tokens of love or friendship." Be it said to their credit, such practices were never indulged in by the English gift-book publishers.

## II

## PHYSICAL APPEARANCE AND MAKE-UP

The "really truly" gift-books had an appearance and make-up all their own, very different from any other volumes. At first they were the small duodecimos, then octavos, and finally some of them appeared as quartos. Their bindings were ornate, often to the point of gaudiness. If of leather the covers were heavily embossed, or profusely gilt, or if a cloth was desired, a watered silk dress gave distinction to the volumes. Some of the earlier ones had engraved paper sides, usually green. Some had bindings with a floral design inlaid with mother-of-pearl. A few had slip-cases to protect their bindings, a ribbon being attached with which to pull forth the volume. Some had large paper editions, sold at a higher price than the regular copies.

The contents consisted of prose — short stories and essays — and selected poetry often with flowery borders about each page. There were illustrations — engravings or colored plates — dignified in the catalogues as embellishments. These numbered anywhere from one to twenty-five or thirty and were either illustrative of the text (though there are suspicions that oftentimes the story was written up to the pictures), or had no connection whatever with the contents. There was, usually, an engraved or colored "inscription plate" upon which the donor was expected to write his name and that of the fortunate recipient-to-be. Many of the later "tokens," especially the spurious ones, had crudely colored inscription plates and illuminated title pages. The pagination almost invariably began in Roman numerals, covering contents pages, list of plates and preface, then Arabic figures for the rest of the book. When there are found two series of pages in a volume, each beginning from page 1, and there are twelve engravings or twelve colored flower plates, it may be taken as a sign that what we have is really a monthly magazine, a year's numbers of which are bound up to look like a new annual, and with an appropriate name.

In their names these literary annuals were especially distinctive. They were gifts, tokens, souvenirs, mementos, keepsakes and offerings, with all conceivable qualifying adjectives, or else they bore the name of some flower, plant or gem. Every phase of every subject had its token, from "Mourner's Chaplet" to "Marriage Ring," from "Mother's Present" and "Young Maiden's Mirror" to "Young Man's Guide" and "Pastor's Gift." There were "Leaflets of Memory" and "Thought Blossoms," "Rainbows" and "Snowflakes," and "Dewdrops." The subtitle was usually "A Christmas, New Year's and Birthday Present." Thus in binding, contents, illustrations, and name these interesting "butterfly books" were easily distinguished from the common run.

They were sold at all prices, some bringing a guinea in England, and $5.00 in America. Then, in a class by themselves, were the little American-printed books, usually in dark cloth bindings, about 4½ x 2¾ inches in size. These were not "annuals," but were "gifts," and most of them had several reissues with various dates, but from the same stereotype plates. Types of these were the "Bouquet," "Casket of Love," "Floral Gems," "Flower Vase," "Hare-bell," "Primrose." They flourished from about 1844 to 1852. C. W. Everest was the editor of many of them. They ordinarily were illustrated by a frontispiece only.

## III

## THE DUPLICATE AND SPURIOUS ISSUES

While there was apparently no reissue of any of the English annuals, with simply a change of date or name, the number of those printed in America, which appeared again under different titles but with practically the same contents, was evidently very large. Except for the few duplications noticed in the New York Public Library list, no one seems to have been aware of this curious practice of some publishers.

In the bibliography which follows it will be noted that nearly every American Annual which was so successful as to run for several years has one or more namesakes, *but without date on title.*

In listing books of the same title undated copies are placed first, followed by the rest chronologically arranged. In reality, however, the undated annual was almost invariably of later issue than those which bore dates. In other words, whenever a successful series ended there were publishers ready to enter the field with a spurious "gift-book" of the same name in order to supply the not inconsiderable demand there must have been for "this year's volume" of some old favorite. The stereotyped plates of some unsuccessful venture were purchased for a song, the date was removed, the title changed, and some inferior or worn-out picture plates used. Thus apparently the "Token" or the "Amaranth" still flourished. This renaming was so clumsily done in many cases that the original title still appeared in the preface, thus at once unmasking the book. In other cases the alteration was well done, and even the first article in the book was changed. In some of them the original list of plates still remained, with different pictures inserted in the body of the work. In others this page of the contents was omitted, leaving a break in pagination, or a new list of plates was made and substituted.

For example: the "Snow Flake" was published from 1849 to 1855 in Philadelphia, by E. H. Butler & Co. In 1855 Leavitt & Allen New York, brought out an undated "Snow Flake" that was really "Moss Rose" with slight changes. In 1856 the same firm appears with a "Snow Flake," this time the "Magnolia" of 1836, with new plates and the final pages omitted. By not having any date visible, these spurious volumes could often be used over and over again in successive years by simply using a different colored leather binding. Leavitt & Allen, and Cornish, Lamport & Co. seem to have done most of this work of issuing spurious or false tokens.

The opposite of the above practice is also common. That is, a gift-book of high merit was used in later years under other names. For instance "The Token and Atlantic Souvenir" of 1840 appears both as "Honeysuckle" and as "Moss Rose" in 1848, as "Atlantic Souvenir" about 1853, and as "Token of Friendship" and "Friendship's Gift" in some other years. In nearly every case the plates vary, but the text is identical. Evidently the quality of contents was intended to sell these, the old type having been secured for little or nothing.

Another peculiarity is the appearance of the same volume with different imprints. "The American Juvenile Keepsake" of 1834, New York, appears from Bristol, R. I., and from Brockville, N. C., and was also issued under the titles of "Gift," "Gem," and "Youth's Keepsake," in later years.

One wonders if a confiding public was willing to buy "Amaranth" in 1849, and "Garland" in 1850, "Keepsake of Friendship" in 1851, "Magnolia" in 1852, "Token of Friendship" in 1853, "Casket" in 1854, and "Memory's Gift," in 1869, when all these seven were one and the same inside. Did the fair recipient of the same stories and poems each year under a different name modestly refrain from telling of her discovery when next the admirer called? We may ask how, if Emily Percival really edited the "Amaranth," 1852, G. S. Monroe could edit the same work in 1854 under title of "Keepsake of Friendship," and Clara Arnold in 1855 as the "Magnolia." Were G. S. Monroe and Clara Arnold *noms de plume* of Emily? We imagine not; those worthy people never knew they had edited these works, but they were the editors of previous successful volumes of those names, and the publisher of these bastard gifts did not hesitate to adopt both name and editor.

The case of "The Wreath of Wild Flowers," a book of miscellanies, by John Milton Stearns, published in New York in 1846, and copyrighted in that year, will serve as a final example of how some publishers met the demand for a new annual each year. With the addition of a preliminary poem, and some extra plates, Mr. Stearn's work was used as "Amaranth" in 1851, Boston; "Garland" in 1852, Boston, edited by Emily Percival; "Keepsake of Friendship," in 1853, Boston, edited by G. S. Monroe; "Token of Friendship" [1854], Boston, and also New York, and finally as "Magnolia" with a preface date of 1853. Nearly all these books vary in the unpaged poem at the beginning, and in the plates.

Enough has doubtless been said here to show the advantage of a bibliography which might prevent collectors from duplicating material, though there must still be cases in which I have failed to note the repetition of contents.

## IV

## LITERARY AND ARTISTIC WORTH

The literature of the "gift-books" was remarkable for its freedom from the slightest taint of impropriety. There was never a contribution that savored of the lack of refinement. These volumes were intended as gifts, and were such that they might ornament the drawing-room table of the most fastidious without offense either to mind or eye. The list of contributors to the English Annuals included all the foremost writers of the time. We find such names as Byron, Southey, the Howitts, Macaulay, Scott, Wordsworth, Lamb, Coleridge, Praed, Hood, Ruskin, Lytton, Landor, Shelley, Campbell, the Brownings, Moore, Tennyson, Dickens, Thackeray, and many more. It was the proper thing to write for these "tokens."

Toward the end of the "annual" fad, it became beneath the dignity of famous authors to contribute and the favor of royal and titled persons was withdrawn. The Countess of Blessington probably did much to stay the approaching oblivion by lending her name and giving of her time as editor to several successful series, notably the "Keepsake" and "Book of Beauty." From her position and her wide acquaintance in literary and art circles she was enabled to command contributions from authors and artists of high repute. Her presence did much also to keep "annuals" in vogue among the aristocracy.

All the better class of "gift-books" throughout their

existence diluted their good things with many a mediocre article by unknown or unnamed authors.

As early as 1828 *The Quarterly Review* asks, "Why, when there are in the country men able and willing to contribute such things [referring to quotations made from several current 'gift-books'] to literary pocketbooks, is there no one production of this class which it is possible to point out as distinguished throughout for its literary excellence? Are the classics of our age to continue to see their beautiful fragments doled out year after year in the midst of such miserable and mawkish trash as fills at least nineteen pages out of every twenty in the best of the gaudy duodecimos now before us?" This is perhaps putting it too strongly, but it shows the tendency to make a few good essays and a sprinkling of true poetry carry off the whole book. Whatever may be said of the literary contributions, the illustrations were usually of a very high order in the early years before the field was overfilled and both pictures and text suffered from the competition and consequent cheapening of price.

Engravers were paid, it is said, as high as £150 for a single plate, and the artist or owner of the painting to be engraved received at times a like sum for permission to use it.

Engravings of pictures by Turner, Clarkson, Stanfield, Stothard, Samuel Prout, Martin, Mulready, Landseer, Cattermole, Eastlake, Wilkie and others were included. A favorite method was to give illustrations from Shakespeare or Milton, the Waverley Novels, Pilgrim's Progress, or Don Quixote, and then have these written up to by nameless authors.

In the United States much the same course was followed by the "gift-book" publishers. At first the little volumes were below the English standard of excellence, the field being new and untried and the publishers timid about such great expenditures as were made across the water. In fact most of the plates were from paintings by English artists, but the text from the first was all American. The foremost writers found a place in the contents of many of the American "gifts," and hence collectors of first editions of the works of such men are eagerly seeking "annuals" at the present time. Many of the best American engravers are represented by fine plates in these "presents." Sartain contributed many illustrations, while those books illustrated with one or more plates by John Cheney are much in demand.

To show the extent to which the foremost American authors of the time are represented in this class of literature, a few are here cited, rather at random, and with no attempt to make an exhaustive list: —

Nathaniel Hawthorne has his first published production in the "Token" of 1830, and contributions in the same publication in 1831, 1832, 1833, 1835 to 1838, inclusive. He also appears in the "Boston Book," 1841; "Youth's Keepsake," 1835; "Memorial," 1851; and "Scenes in the Life of the Saviour," 1845.

Edgar Allen Poe contributed his "Manuscript found in a bottle" to the "Gift" of 1836, and had other pieces in 1842, 1843 and 1845. He also contributed to "Mayflower," 1846; "Missionary Memorial," 1846; "Opal," 1844 and 1845; "Leaflets of Memory," 1850; and "Irving Offering," 1851.

The first of Whittier's writings to appear in book form was his "Light in the Binnacle," in the "Memorial," 1827. There are contributions by him also in "Oasis," 1834; "Literary Souvenir," 1831; "Laurel," 1837; "Youth's Keepsake," 1835; "Scenes in the Life of the Saviour," 1845; "Fountain," 1847; "Bouquet of Flowers," 1845; "Christian Keepsake," 1840; "Liberty Bell," 1846; "Missionary Memorial," 1846; "Opal," 1846, 1847; "Christian Souvenir," 1851; "Young Lady's Cabinet of Gems," 1854; "Cloud Crystals," 1864, and "Evergreen," n.d.

Bryant had contributions in the "Album," 1824; "Beauties of Sacred Literature," 1852; "Cloud Crystals," 1864; "Lady's Book of Flowers," 1846; "Laurel," 1837; "Literary Souvenir," 1831; "Masonic Token," 1868; "Premium," 1833; "Talisman," 1828, 1829, 1830; "Thought Blossom," n.d. and 1855; "Wide Awake Gift," 1855.

Emerson will be found in the "Gift," 1844, 1845; "Marriage Offering," 1848; "Liberty Bell," 1851; "Wide Awake Gift," 1855; "Cloud Crystals," 1864.

O. W. Holmes added his contributions to help make up "Youth's Keepsake," 1831; "Token," 1831, 1833, 1837; "Laurel," 1837; "Boston Book," 1841; "Bouquet of Flowers," 1845; "Lady's Book of Flowers," 1846; "Fountain," 1847; "Memory and Hope," 1851; "Young Lady's Cabinet of Gems," 1854; "Wide Awake Gift," 1855.

Longfellow had a good share in the "annual" craze, though doubtless, as with other authors, he appears in many without his knowledge. We find pieces by him in "Atlantic Souvenir," 1828; "Token," 1833, 1842; "Boston Book," 1841; "Laurel," 1837;

"Liberty Bell," 1845, 1846; "Opal," 1847; "Scenes in the Life of the Saviour," 1845; "Gift," 1845; "Bouquet of Flowers," 1845; "Irving Offering," 1851; "Dew Drop," 1852; "Young Lady's Cabinet of Gems," 1854; "Wide Awake Gift," 1855; "Christian's Gift," 1857; "Cloud Crystals," 1864.

Lowell appears in the "Token," 1842; "Gift," 1844; "Missionary Memorial," 1846; "Fountain," 1847; "Liberty Bell," 1843, 1844, 1845, 1846, 1848, 1849, 1851; "Memory and Hope," 1851; "Christian Souvenir," 1851; "Dew Drop," 1852; "Cloud Crystals," 1864; and "Evergreen," n.d.

We find contributions by Irving, J. G. Percival, N. P. Willis, FitzGreene Halleck, Mrs. Sigourney, Edward Everett, Mrs. Stowe, Goodrich (Peter Parley), Cooper, Catherine Sedgwick. In short, all the American authors may be found in the pages of these annuals.

The work of American engravers in these annuals is notable. John Cheney, for example, who was perhaps the foremost engraver of portraits of his time, contributed to many volumes, until they had so deteriorated that there was no longer a place for work of such quality as his. His plates appear in "Juvenile Souvenir," 1828; "Token," 1828, 1830 to 38, inclusive; "Memorial," 1828, 1851; "Casket," 1829, 1830; "Moral and Religious Souvenir," 1828; "Lady's Cabinet Album," 1832, 1835, etc.; "Moss Rose," 1854; "Youth's Keepsake," 1830; "Lily," 1839; "Coral," n.d.; "Token of Friendship," n.d.; "Token or Affection's Gift," n.d.; "Gift," 1836, 1837, 1839, 1840, 1842 to 1845; "Literary Souvenir," 1838, 1840, 1844, 1845; "Magnolia," 1837; "Christian Keepsake," 1838, 1839, 1840; "Friendship's Offering," 1841; "Remember!" n.d.; "Ladies' Scrap Book," 1845; "Opal," 1845; "Dew Drop," 1852; "String of Diamonds," 1857.

Cheney's plates were in some cases used over and over again in various volumes, sometimes with the title changed, sometimes with it omitted. The plate entitled *Love Letters* in the "Gift," 1837, was also in "Literary Souvenir," 1838. "Magnolia," 1837, had *Esperanza*, but this same picture appears in "Token or Affection's Gift" (n.d.) as *The Bridge*. *Reflection* in "Christian Keepsake," 1838, becomes *Night* in "Friendship's Offering," 1841. "The Gift," 1839, has *Helen;* "Literary Souvenir," 1840, calls her *La Jeune Jaquette*, and in 1844 she appears a third time, but now as *Isabel*.

Enough has been said to show what an interesting field for a Cheney collector is here spread before us. Several of the "annuals" mentioned above do not appear in Mr. Koehler's exhaustive catalogue of Cheney plates.

Is it to be wondered at that certain volumes of the "Atlantic Souvenir," "Gift" or "Token" sell at auction as high as $16.00, when they contain articles there first printed, or poems "not to be found in the collected works" of some favorite author, or perchance fine impressions of a master-engraver's work?

Sometimes contributors did not sign their articles, and discoveries can doubtless yet be made in this fascinating field by those who have made a study of the style in which Poe or Whittier wrote.

I hope that this introduction to the bibliography which follows may be the means of still further awakening the interest of book-lovers in this almost forgotten fad of a past generation.

A contributor to the *Atlantic Monthly* in 1893, in an article reminiscent of his boyhood acquaintance with these little volumes, says:—

"These books were not to be resold; a last year's Annual was not to be thought of as a present however attractive in itself. Its date betrayed it. They were gifts, and often treasured up as the faded rose and the ivory Malbone miniature of her bridal days are treasured in the matron's cabinet, because they were haunted with the secret and subtle fragrance of bygone memories. If an old Annual could tell its own life-story, and if I could write it down as it should be written, what pages I should proudly aspire to in the best American periodical! But I fear that they are gone, and that my dream of filling a college library shelf with a complete collection of them is only a dream."

Would not this writer be surprised to learn that his library shelf would have to be much longer than the popular five feet to hold the collections now existing? The New York Public Library has a very large collection; the Library of Congress nearly as many. Other libraries are collecting them as opportunity offers. The following bibliography includes mention of two thousand volumes, most of which have been seen by the compiler.

The day of the new "annual" may have passed long ago, but assuredly the "old annuals" are with us to remain.

## ABBREVIATIONS USED AND EXPLANATION OF ENTRIES

For convenience of reference a running number is given each volume.

In cases where there are different editions, or different titles to same work, the title of first article is added in quotation marks as an aid to identification. The size is given in inches and fractions of an inch, but always measured by the page, not the cover.

The number of plates includes not only engravings, but also the engraved or illuminated titles and inscription plates, as these are usually listed with the engravings in the books.

Brackets around the number of plates signify that no list of plates was given in volume.

In alphabetical arrangement the titles beginning with "Lady's" and "Ladies' " are placed as if spelled the same way because in several instances the same volume appears under both spellings.

The volumes listed may be referred to in the libraries indicated by the initials which follow each entry, though the absence of reference to any of these libraries does not necessarily mean that the volume is not there to be found.

Library abbreviations are as follows: —

B. A. Boston Athenæum.
B. M. British Museum (entry made from catalogue only).
B. P. Boston Public Library.
C. U. Columbia University Library.

| | |
|---|---|
| F. | Examined by compiler in private collections, or bookstores. |
| H. U. | Harvard University Library. |
| L. C. | Library of Congress, Washington. |
| N. Y. | New York Public Library. |
| N. Y. S. | New York State Library, Albany (collection destroyed by fire, 1911). |
| P. M. | Philadelphia Mercantile Library. |
| T.-B. | Title supplied by Mr. C. T. Tallent-Bateman. |
| U. M. | University of Michigan Library, Ann Arbor. |
| U. W. | University of Wisconsin Library, Madison. |
| * | Titles not found by compiler, but notice of such publication found. |

Abbreviations used: —

| | |
|---|---|
| c. | copyright. |
| col. | colored. |
| ed. | edited, edition, editor. |
| engr. | engraved. |
| front. | frontispiece. |
| illum. | illuminated. |
| illus. | illustrations paged with text. |
| l. | leaf, leaves. |
| n. d. | no date. |
| n. p. | no place. |
| p. | page, pages. |
| p. l. | preliminary leaf or leaves. |
| pl. | plate, plates. |
| pref. | preface. |
| v. | volume. |
| vig. t. | vignette title. |

# BIBLIOGRAPHY.

# PART I.

## AMERICAN.

**Affection's gift**; a Christmas, New Year and birthday present. New York, Leavitt & Allen, 27 Dey St., **n. d.** [1854 or 55]. 4 p. l. viii, 9–81, 2 l., 5–175 p., [6 pl.,] 7 x 5. "Appropriate sphere of woman." U.W. (1)

This is "Lady's manual," 1854.
Also issued as "Token and Atlantic souvenir," N. Y., n. d., and "Memory's gift," n. d.

—— ——: or, a holiday present. New York, J. C. Riker, **1832**, c. 1831. 3 p. l., 13–288 p., 10 pl., 6½ x 4¼. N.Y. (2)

—— ——; a Christmas, New Year, and birthday present for **1854**. Philadelphia, E. H Butler & Co., c. 1853. x p., 1 l., 13–328 p., 8 pl., 7¼ x 4¾. L.C., N.Y., U.W. (3)

—— ——, a Christmas, New Year and birthday present for **1855**. Philadelphia, E. H. Butler & Co., 1855, c. 1854. x p., 1 l., 13–328 p., 8 pl., 7¼ x 4¾. B.P., L.C., N.Y. (4)

—— —— for the loving and the loved, by John Cole Hagen. Philadelphia, John E. Potter, **1859**, c. 1859. iv., 5–144 p., [3 pl.,] 7¼ x 4¾. U.W. (5)

**Affection's keepsake.** New York. * (6)

**Album, The.** New York, F. R. Lockwood, **1824**, c. 1823. x p., 1 l., 13–156 p., engr. title, 7 x 4⅝. B.A. (7)

Also copies 8⅛ x 5¼.

**Album, The**; see **Lady's Album.**

**Album of love, The.** New York, Leavitt & Allen., **1853.** 128 p., 4⅝ x 2¾. N.Y. (8)

**Aloe, The,** a gift for all seasons. Ed. by Henry W, Herbert. New York, Lamport, Blakeman & Law. **1854.** 3 p.l., 11–260, 2 l. 7¼ x 4⅞. "The magnolia. 'Not in the autumn.'" H.U. (9)

This is "Magnolia." 1836, with changed pl. and p. (264)–300 omitted. See also "Friendship's token," N. Y., n. d., "Gift of affection," n. d., "Morning glory," n. d., "Memory," c. 1854, "Snow flake," n. d.

**Amaranth, The,** or token of remembrance; a Christmas and New Year's gift, ed. by Emily Percival. Boston, Phillips, Sampson & Co. **n. d.** 288 p., 7 pl., 7¼ x 4¾. "To Juliet." U.W. (10)

Same as 1855.

**Amaranth, The,** or token of remembrance; a Christmas and New Year's gift, ed. by Emily Percival. New York, Leavitt & Allen. **n. d.** 5–6, 9–288 p., [6 pl.,] 7¼ x 5. " To Juliet." B.A., B.P., U.W. (11)

Same as N. Y., 1869.
Same as Boston, 1855 edition, except different plates, and pages 7–8, the list of plates, omitted. There are at least two editions of this N. Y., n. d. issue, each with different plates.

—— ——. Philadelphia, Thomas J. Ash. **n. d.** 1 p.l., 296 p., [5 pl.,] 5¾ x 3½. "The two smugglers." B.P. (12)

—— ——; or masonic garland; ed by C. W. Moore. v. 1, Boston, 5828–9 [**1828–9**]. * (13)

—— ——, a literary and religious offering designed as a Christmas and New Year's present, ed. by J. H. Buckingham. Newburyport, Charles Whipple. **c. 1831**, 2 p. l., 7–180 p., front., 5⅞ x 3½. N.Y., L. C. (14)

—— ——. Philadelphia, **1840.** See **Literary Amaranth, 1840.**

—— ——; a gift for all seasons. Philadelphia, American Sunday School Union, **c. 1841.** 235 p., 9 pl., 5¾ x 3¾. N.Y., P.M. (15)

—— —— a gift for all seasons. Philadelphia, American Sunday School Union, **1842,** c. 1841. 235 p., 9 pl., 7 x 4½. N.Y., U.W., P.M. (16)

Same as c. 1841 above, except on large paper, and two of plates transposed.

—— ——. Philadelphia, **1845.** See **Literary Amaranth, 1845.**

—— ——, or token of remembrance, a Christmas and New Year's gift for **1847.** [v. 1.] Boston, Phillips & Sampson, 1847, c.1846. viii p., 1 l., 11–324 p., 7 pl., 6¾ x 4½. " The Amaranth." U.W., N.Y., B.P., L.C. (17)

Issued as " Garland," 1848, with first article changed to " The Garland "; issued as " Keepsake of friendship," 1849, with another change in first article; issued as " Ladies' gift," N. Y., n. d., also 1850, and 1851; and as " Gift of affection," N. Y., n. d. Pl. vary in all editions.

—— ——, or token of remembrance, a Christmas and New Year's gift for **1848.** [v. 2.] Boston, N. C. Barton, 1848, c. 1847. vi p., 1 l., 9–288 p., 6 pl., 7½ x 4¾. " Immortality." N.Y., B.P., L.C. (18)

Issued as " Garland," 1849, with first article changed; as " Keepsake of friendship," 1850, with still another substitution of first article.

—— ——, or token of remembrance, a Christmas and New Year's gift for **1849.** [v. 3.] Boston, Phillips & Sampson, 1849, c. 1848. vi p., 1 l., 9–322 p., 6 pl., 7 x 4⅝. " Medora." B.A., N.Y. (19)

Also issued with imprint Worcester, E. Livermore, 1849. P.M.

Issued as " Garland," 1850, with first article changed to " Song," and different front. A col. t. is added.
The " Casket," Boston, pref. d. 1853, and " Casket," N.Y., n. d., are same except first article changed to " The quiet eye," etc., and the front. and engr. t. replaced by col. presentation pl., and col. t.
" Memory's gift," N. Y., 1869, and " Memory's gift," N. Y., n. d., 322 p., are same except pl. and first article, " The quiet eye," pref. is that of " Casket."
" Token of friendship," Boston, pref. d. Aug., 1852, is same except first article, " The new year."
" Keepsake of friendship," Worcester, 1851, is same, except that first article is " Friendship," and front. and engr. t. are replaced by col. presentation pl., and col. t.
" Magnolia," 1852, is same with first article changed to " Love of nature."

—— ——, or token of remembrance, a Christmas and New Year's gift for **1850**. [v. 4.] New York, Gates, Stedman & Co., 1850. 288 p., [4 pl. and engr. t.,] 7 x 4¾. " To Kate." L.C., C.U. (20)

Issued as " Garland," 1851, with first article changed and 2 pl. substituted. Issued as "Magnolia" [1853] with front article changed and only 2 pl. the same.

—— ——, or token of remembrance, a Christmas and New Year's gift for **1851**. [v. 5.] Boston, Phillips, Sampson & Co., 1851, c. 1850. 5 p. l., 276 p., 6 pl., 7 x 4¾. " Forest maid " on first unpaged leaf. " The Refugee," first paged article.
N.Y., B.P., U.W., L.C. (21)

This is " Wreath of wild flowers," 1846, with addition of pl. and preliminary unpaged l.
The " Garland," 1852, and " Keepsake of friendship," Boston, 1853, are same as this except the preliminary unpaged article" Forest maid " is replaced by " Humility," and the engr. t. gives place to a col. t.
"Token of friendship," Boston, n. d., [pref. d. Aug., 1854,] and " Token of friendship," N. Y., n. d., are same except preliminary unpaged article "Forest maid " is replaced by " Who are the happy," and front. and engr. t. are replaced by col. front. and col. t.
The " Magnolia" [pref. d. 1853,] is same, except " Forest maid" is replaced by " Who are the happy."

—— ——, or token of remembrance, a Christmas and New Year's gift for **1852**, ed. by Emily Percival. [v. 6.] Boston, Phillips, Sampson & Co., 1852, c. 1851. 288 p., 7 pl., 7¼ x 4¾. " Heather bell."
N.Y., B.P., U.W. (22)

Also issued as " Garland," 1853," " Magnolia," 1855, and " Keepsake of friendship," 1854, which are the same except first article.

—— ——, or token of remembrance, a Christmas and New Year's gift for **1853**, ed. by Emily Percival. [v. 7.] Boston, Phillips, Sampson & Co., 1853, c 1852. 288 p., 7 pl., 7¼ x 4¾. " Desdemona."
N.Y., B.P. (23)

Also issued as " Garland," 1854, and "Keepsake of friendship," 1855, with change in first article.

**Amaranth, The**, or token of remembrance, a Christmas and New Year's gift for **1854**, ed. by Emily Percival. [v. 8.] Boston, Phillips, Sampson & Co 1854, c. 1853. 288 p., 6 pl., 7¼ x 4¾. "Daughter of the Bardi." N.Y., B.P., C.U., U.W. (24)

"The Garland," Boston, 1855, "The Garland," Boston c. 1854, "The Garland," N. Y., n. d., are same as this, except that they have an added engr. t.
"The Garland," N. Y., 1869, is same, except it has only engr. t., and no pl., and omits p. 7–8, the list of pl.

—— ——, or token of remembrance, a Christmas and New Year's gift for **1855**, ed. by Emily Percival. [v. 9.] Boston, Phillips, Sampson & Co., 1855, c. 1854. 1 p. l., 5–288 p., 7 pl., 7¼ x 4¾. N.Y., B.P., U.W. (25)

Also issued with imprint, Boston, n. d., c. 1854, and Boston entirely without date, and N. Y., n. d., with plates changed and p. 7–8, list of plates, omitted; and N. Y., 1869, plates changed and p. 7–8 omitted.

—— ——, or token of remembrance, a Christmas and New Year's gift, ed. by Emily Percival. New York, Geo. A. Leavitt, **1869**. 1–6, 9–288 p., [6 pl.,] 7 x 4¾ F. (26)

This is the same as "Amaranth," Boston, 1855, with plates changed and p. 7–8, list of plates, omitted.

**American book of beauty**, The, or token of friendship, a gift for all seasons, ed. by a lady. Hartford, Silas Andrus & Son, **n. d.** 2 p. l., 7–128 p., 8 pl. [7 in list], 10 x 6¾. L.C. (27)

**American comic annual**, ed. by Henry J. Finn. Boston, Richardson, Lord & Holbrook, **1831**, c. 1830. viii) 220 p., [13 pl., and many illus.,] 6⅝ x 4⅛. F. (28,

**American cottage life.** See **Fireside poetical readings.**

**American gift book, The.** See **Rough and ready annual, 1848.**

—— ——, a perpetual souvenir. New York, J. C. Derby, **1856**, c. 1855. xii, 13–312 p., 7¼ x 5. U.W. (29)

The issues by Derby and Jackson, 1858, c. 1855, and 1859, c. 1855, are identical with above. L.C.

**American juvenile keepsake, The,** ed. by Mrs. Hofland. Bristol, R. I., J. Gladding & Co., **n. d.** 252 p., 9 pl., 5¾ x 3⅝. "London cousin and country cousin." L.C. (30)

This is same as New York issue, c. 1834.

—— ——, ed. by Mrs. Hofland. New York, C. Wells, **c. 1834.** 2 p. l., iii–iv, vii–x, 1–252 p., 9 pl., 6 x 3¾. N. Y., U. W. (31)

This was also issued with imprint Bristol, R. I., n. d., and with imprint Brockville, N. C., 1835.
The Gift, New York, 1847, is reprint of this, omitting list of pl., all but a few pl., omitting two articles and rearranging others.
"The Youth's keepsake," New York, n. d., of which at least two editions were issued, one of them 1846, or after, is reprint of this, with but 6 pl.
"The Gem," 1849, is same, except it has 8 pl.

**American juvenile keepsake, The**, ed. by Mrs. Hofland. Brockville, N. C., **1835.** * (32)

This is the same as New York, c. 1834.

—— ——, for **1836,** ed by Mrs. Hofland. New York, C. Wells, c. 1834. 2 p. l., iii–iv, vii–x, 1–252 p., 9 pl., 5¾ x 3¾. N. Y., L. C. (33)

This is the same as New York, c. 1834.

—— ——, ed. by Mrs. Hofland. Bristol, R. I., J. Gladding & Co., n. d. [**1837** on back of original pub. binding.] 5⅞ x 3¾. F. (34)

This is the same as New York, c. 1834.

—— ——, ed. by Mrs. Hofland. New York, C. Wells, c. 1834 [**1840** on back of binding]. L.C. (35)

This is the same as New York, c. 1834.

**American keepsake** for all seasons, ed. by Anna Wilmot New York, **n. d.** * (36)

This is the same as 1851.

—— —— for **1851,** ed. by Anna Wilmot. New York, Cornish, Lamport & Co., c. 1850. vi p., 1 l., 9–312 p., 7 pl., 7¼ x 5. N.Y., B.P., L.C., U W. (37)

—— —— for all seasons, ed. by Anna Wilmot. New York, Cornish, Lamport & Co., **c. 1851.** vi p., 1 l., 9–312 p., 7 pl., 7½ x 4⅞. B.A. (38)

Same as 1851.

**American poets' gift.** Title on publisher's binding of **Poet's gift,** 1845. which see.

**Amethyst, The,** an annual of literature, ed. and pub. by N. C. Brooks. Baltimore, Wm. A. Francis, **1831,** c. 64th year of independence. 1 p. l., 5–6, vii–x, 11–290 p., 8 pl., 5½ x 3½. N.Y., B.A. (40)

—— ——, or poetical gems, a gift book for all seasons, ed. by Mrs. M. P. James. Boston, James French, **1850.** iv., 5–128 p., 4½ x 2¾. N.Y (41)

**Amulet.** Boston, Otis, Broaders & Co., **n. d.,** vi p., 1 l., 9–296 p., 9 pl., 6¾ x 4½. L.C. (42)

Same as 1846.

——. A Christmas and New Year's or holiday present, with nine beautiful engravings. Boston, Otis, Broaders & Co., **1846.** vi p., 1 l., 9–296 p., 9 pl., 6¾ x 4½. L.C., N.Y., C.U., B.P., U.W. (43)

In some copies sub-title reads "A Christmas and New Year's present for 1846."
This has old Token plates.
There is an edition exactly like this but without date. L. C. (43a)

**Annual, The,** of the Board of Education of the General Assembly of the Presbyterian church in the U. S., ed. by John Breckinridge. [v. 1.] Philadelphia, Russell & Martien, **1832,** c. 1832. iv, 5–318 p., [5 pl.,] 5⅝ x 3½. F. (44)

**Annual, The,** [v. 2], **1833.** * (45)

—— —— [v. 3], **1834.** * (46)

—— ——, of the Board of Education of the Presbyterian church in the U. S., a New Year's offering for **1835,** ed. by John Breckinridge. Philadelphia, Joseph Whetham, 1835, c. 1834. 352 p., 6 pl., 5⅞ x 3¾. B.P. (47)

Engr. t. reads, Philadelphia, Russell & Martien, 1834.

**Annual souvenir gallery,** an illustrated gift book for all seasons, ed. by Emily Percival. Boston, Phillips, Sampson & Co., **1852,** c. 1851. 1 p. l., 294 p., 13 pl., 10½ x 7. F. (47a)

This is "Souvenir gallery," 1850, with last 2 p. omitted. See also "Souvenir annual," n. d.

**Annualette, The,** a Christmas and New Year's gift for children. Boston, Samuel G. Simpkins, **1840,** c. 1839. iv p., 1 l., 7–137 p., [4 pl. and engraved t., illus.,] 5⅞ x 3¾. N Y., B.P. (48)

—— ——, a Christmas and New Year's gift for children. Boston, William Crosby & Co., **1841,** c. 1840. 140 p., 1 l., [illus.,] 5¾ x 3⅝. N.Y. (49)

—— ——, a Christmas and New Year's gift for children. Boston, Wm. Crosby & Co., **1842,** c. 1842. iv, 5–137 p., [3 pl.,] 5⅝ x 3½. F. (50)

—— ——, a Christmas and New Year's gift for children Boston, T. H. Carter, **1843.** iv, 9–160 p., [3 pl.,] 5⅝ x 3½. B. P. (51)

—— ——, a Christmas and New Year's gift, ed. by a lady. Boston, T. H. Carter & Co., **1844,** c. 1843. xii, 13–142 p., 1 l., [colored front., illum. t 6 pl.,] 5¾ x 3½. N. Y. (52)

—— ——, a Christmas and New Year's gift, ed. by a lady. Boston, T. H. Carter & Co., **1845.** viii, 9–141 p., 6 pl., 6 x 3⅝. C.U. (53)
[There was no issue for 1846.]

—— ——, a Christmas and New Year's gift, ed. by a lady. Boston, Benjamin B. Mussey, **1847.** viii, 9–144 p., 4 pl., 6 x 4. F. (53a)

**Apples of gold** in pictures of silver, ed. by Edward B. Fellows. New York, Nafis & Cornish, **c. 1848.** xii, 13–264 p., 9 pl., 6 x 4. F. (54)

**Appleton's juvenile annual** for **1869,** a Christmas and New Year's gift for young people. New York, D. Appleton & Co., 1869, c. 1868. 382 p., 7 pl., 7 x 4¾. P.M. (55)

**Atkinson's casket.** See "Casket," 1826–1840.

**Atlantic souvenir, The,** a Christmas and New Year's gift. New York, Leavitt & Allen, **n. d.** [1853, 54 or 55]. viii 9–264 p., [6 pl.,] 7¼ x 5. "Rainbow bridge." N.Y., U W (56)

This is really "The token and Atlantic souvenir," Boston, 1840, with p. 265–304 omitted, and plates changed. See also "Honeysuckle," 1848, "Token of friendship," n. d., "Friendship's gift," n. d., "Moss rose," 1848.

—— ——, a Christmas and New Year's offering. **1826.** [v. 1.] Philadelphia, H. C. Carey & I. Lea. 2 p. l., 353 p., [engr. presentation pl., 7 pl.,] 5½ x 3½. N.Y., B.P. (57)

In slip case.

—— ——, a Christmas and New Year's offering. **1827.** [v. 2.] Philadelphia, H. C. Carey & I. Lea. x p., 1 l., 360 p., 10 pl., 5½ x 3½. N.Y., B.A., L.C. (58)

—— ——, a Christmas and New Year's offering. **1828.** [v. 3.] Philadelphia, Carey, Lea & Carey, c. 1827. xii, 384 p., 14 pl., 5½ x 3½. N.Y., B.P., L.C. (59)

Portions of 1827, 1828, reprinted in Spanish as El Aguinaldo, Filadelphia, 1829.

—— ——, a Christmas and New Year's offering. **1829.** [v. 4.] Philadelphia, Carey, Lea & Carey. c 1828. x p., 1 l., 360 p., 12 pl., 5½ x 3½. N.Y., B.P., L.C., U.W. (60)

—— ——, for **1830.** [v 5.] Philadelphia, Carey, Lea & Carey, 1830, c. 1829. xii, 13–328 p., 12 pl., 5¾ x 3¾. N.Y., B.P., L.C., U.W. (61)

—— ——, for **1831.** [v. 6.] Philadelphia, Carey & Lea, 1831. xii, 13–328 p., 13 pl. [including presentation pl.], 5¾ x 3¾. N.Y., B.P., U.W. (62)

—— ——, for **1832.** [v. 7.] Philadelphia, Carey & Lea, c. 1831. xii, 13–328 p., 12 pl., 6 x 3¾. N.Y., B.P., L.C., U.W. (63)

After 1832 The Atlantic souvenir was merged in "The Token."

**Atlantic souvenir, The,** for **1859.** New York, Derby & Jackson, 1859. viii p., 1 l., 11–288 p., 12 pl., 9¼ x 6¾. N.Y., B.A. (64)

**Autumn leaves.** Original pieces in prose and verse [ed by Anne W. Abbot]. Cambridge, John Bartlett, **1853,** c. 1853. vi p., 1 l., 200 p., 7 x 4⅝. B.A. (65)

**Baltimore book, The,** a Christmas and New Year's present, ed. by W. H. Carpenter and T. S. Arthur. Baltimore, Bayly & Burns, **1838.** viii, 9–296 p., 6 pl., 7¼ x 4½. N.Y. (66)

There is an edition with date erased on title, but with 1839 on back of publisher's cover. N.Y. (66a)

**Beauties of sacred literature,** ed. by Thomas Wyatt, Charlestown [Mass.], Ladies New England Art Union, **1852,** c. 1848. vi p., 1 l., 220 p., 8 pl., 9⅛x5¾. F. (67)

**Beauties, The, of the English annuals for 1835.** Hartford, Silas Andrus & Son, 1846. 2 p. l., 192 p., 7½ x 4½. P.M. (68)

Selections from Forget-me-not, Gem, Friendship's offering, and English annual, for 1835.

**Benison, The.** Name on back of publisher's leather cover of Lady's manual, N. Y., **1854.** B.P.

**Biographical annual,** containing memoirs of eminent persons recently deceased, ed. by R. W. Griswold. New York, Linen & Fennell. **1841.** c. 1840. xii., 13–307 p., front, 7⅜x4½. 12 mo. F (69)

**Book of beauty, The.** New York, Leavitt & Allen, **c. 1855.** 3 p. l., 17–290 p., 1 l., 8 pl., 9¼ x 6¾. C.U. (70)

—— ——. Late Victorian era, ed. and arranged by Mrs. F. Harcourt Williamson. New York and London, 2 vols, **1896.** (71)

—— ——. The era of King Edward VII, ed. by Mrs. F. H. Williamson. Philadelphia, J. B. Lippincott & Co., **1902.** (72)

**Book of flowers.** Title on back of "Flora and Thalia," Phila., 1836.

**Book of gems, The,** a gift for all seasons, by Eugene Sinclair. Manchester, N. H., Wm. H. Fisk, **1854,** c. 1850. x, 11–312 p., [3 pl. and illum. t.,] 6⅞ x 4¼. B.A. (73)

This is a reprint of " Gems for you," 1850.
Also reprinted in **1856.** * (73a)

**Book of pearls, The.** A choice garland of prose, poetry and art. New York, D. Appleton & Co. **1849.** 11–280 p., 20 pl., 9 x 6. L.C. (74)

**Book of the boudoir,** or memento of friendship. A gift for all seasons, ed. by Ellen Louise [Louise Chandler Moulton]. Boston, Phillips, Sampson & Co. **c. 1853.** viii, 9–400 p., 6 pl., 9½ x 7. N.Y., P.M. (75) There was also an issue of this, New York, W. H. Appleton, n. d. iv, vii–viii, 9–400 p., [8 pl. and illum. t.,] 8½ x 6¼. F. (76)

—— ——. N. Y. **1855.** * (77)

**Boston book, The,** being specimens of metropolitan literature, occasional and periodical, [ed. by Henry T. Tuckerman]. [v. 1.] Boston, Light & Haton, **1836,** c. 1835. xii, 13–312 p., 7½ x 4½. N.Y., C.U. (78)

—— ——, for **1837,** being specimens of metropolitan literature, ed. by B. B. Thatcher. [v. 2.] Boston, Light & Stearns, 1837, c. 1836. xii, 13–360 p., 7 x 4½. N.Y. (79)

—— ——, being specimens of metropolitan literature, [ed. by Geo. S. Hillard]. [v. 3.] Boston, George W. Light, **1841,** c. 1840. xii, 13–352 p., 7 x 4½. N.Y., C.U. (80)

—— ——, being specimens of metropolitan literature. [v. 4.] Boston, Ticknor, Reed & Fields, **1850,** c. 1849, viii, 364 p., front., 7¼ x 5½. N.Y., P.M. (81)

**Boudoir annual, The,** a Christmas, New Year and birthday present for **1846.** Boston, Phillips & Sampson, 1846, c. 1845. 4 p. l., 13–100 p., 16 pl., 11¼ x 9. N.Y. (82)

**Bouquet, The,** containing the language of flowers and their poetic sentiments, by a lady. Boston, Oliver L. Perkins, **1844,** c. 1844., 128 p. [5 pl.,] 4¼ x 2¾. F. (83)

—— ——, containing the poetry and language of flowers, by a lady. Boston, O. L. Perkins, **1845.** 1 p.l., 128 p., 1 pl., 4¼ x 2¾. L. (84)

Same as 1844. Also issued with imprint Benj. B. Mussey, 1845.

Also issued as "Bouquet of flowers," 1845.

**Bouquet of flowers, 1845.** Same as (83). * (84a)

**Boys' scrap book, The, 1839.** [Philadelphia] American Sunday school union. viii p., 1 l., 11–255 p., 6½ x 5⅛. L.C. (85)

**Bridal token, The,** or a hint to husbands. Pawtucket [R. I.], Smith & Stanley, **1846.** vi, 7–92 p., 4½ x 3 F. (86)

**Bridal wreath, The,** a wedding souvenir. Boston, **1848.** * (87)

**Brilliant, The,** a gift book, ed. by T. S. Arthur. New York, Charles Scribner, **n. d.** viii, 9–304 p., [15 pl.,] 8¼ x 6. F. (88)

Same as 1850.

—— ——, a gift book for **1850,** ed. by T. S. Arthur. [v. 1.] New York, Baker & Scribner, 1850. viii, 9–304 p., 15 pl., 8¼ x 6. H.U., U.W. (89)

Issued later by Charles Scribner, n. d.

Also issued for 1851 and identical with 1850, has list of 15 pl., and engr. front. not listed. N.Y. (89a)

**Buds and blossoms** for the young, by Mrs. Hughs. Philadelphia, Lindsay & Blakiston, **1850,** c. 1848. 205 p., [9 pl.,] 6¾ x 5¼. F. (90)

**Cabinet.** Philadelphia, J. Laval & S. F. Bradford, **c. 1829.** vi, 18, 13, 34, 20, 4, 3 p., 9 pl., 5⅞ x 3¾. F. (91)

A series of sketches of members of the national administration, each paged separately. This is also bound up with "Talisman," 1830, and lettered on back of pub. [?] cloth case, "Cabinet and talisman." F.

**Cabinet annual, The,** a Christmas and New Year's gift for **1855.** Philadelphia, E. H. Butler & Co., 1855, c. 1854. xiv p, 1 l., 19–264 p., 24 pl., 7¾ x 5½. H.U., C.U. (92)

**Cabinet of modern art.** Philadelphia, E. H. Butler & Co., **n. d.** [1st series.] 264 p., 25 pl., 7¾ x 5½. "Mary of our village." F. (93)

—— ——. Second series. Philadelphia, E. H. Butler & Co., **1852,** c. 1851. xiv p., 1 l., 17–264 p., 25 pl., 7¾ x 5⅝. F. (94)

**Casket, The,** or flowers of literature, wit, and sentiment for 1826–40. Philadelphia, S. C. Atkinson. (95)

These are really magazines, not annuals.

**Casket, The,** a gift book for all seasons, illustrated. Boston, Phillips & Sampson, **n. d.** vi p., 1 l., 9–322 p., 6 pl., 7¼ x 5. "The quiet eye." N.Y., B.A. (96)

Also issued by Leavitt & Allen, New York, n. d. Same as "Casket" [1853]. N. Y.

See note under "Amaranth," 1849, which this really is, with change of first pages [9–12] and plates.

—— ——, a Christmas and New Year's present for children and young persons, **1829.** Boston, Bowles & Dearborn, c. 1828. viii, 268 p., 7 pl. [only 5 listed], 5¾ x 3½. B.P. (97)

—— ——, or youth's pocket library. Hingham [Mass.], C. & E. B. Gill, **1834**, c. 1829. 4th ed. improved. 256 p., [6 pl.,] 5¼ x 3¼. F. (98)

—— —— of entertaining and useful reading. New York, Chas. S. Francis & Co., **1843.** 287 p., pl., 6¾ x 4. P.M. (99)

This is the third series of the library of entertaining and useful knowledge, each having a different name.

—— ——, a souvenir for **1845.** New York, Edward Kearny. xxiv, 25–395 p., [6 pl.,] 7 x 4¼. U.W. (100)

—— ——, a gift book for all seasons, illustrated, Boston, Phillips, Sampson & Co., n. d. [**pref. Aug.. 1853**]. vi p., 1 l., 9–322 p., 6 pl., 7¼ x 4½. "The quiet eye." P.M. (101)

This is really "Amaranth," 1849 [which see] with p. 9–12 replaced with two poems, and with variations in plates. This "Casket" was also issued entirely without date both by Phillips, Sampson & Co., Boston, and by Leavitt & Allen, New York, also by Phillips, Sampson & Co., Boston, with preface dated Aug., 1854.

See also "Garland," 1850, "Token of friendship" [1852], "Keepsake of friendship 1851, "Memory's gift," N. Y., n. d., and N. Y., 1869, "Magnolia," 1852.

**Casket of gems, The,** a gift for all seasons, **1863.** Boston, William H. Hill, Jr., 1863. 5–93 p. incl. 9 illus., 5¾ x 4½. F. (102)

**Casket of love, The,** from the most celebrated authors. Philadelphia, Henry F. Anners, **n. d.** 7–120 p., 4½ x 2¾. F. (103)

**Catholic keepsake, The,** ed. by Prof. Walter. Philadelphia, M. Fithian, Aug. 16, **1845.** vi. 9–252 p., 9 pl., 7½ x 3¾. * (104)

Also issued from Baltimore, Murphy & Co., n. d., with same text, but none of the pl. except illum. t. "A legacy regained." L.C. (104a)

**Cecilian gift, The,** or romances of the musicians. New York, Leavitt & Allen, **n. d.** 259 p., 7 pl., 7½ x 5½. * (105)

**Centre table, The,** illustrated by 50 fine engravings. New York, Leavitt & Allen, **1860.** 5–264 p, 50 pl. 9⅞ x 7½. U.M. (106)

**Charleston book, The,** a miscellany of prose and verse Charleston, Samuel Hart, Sen., **1845**, c. 1844. viii, 404 p., 7½ x 4½. N.Y., L.C. (107)

**Charm,** a book for boys and girls, illustrated. Boston, Phillips, Sampson & Co., **c. 1854.** iv p., 1 l., 7–167 p. 7 pl., 6½ x 4¾. F. (108)

**Children's annual,** a Christmas, New-Year and every-day gift book for **1853,** by Mrs. Colman. New York, S. Raynor, 1853, c. 1852. 216 p., 10 pl., 6 x 3½. P.M. (109)

**Children's garland, The,** from the best poets. Selected and arranged by Coventry Patmore, **1863.** Cambridge [Mass.], Sever & Francis, 1863. xii, 354 p., illum. t., 6⅝ x 4¼. F. (110)

**Child's annual, The,** or conversations instructive and entertaining for the use of children, by a lady. Philadelphia, Thos. T. Ash, **1831.** 190 p., 12 col. pl., 5¾ x 3½. H.U. (111)

—— ——. Boston, Allen & Ticknor, **1834,** c. 1833. vi, 192 p., [16 pl.,] 5¾ x 3½. H.U., L.C. (112)

—— ——. Boston, William D. Ticknor, **1837.** vi, 192 p., 17 pl., 5¾ x 3⅝. F. (113)

**Child's first gift, The,** for **1848.** Collected and prepared by Amos Smith, Jr. Boston, Edwin J. Mann, 1848. 1 p. l., 5–48 p., 5⅝ x 4⅜. F. (114)

**Child's gem, The.** New York, **1833.** * (115)

—— ——. New York, Samuel Colman, **c. 1838.** [v. 2.] 2 p. l., 7–144 p., 3½ x 2⅞. F. (116)

—— ——, for **1842,** ed. by a lady. New York, S. Colman, c. 1841. x p, 1 l., 13–144 p., 12 pl., 4½ x 3¾. L.C. (117)

—— ——, for **1844.** Ed. by Mrs. S. Colman. * (118)

—— ——. Boston, T. H. Carter & Co., **1845.** * (119)

**Child's keepsake, The.** 1st ed. * (120)

—— ——, a book of original poems for the young, by E. Porter Dyer. 2d ed. enlarged. Boston, C. Stone, **1854,** c. 1852. viii, 9–128 p., front., 4½ x 3. F (120a)

**Child's Token.** New York, S. Colman, **1842.** * (121)

**Christian comforter, The.** 1st ed. * (121a)

**Christian diadem, The,** and family keepsake, a repository of religious and literary gems, ed. by Z. Paten Hatch. New York, v. 1, **1851.** iv, 5–308 p., 12 pl. 9 x 5¾. B.A. (122)

Really a magazine.

—— ——, and family keepsake, a gift book for all seasons. In two parts. Ed. by Z. Paten Hatch. New York, **1853.** 11–212, 5–202, iii–iv p., 13 pl., 8⅞ x 5¾. B.A. (123)

Really a magazine.
Also pub. in 1855.

**Christian family annual,** by Rev. Daniel Newell. New York, [v. 1,] **1843.** vii, 300 p., pl., 8½ x 5½. B.P. (124)

Really "The Christian family magazine," which is issued at end of year as an annual, v. 1, Sept. 1841 — Ag. 42. Also issued as "Christian family magazine or parents' and children's annual," 1842, c. 1842.

—— ——, **1844.** New York. [v. 2.] 302 p. (125)

This is vol. 2 of "Christian family magazine," Sept., 1842 — Ag. 1843.

—— ——, for **1845,** ed. by Rev. Daniel Newell. [v. 3.] New York. 432 p., 24 pl., 8¾ x 5¾. F. (126)

This is also issued without date. It is the "Christian family magazine," vol. 3.

**Christian keepsake, The,** a Christmas & New Year's gift, ed by Mrs. L. H. Sigourney. New York, Leavitt & Allen, **n. d.** [1856 or after]. 262 p., 6 pl., 7 x 5. "The infant St. John." C.U. (127)

This is "Religious souvenir," 1839, with different pl. and p. 263–88 omitted.

—— ——, and missionary annual, ed. by Rev. John A. Clark, **1838.** [v. 1.] Philadelphia, Wm. Marshall & Co., c. 1837. viii, 9–312 p., 11 pl., 6½ x 4½. N.Y., B.A., U.W. (128)

—— —— and missionary annual, ed. by Rev. John A. Clark, **1839.** [v. 2.] Philadelphia, Wm. Marshall & Co., c. 1838. viii, 9–312 p., 10 pl., 7½ x 5. N.Y., B.P., U.W. (129)

—— —— and missionary annual, ed. by Rev. John A. Clark, **1840.** [v. 3.] Philadelphia, Wm. Marshall & Co., c. 1839. viii, 9–320 p., 9 pl., 7¼ x 4¾. N.Y., B.A., U.W. (130)

—— —— and missionary annual for **1847.** Boston, Phillips, Sampson & Co., 1847, c. 1846. viii, 13–316 p., 9 pl., 7¼ x 4¾. N.Y., B.P., U.W. (131)

—— ——, and missionary annual for **1848.** Philadelphia, Brower, Hayes & Co., 1848, c. 1847. viii, 13–316 p., 9 pl., 7¼ x 4¾. N.Y., B.P., U.W. (132)

—— —— and missionary annual for **1849.** Philadelphia, Brower, Hayes & Co., 1849, c. 1848. vi p., 1 l., 13–330 p., 9 pl., 7 x 4½. N.Y., B.P., U.W. (133)

—— ——, or friendship's memorial, a gift for all seasons ed. by Rev. Enoch Hutchinson. Nashua, N. H., J. M. Fletcher, **1850.** vi, 7–338 p. [7 pl.,] 9 x 5½. F. (133a)

**Christian offering** for **1832.** Boston, Lincoln & Edmands, 1832, c. 1831. viii, 231 p., [7 pl.,] 6¼ x 4¼. N.Y., B.P., (134)

Reprinted in 1837 and 1844 with slight change. See below.

**Christian Offering.** Boston, James B. Dow, **1837,** c. 1831. viii 231 p., front., engr. t., 6 x 3¾. B.P. (135)

Reprint of 1832 except front. is different and all other plates except engr. t. omitted. See also 1844.

—— —— and churchman's annual, ed. by Rev. John W. Brown. New York, Sherman & Trevett, **1839,** c. 1838. x p., 1 l., 13–204 p., 7¼ x 4½. N.Y. (136)

—— —— Boston, James B. Dow, **1844,** c. 1831. viii, 231 p., front., engr. t., 6⅛ x 3¾. B.P. (137)

Same as 1837. Engr. t. dated 1843. Reprint of 1832, with different front., and with other pl. except engr. t. omitted.

**Christian parlor book.** New York, **1845** et seq.

This is the title given vols. of "Christian parlor magazine" when issued as an annual.

—— —— Devoted to science, literature and religion. New York, George Pratt, **1851.** iv, 358 p., 25 pl., 9¾ x 6½. N.Y. (138)

—— ——, **1852.** * (139)

**Christian souvenir, The,** an offering for Christmas and the New Year, ed. by Isaac F. Shepard. [v. 1.] Boston, Henry B. Williams, **1843,** c. 1842. 304 p., 6 pl., 6¾ x 4¼. N.Y., L.C., U.W. (140)
This was also issued with 1844 on the back of cover, otherwise identical. H.U., B.P., B.A. (141)

—— ——, ed. by Rev. H. D. Moore. v. 1, Philadelphia, F. C. Wilson, **1847.** 384 p., pl., 8 x 5¼. (142)

Really a magazine. See "Christian wreath."

—— —— and missionary annual for **1851.** Auburn [N. Y.], Derby & Miller, 1851. 4 p.l., 372 p., [6 pl.,] 7⅜ x 4¾. N.Y., B.P. (143)

Illum. t. reads "Christian souvenir and missionary memorial."

This is "Missionary memorial," N. Y. 1846, with different pl.

Also issued as "Christ's messenger," 1848, and "The Evergreen," N. Y., n. d.

—— ——, an illustrated annual, New York, **1858.** * (144)

**Christian wreath.** Philadelphia, **1847.** [vol. 1.] N. Y. (144a)

Really a monthly periodical.

**Christian year, The,** or thoughts in verse for the Sundays and holydays throughout the year. 3d Amer. ed. Philadelphia, Lee & Blanchard, **1842,** c. 1834. xvi, 17–320 p., 6½ x 4⅛. L.C. (145)

**Christian's annual, The,** a miscellany for **1846.** Philadelphia, Henry F. Anners, 1846. 288 p., 9 pl., 6 x 4. L.C., B.P., C U. (146)

**Christian's gift, The,** ed. by Rufus W. Clark. Boston John P. Jewett & Co., **1857,** c. 1856. vi p., 1 l., 9–308 p., 7 pl., 8¼ x 5½. N.Y. (147)

**Christmas blossoms** and New Year's wreath for **1847.** [v. 1.] Boston, Phillips & Sampson, 1847, c. 1846. iv p., 2 l., 7–168 p., 6 pl., 7 x 5¼. B.P., L.C., U.W. (148)

—— ——, and New Year's wreath for **1848,** by Uncle Thomas. [v. 2.] Boston, Phillips & Sampson, 1848, c. 1847. 3 p. l., 17–168 p., 6 pl., 7 x 5. L.C., B.A. (149)

Phillips & Sampson continued their series by issuing in 1849 "Christmas roses," Boston, while "Christmas blossoms" was taken over by a Philadelphia publisher for 1849.

—— ——, and New Year's wreath for **1849,** by Uncle Thomas. [v. 3.] Philadelphia, E. H. Butler & Co., 1849, c. 1848. 3 p.l., 17–176 p., 6 pl., 7 x 5. P.M. (150)

—— ——, and New Year's wreath for **1855,** by Uncle Thomas. [v. 4.] Philadelphia, E. H. Butler & Co., 1850, c. 1849. 3 p.l., 17–176 p., 6 pl., 7 x 4¼. L.C. (151)

—— ——, and New Year's wreath for **1851,** by Uncle Thomas. [v. 5.] Philadelphia, E. H. Butler & Co., 1851, c. 1850. 3 p.l., 17–256 p., 6 pl., 7 x 5. N.Y., L.C., B.A., U.W. (152)

—— ——, and New Year's wreath for **1852,** by Uncle Thomas. [v. 6.] Philadelphia, E. H. Butler & Co., 1852, c. 1851. xiv p., 1 l., 17–256 p., 6 pl., 7 x 5¼. L.C., U.W. (153)

—— ——, and New Year's wreath for **1854.** Philadelphia, E. H. Butler & Co., 1854, c. 1853. xiii–xiv p., 1 l., 17–256 p., 6 pl., 6⅞ x 5¼. L.C., N.Y. (154)

**Christmas garland,** a miscellany of verses, stories and essays. Chicago, H. Stone & Co., **1901.** (155)

**Christmas roses** and New Year's gift for **1849.** Boston, Phillips & Sampson, 1849, c. 1848. 3 p. l., 17–180 p., 6 pl., 7 x 5¼. H.U., B.A. (156)

Follows v. 2 of "Christmas blossoms," 1848, as that series had been taken over by a Phila. publisher.

—— —— and New Year's gift, a present for young people. Boston, Phillips & Sampson, n. d., **c. 1848.** 3 p. l., 17–180 p., 3 pl., 7 x 5½. C.U. (157)

"A second edition [of 1849] from same plates, with a slight change in title, and lessening somewhat the number of engravings." (Advertisement.)

**Christmas tales.** Boston, Munroe & Francis, **n. d.** 288 p., 5½ x 3½. N.Y. (158)

Made up from articles destined for "Forget me not," but crowded out.

**Christmas tribute, The,** and New Year's gift, a souvenir for **1851.** Philadelphia, E. H. Butler & Co., 1851, c. 1850. 3 p. l., 13–329 p., 9 pl., 7¼ x 4½. N.Y., B. P., U.W. (159)

Also issued without date.

**Christmastide.** Boston, **1878.** * (160)

**Christ's messenger,** or The Missionary memorial. New York, E. Walker, **1848,** c. 1845. 4 p. l., 372 p., [6 pl.,] 7⅜ x 4½. F. (160a)

This is "Missionary memorial," 1846, with different pl. Also issued as "Christian souvenir," 1851, and "The Evergreen," N. Y., n. d.

**Churchman's annual.** Title on back of "Christian offering," 1839.

**Cloud crystals,** a snow flake album collected and edited by a lady. New York, Appleton & Co., **1864,** c. 1863. 158 p., 28 pl. and illum. t., 10 x 7½. L.C., B.A., U.W. (161)

Also issued with date, 1865; and reprinted in 1883.

**Comic annual.** Title on back of "American comic annual," 1831.

**Companion and token.** Title on back of "Young lady's companion."

**Compliment for the season, A. 1832.** New York, N. B. Holmes. viii, 9–216 p., [4 pl.,] 5⅞ x 3¾. B.A. (161a)

**Coral, The,** a gift for all seasons, illus. with 8 beautiful steel engravings, ed. by Henry W. Herbert. New York, Cornish, Lamport & Co. **n. d.** v, 9–300 p., 8 pl., 7¼ x 4½. "The magnolia. 'Not in the autumn.'" N.Y. (162)

Some copies have 1851 on back of cover. P.M.
This is "Magnolia," 1836, with changed plates. See also "Aloe," 1854, "Friendship's token," N. Y., n. d., "Gift of affection," n. d., "Morning Glory," n. d., "Memory," c. 1854, "Snow flake," n. d.

**Coronal, The,** and young lady's remembrancer, ed. by Rev. Frederic Janes. New York, James H. Pratt & Co., **1853,** c. 1852. vi p., 1 l., 9–384 p., 10 pl., 8¼ x 5¾. B.A., P.M. (163)

**Coronet, The,** or choice gems for the home circle. Philadelphia, J. B. Lippincott & Co., **n. d.** viii, 9–304 p., 10 pl., 9 x 6⅛. "Blanche Evelyn." F. (164)

**Crystal fount, The,** for all seasons, ed. by T. S. Arthur, New York, Cornish, Lamport & Co., **n. d.** [circ. 1854.] viii, 9–320 p., 10 pl., 7¾ x 5½. "The fountain." U.W. (165)

**Crystal gem, The,** John S. Adams, ed. Boston, J. Buffum, **c. 1853.** 96 p., 3 x 2. "Water." L.C. (166)

**Dahlia, The,** a memorial of affection for **1842,** ed. by a lady. New York, James P. Giffing, c. 1841. 180 p., 6 pl., 6 x 3¾. F. (167)

**Dew drop, The,** a tribute of affection, for **1852.** [v. 1.] Philadelphia, Lippincott, Grambo & Co., 1852, c. 1851. x p., 1 l., 13–316 p., 9 pl., 7¼ x 4½. B.P. (168)

—— ——, a tribute of affection for **1853.** Philadelphia, Lippincott, Grambo & Co., 1853, c. 1852. x p., 1 l., 13–328 p., 8 pl., 7¼ x 4¾. N.Y., B.A. (169)

—— ——. Title on cover of "Dew-drops of the nineteenth century," 1854.

**Dew-drops of the nineteenth century,** gathered and presented in their brightness and purity by Seba Smith. Floral department by John B. Newman. New York, J. K. Wellman, **1846–7,** c. 1845. viii,9–216 p., [8 col pl. of flowers,] 7½ x 4½. B.A. (170)

This was reissued as "Gift of friendship," for 1848, N. Y., with 6 steel plates, but no flower plates, though floral department is present. Also reissued as "Keepsake," 1848.

Also issued without "The floral department," and without plates, N. Y., 1846, c. 1845, 203 p. B. P. (170a)

—— ——, gathered and preserved in their brightness and purity by Seba Smith. Floral department by John B. Newman. New York, Lamport, Blakeman & Law, **1854.** viii, 9–216 p., 5 steel pl. and col. t., 7¼ x 4¾. B.P. (171)

This is same as 1846–7, except by different publisher and having 5 pl. added. and the col. flower pl. omitted. Back of cover reads, "Dew drop."

See also "Gift of friendship," N. Y., 1848, "Keepsake," 1848.

**Diadem, The,** for **1845,** a present for all seasons, with splendid engravings. [v. 1.] Philadelphia, Carey & Hart, 1845. 2 p.l., 9–100 p., [11 pl. and engr. t.,] 11 x 8¾. N.Y., B.P. (172)

—— ——, for **1846,** a present for all seasons, with ten engravings. [v. 2.] Philadelphia, Carey & Hart, 1846, c. 1845. 96 p., 10 pl., 10¾ x 8½. B.P., P.M. (173)

—— ——, for **1847,** a present for all seasons, with ten engravings. [v. 3.] Philadelphia, Carey & Hart, 1847, c. 1846. 100 p., [10 pl.,] 10¾ x 9. N.Y., B.A. (174)

—— ——, a souvenir for the drawing room and parlor and gift book for all seasons, illustrated with twelve steel engravings by first artists, ed. by Emily Percival. Boston, Phillips, Sampson & Co., n. d., **c. 1853.** 4 p. l., 11–288 p., 12 pl., 9¾ x 7½. N.Y., B.P. (175)

Also issued without date or c. date. H.U. (175a)

**Diadem, The,** a souvenir for the drawing room and parlor, and gift book for all seasons, ed. by Emily Percival. New York, W. H. Appleton, **n. d.** 4 p. l., 11–288 p., [10 pl. and illum. t.,] 8½ x 6¼. N.Y. (176)

This is identical with 1853, except smaller size, and omitting 2 pl. and adding illum. t.
Also issued by Leavitt & Allen, New York, n. d. 3 p. l., 11–288 p., [12 pl.,] 9¾ x 7¾. F.

**Dial of love, The,** a Christmas book for the young, by Mary Howitt, illustrated. Philadelphia, Lindsay & Blakiston, **1857.** 4 p. l., 13–189 p., 9 pl., 7 x 4⅝. F. (177)

Probably American reprint of English magazine of this name.

**Domestic and religious offering.** Sub-title and title on back of cover of "Fireside poetical readings," 1843.

**Drawing-room annual, The,** a present for all seasons. Philadelphia, Lindsay & Blakiston, n. d. [**1843**]. vi p., 1 l., 9–64 p., 15 pl., 8⅛ x 8⅛. "Ella." L.C. (178)

**Drawing room scrap-book, The,** with twenty illustrations, ed. by Amelia W. Lawrence. Philadelphia, Carey & Hart, **1850,** c. 1850. 102 p., [20 pl.,] 10½ x 8¼. N.Y. (179)

**Drops from Flora's cup,** or the poetry of flowers. Boston, G. W. Cottrell & Co., **c. 1845.** x, 11–160 p., col. front., col. t., 5⅝ x 3½. L.C. (180)

Also issued by Oliver L. Perkins, Boston, 1846, c. 1845, otherwise identical except col. front. is different, and size 4½ x 2⅞.

**Eclectic gift-book, The,** for the holidays, **1859–60.** New York, W. H. Bidwell, 1859-60. 1–12, 1–284 p. F. (181)

This is "Eclectic magazine," v. 48, 1859 with 6 p. l. [p. 1–12], and 5 pl. inserted at beginning.

**Educational annual.** Title on back of "Annual of the board of education of the general assembly of the Presbyterian church in the United States."

**El Aguinaldo.** See note under "Atlantic souvenir," 1828.

**Emblem, The,** a gift for all seasons, with new and elegant illustrations. New York, Leavitt & Allen, **n. d.** [1856 or after]. viii, 9–263 p., 6 pl., 7¼ x 4¾. P.M., B.A. (182)

**Emerald, The,** a collection of graphic and entertaining tales, brilliant poems and essays gleaned chiefly from fugitive literature of the nineteenth century, ed. by Epes Sargent. Boston, John L. Shorey, **1866.** vi, 3–316 p., 6¾ x 4¼. P. M. (183)

The "Gem" series began with this and pub. announce it will be followed by Sapphire, Amethyst, Topaz, Diamond, etc.

**Evergreen, The,** a Christmas, New Year and birthday gift. New York, Leavitt & Allen, **n. d.** [circa 1858]. 4 p. l., 252 p., 6 pl., 7¼ x 5. N.Y., B.A., U.W. (184)

This is "Missionary memorial," 1846, with p. 253–372 omitted, a proem added, and pl. added.

See also "Christ's messenger," and "Christian souvenir,' 1851.

—— ——, Philadelphia, American Sunday School Union, **1837.** vi p., 1 l., 9–159 p., 8 pl., 5⅝ x 4⅜. P.M., U.W. (185)

—— ——, or church offering for all seasons, ed. by Joseph Salkeld. v. 1. New Haven, **1844.** 380 p., illus. U.W. (185a)

Really a monthly magazine, issued at end of year as an annual, 1843-53.

—— ——, for **1847,** a present for all seasons, embellished with ten elegant steel engravings. Philadelphia, Carey & Hart, 1847, c. 1846. xii, 13–300 p., 10 pl., 9¼ x 6. N.Y., B.A. (186)

—— ——, or gems of literature for **1850,** ed. by Rev. Edward A. Rice. New York, J. C. Burdick, 1850. iv, 7-308 p., 12 pl.,[8 pl.,] 8¾ x 5¾. N.Y. (186a)

A magazine. Plates vary from list.

**Excelsior annual, The,** or pupils' gift for **1849,** ed. by Edward B. Fellows. New York, Nafis & Cornish, c. 1848. xii, 13–264 p., 10 pl., 6½ x 4½. N.Y., L.C., U.W. (187)

All written by pupils in New York City.

**Fables of Flora,** ed. by Miss S. C. Edgarton. Lowell, Powers & Bagley, **c. 1844.** iv, 5–144 p., col. front., 4⅜ x 2¾. L.C. (188)

**Family circle, The,** its affections and pleasures, ed. by H. A. Graves. Boston, Gould, Kendall & Lincoln. **c. 1843.** vi, 7–128 p., 4½ x 2¾. F. (188a)

Also issued with **1845,** on title, c. 1843, and also with only date c. 1843. F (188b)

This with "Marriage ring," and a special t. and preface prefixed, was issued as "Wedding gift."

**Family circle** and parlor annual, N.Y. vols. 1-14 1843–1856, ed. by Rev. D. Newell, and later by Mrs D. Newell. Really was a magazine, "Family circle." B.P.

See "Parlor annual," another of its annual titles, and "Youth's parlor annual."

**Fireside poetical readings,** . . . designed as a domestic and religious offering. Collected and pub. by Dexter S. King. Boston, **1843,** c. 1842. ii, 3–313 p., [1 pl.,] 7½ x 4½. In two parts. Part I, Domestic offering; Part II., Religious offering. B.P., C.U. (189)

Back of book reads "Domestic and religious offering."

**Flora and Thalia,** or gems of flowers and poetry, by a lady. Philadelphia, Carey, Lea & Blanchard, **1836.** 7–240 p., many col. pl. of flowers, 5¼ x 3½. F. (190).

Back of book reads, "Book of flowers."

**Floral fortune teller,** a game for the season of flowers, by Miss S. C. Edgarton. Boston, A. Tompkins, **1848,** c. 1846, vi p., 1 l., 9–160 p., illum. t., 4⅝ x 2½. F. (190a)

**Floral gems,** or the songs of the flowers, by Mrs. J. Thayer. 3d ed. Boston, James French, **1847,** c. 1846. iv, 5–128 p., front., 4¼ x 2¾. F. (190b)

**Floral keepsake, The,** with 30 engravings elegantly colored from nature, ed. by John Keese. New York, Leavitt & Allen, **n. d.** [1853, 54, or 55]. 112 p., 30 pl., 10 x 7¾. L.C., U.W. (191)

Same as 1850, but with less plates. Reissued Leavitt & Allen, 1854. Also reissued n. d. [1856, or a little later], Leavitt & Allen, New York. F. (191a)

—— ——, for **1850,** with 46 colored engravings, ed. by John Keese. New York, Leavitt & Co., 1850. 112 p., 46 pl., 9½ x 7⅛. F. (192)

—— ——, with 30 engravings . . . etc. New York, Leavitt & Allen, **1854.** Same as n. d. above. F. (192a)

**Floral offering, The,** a token of friendship, ed. by Frances S. Osgood. Philadelphia, Carey & Hart, **1847,** c. 1846. 1 p. l., signatures 3–32 [each 4 p.], 10½ x 8¾. B.A. (193)

—— ——, a token of affection and esteem . . . by Henrietta Dumont. Philadelphia, H. C. Peck & Theo. Bliss, **1853,** c. 1851. 300 p., [6 col. pl. of flowers]. C.U. (194)

Also an ed. identical except imprint, Theodore Bliss & Co., 1863, c. 1851. C.U. (194a)

**Floral wreath, The,** an offering of friendship, John S. Adams, ed. Boston, J. Buffum, **c. 1851.** 96 p., 3 x 2. L.C. (195)

**Floral wreath** and treasury of entertaining and useful knowledge. v. 1, **1848,** New York, ed. and pub. by Rev. D. Newell.

Really a magazine.

**Floral year, The,** by Mrs. Anna Peyre Dinnies. Boston, Benj. B. Mussey, **1847,** c. 1845. xii, 13–265, 12 pl., 7¾ x 5¾. U.W. (196)

**Flora's album,** ed. by John S. Adams. New York, Leavitt, Trow & Co., **1848.** 128 p., col. front. 32mo. L.C. (197)

**Flora's gem,** or the bouquet for all seasons, ed. by A. A Phillips. New York, Nafis, Cornish & Co., [circa **1848**]. viii, 103 p., 10 pl., 9⅜ x 7⅝. * (198)

**Flora's interpreter,** or the American book of flowers and sentiments, by Mrs. Sarah Josepha Hale. 14th ed. improved. Boston, Thomas H. Webb. [circa **1847**]. c. 1833. x p., 1 l., 13–262 p., 1 l. [2 pl.,] 7¼ x 4½. F. (199)

The 1st ed. was c. 1833; the 6th had new preface date, 1837, and "improved" added to title.
This was republished in London as "Book of flowers," without permission.

—— ——, and fortuna flora, by Mrs. Sarah Josepha Hale. Boston, Sanborn, Carter, Bazin & Co., **c. 1848.** x p., 1 l., 13–288 p., 4 pl., 7¼ x 4¼. U.W. (199a)

A new edition of "Flora's interpreter" published 16 years before, with "Fortuna flora" added.

**Flora's lexicon,** an interpretation of the language of flowers with an outline of botany and a poetical introduction by Catharine H. Waterman. Boston, Phillips, Sampson & Co., **1852**, c. 1839. 252 p., 4 pl., 7½ x 4¾. F. (200)

Reissued in 1857 without change. F.

**Flower garden, The,** or chapters on flowers, a sequel to "Floral biography," by Charlotte Elizabeth. New York, M. W. Dodd, **1840.** iv, 5–330 p., engr. t., 7¼ x 4½. F. (201)

**Flower vase, The,** containing the language of flowers and their poetic sentiments by Miss S. C. Edgarton. Lowell, Powers & Bagley, **1844,** c. 1843. iv p., 1 l., 7–157 p., col. front., 4⅜ x 2¾ U.W. (202)

The same was issued in 1847 and again in 1848. Lowell, c. 1843, Merrill & Heywood, and in 1850, Lowell, Joshua Merrill. F.

**Floweret, The,** a gift of love, by Miss A. M. Wells. Boston, T. H. Carter & Co. * (203)

**Flowers of literature** and ladies' keepsake, a selection from some of the best authors of England, Scotland, Swisserland [sic] and America, by a lady of Rhode Island. Providence, Albert C. Greene, **1850,** c. 1850. 142 p., 7 x 4⅛. N.Y. (204)

**Flowers of loveliness,** a token of remembrance for **1852.** Philadelphia, Henry F. Anners, c. 1851. 288 p., 9 pl., 9¼ x 6½. L.C. (205)

**Forget-me-not,** or the philipena, Lowell, **n. d.** * (206)
Same as 1846.

—— ——, a Christmas, New Year and birthday gift. New York, Leavitt & Allen, **n. d.** 2 p. l., 7–260 p., [6 pl.,] 7⅞ x 5¾. "The prior of St. Michael." C.U., P.M., U.W. (207)

This is "Pearl," Phila. 1853, with p. 261–70 omitted and variation in plates.

There is also an ed. pub. by Geo. A. Leavitt, n. d. [circa 1869]. F (207a)
Also issued as "Passion flower," c.1854, "Pearl Gift," n. d., and "Philopœna," n. d.

**Forget me not, The,** a gift for all seasons. New York. Nafis & Cornish, **n. d.** [circa 1845]. vi, 7–232 p., [9 pl.,] 5⅞ x 3¾. "The young Tyrolese." H.U., U.W. (208)

This is "The lily," 1831, with pl. changed, otherwise the same throughout. Even the preface speaks of it as "Lily."

**Forget-me-not,** a gift for **1846,** ed. by Alfred A. Phillips. New York, Nafis & Cornish, c. 1845. xii, 9–282 p., 7 pl., 6 x 3¾. N.Y. (209)

—— ——, or the philopene by Mrs. J. S. F. Lunt, Lowell, Nathaniel L. Dayton, **1846,** c. 1845. vi., 7-128 p. col. t. 4½ x 2¾. F. (209a)

Reissued in 1847, and 1852 with change in spelling of sub-t.

**Forget-me-not, The,** or the philipena, by Mrs. Lunt. Lowell, Nathaniel L. Dayton, **1847,** c. 1845. vi, 7–128 p., col. front., 4½ x 2¾. U.W. (210)

Lettered "Philipena" on back of cover. Same as 1846.
Also issued without d. P.M. (210a)
There is an ed. d. 1852. F.
This was also pub. under title "Philipena," 1847.

—— —— for **1848,** ed. by Alfred A. Phillips. Nafis & Cornish, 1848, c. 1847. vi p., 1 l., 9–307 p., 9 pl., 7½ x 4¼. N.Y., P.M. (211)

—— —— for **1849,** ed. by Alfred A. Phillips. New York, Nafis & Cornish, 1849, c. 1848. viii, 9–318 p., 1 l., 8 pl., 7⅛ x 4½. N.Y. (212)

—— —— for **1850,** ed. by Mrs. Emeline S. Smith. New York, Nafis & Cornish, c. 1849. x, 11–310 p., 8 pl. [only 7 on list], 7¼ x 4¾. N.Y., L.C., U.W. (213)

—— —— for **1851,** ed. by Mrs. Emeline S. Smith. New York, Cornish, Lamport & Co., c. 1850. vi p., 1 l., 9–312 p., 8 pl., 7¼ x 4¼. B.P., U.W. (214)

—— ——, for all seasons, ed. by Ida Maitland. New York, Lamport, Blakeman & Law, **c. 1851.** 264 p., 7 pl., 6⅛ x 4½. N.Y., C.U. (215)

—— ——, or the philipena, by Mrs. Lunt. Lowell, Nathaniel L. Dayton, **1852,** c. 1845. vi, 7–128 p., 5⅜ x 3⅝. F. (216)

Same as 1846, except larger in size.

—— ——, a Christmas, New Year and birthday gift. New York, Leavitt & Allen, **c. 1855.** 5–264 p., 7 pl., 7¼ x 5. "The seaman's wife." N.Y., B.P. (217)

Also issued as "Philopœna," n. d. and "Glen annual," n. d.

**Fountain, The,** a gift, ed. by H. Hastings Weld. Philadelphia, William Sloanaker, **1847,** c. 1846. iv p., 1 l., 7–252 p., 8 pl., 8¼ x 5¼. L.C., B.P. (218)

**Freedom's gift,** or sentiments of the free. Hartford, S. S. Cowles, **1840,** c. 1840. viii, 9–108 p., engr front., 7⅛ x 4¼. F. (219)

**Freemason's gift,** a Christmas and New Year's offering. New York, Leavitt & Allen, **n. d.** [1853, 54 or 55]. viii, 9–263 p., 4 pl., 7⅛ x 5. L.C. (220)

Called "Masonic offering" at top of p. 9.

**Friendship.** New York, Leavitt & Allen, **c. 1854.** 2 p. l., vii–viii, 9–264 p., 8 pl., 7¼ x 4¾. "Cecelia." C.U. (221)

Illuminated title reads "Friendship, a souvenir," and back of cover, "Friendship's token."
Also issued as "Passion flower," n. d., "Moss rose," n. d. Pl. vary.

**Friendship's gift,** a Christmas and New Year's annual. New York, Leavitt & Allen, **n. d.** 2 p. l., 11–264 p. [6 pl.,] 7¼ x 5⅞. "The carpenter's daughter." L.C. (222)

The same is issued with Pub. George A. Leavitt, n. d. [circa 1869]. C.U.
This is "Friendship's offering," c. 1855, with different pl. and list of illus. omitted.
See also "Gem annual," n. d., "Lady's annual," n. d

—— ——, a Christmas and New Year's annual. New York, Leavitt & Allen, **n. d.** [circa 1856]. viii, 9–264 p., 6 pl., 7¼ x 5. "Rainbow bridge." U.W. (223)

This is really the "Token and Atlantic souvenir," Boston, 1840, with p. 265–304 omitted and pl. changed.
See also "Token of friendship," New York, n. d., "Atlantic souvenir," New York, n. d.; "Honeysuckle," 1848.

—— —— of moral and entertaining literature, ed. by Mrs. M. O. Stevens. Boston and Lowell, Edward A. Rice, [v. 1–2,] **1847.** 1–192, 1–192 p., 8¾ x 5.
A periodical.

—— ——, a souvenir for **1848,** ed. by Walter Percival. Boston, John P. Hill, 1848, c. 1847. vi p., 1 l., 12–312 p., 10 pl., 7¼ x 4¾. C.U., L.C., B.P., U.W. (224)
Also issued as "Lady's gift," 1849.

—— ——, a token of remembrance, ed. by Josephine Gilbert. Lynn, M[as]s., Thomas Herbert, **1852,** c. 1850. 320 p., 7 pl., 7 x 4½. "Gaspar Poussin." P.M. (225)

Pref. speaks of it as "Lily of valley."
Also issued without date, except the pref. date of July, 1850. B.P. (225a)
This is really the "Lily of the valley," for 1851, with its name, and name of ed. changed.
Also issued as "Mignonette," 1856, omitting p. 259–320 and 2 pl.

**Friendship's jewel,** a gift of remembrance, ed. by J. S. A. Boston, J. Buffum, **c. 1851.** 96 p., 3 x 2. N.Y. (226)

**Friendship's memorial** for **1853.** New York, Edward H. Fletcher, 1853. iv, 5–304 p., 10 pl., 9½ x 5¾. N.Y. (227)

**Friendship's offering,** a Christmas, New Year's and birthday gift. New York, Leavitt & Allen, **n. d.** vi, 9–264 p., [5 pl. and col. presentation pl.,] 3¾ x 5¾. "The portrait." N.Y. (228)

Also issued by Geo. A. Leavitt, n. d. [circa 1869]. N.Y., P.M. (228a)
Also issued as "Memory's gift," N. Y., n. d., "Moss rose," c. 1854, and "Philopœna," n. d., with variation in pl.

**Friendship's offering**, ed. by Miss Catharine H. Waterman, **1841.** [ v. 1. ] Philadelphia, Marshall, Williams & Butler, c. 1840. vi p., 1 l., 9–320 p., 10 pl., 6⅛ x 4¼. N.Y., B.P., U.W., L.C. (229)

—— ——, ed. by Mrs. Catharine H. W. Esling, **1842.** [ v. 2. ] Boston, E. Littlefield, c. 1841. vi p. 1 l., 9–320 p., 10 pl., 6¼ x 4¼. N.Y., B.P., L.C. (230)

—— —— and winter's wreath, a Christmas and New Year's present for **1843.** [ v. 3. ] Philadelphia, E. H. Butler & Co., c. 1842. vi p., 1 l., 9–320 p., 10 pl., 6 x 4¼. N.Y.S. (231)

Also issued with imprint, Boston, Lewis & Sampson, 1843, c. 1842. L.C., N.Y. (231a)
Also issued with imprint Phila., Z. Pratt, 1843. B.P. (231b)
Also issued in large paper, 7¼ x 4¾. F. (231c)

—— ——, and winter's wreath, a Christmas, and New Year's present for **1844.** [v. 4.] Boston, Lewis & Sampson, c. 1843. vii p., 1 l., 9–320 p., 6¼ x 4¼. L.C., N.Y., U.W. (232)

—— ——, a Christmas, New Year and birthday present for **1845.** [ v. 5.] Boston, Lewis & Sampson, 1845, c. 1844. vi p., 1 l., 13–340 p., 9 pl., 7¼ x 4¾. N.Y., B.P., C.U., B.A., U.W. (233)

Also issued with imprint Butler & Williams.

—— ——, a Christmas, New Year and birthday present for **1846.** [ v. 6.] Boston, Phillips & Sampson, 1846, c. 1845. vi p., 1 l., 13–292 p., 9 pl., 7¼ x 4¾. N.Y., L.C., B.P., B.A., U.W. (234)

—— ——, a Christmas, New Year and birthday present for **1847.** [v. 7. ] Boston, Phillips & Sampson, 1847 c. 1846. vi p., 1 l., 13–316 p., 9 pl., 7½ x 4¾. N.Y., L.C., B.P., C.U. (235)

—— ——, a Christmas, New Year and birthday present for **1848.** [ v. 8. ] Boston, Phillips & Sampson, 1848. c. 1847. vi p., 1 l., 13–316 p., 9 pl., 7¼ x 4¾. N.Y., L.C., B.P., U.W. (236)

—— ——, a Christmas, New Year and birthday present for **1849.** [ v. 9. ] Boston, Phillips & Sampson 1849, c. 1848. vi p., 1 l., 13–330 p., 9 pl., 7¼ x 4¾. N.Y., B.A., U.W. (237)

—— ——, a Christmas, New Year and birthday present for **1850.** [v. 10.] Boston, Phillips, Sampson & Co., 1850, c. 1849. vi p., 1 l., 13–330 p., 9 pl., 7¼ x 4¾. N.Y., B.P., U.W. (238)

—— ——, a Christmas, New Year and birthday present for **1851.** [ v. 11. ] Boston, Phillips, Sampson & Co., 1851, c. 1850. x p., 1 l., 13–330 p., 9 pl., 7¼ x 4¾. N.Y., L.C., B.P. (239)

—— ——, a Christmas, New Year and birthday present for **1852.** [ v. 12. ] Philadelphia, E. H. Butler & Co., 1852, c. 1851. x p., 1 l., 13–330 p., 9 pl., 7¼ x 4¾. L.C., B.P., C.U. (240)

**Friendship's offering**, a Christmas, New Year and birthday present for **1853.** [v. 13.] Philadelphia, E. H. Butler & Co., 1853, c. 1852. x p., 1 l., 13–328 p., 9 pl., 7⅜ x 4¾. N.Y., L.C., B.P., U.W. (241)

—— ——, a Christmas, New Year and birthday present for **1854.** [v. 14.] Philadelphia, E. H. Butler & Co., 1854, c. 1853. x p., 1 l., 13–328 p., 8 pl., 7¼ x 4¾. L.C., B.P., B.A. (242)

—— ——, a Christmas, New Year and birthday present for **1855.** [v. 15.] Philadelphia, E. H. Butler & Co., 1855, c. 1854. x p., 1 l., 13–328 p., 8 pl., 7¼ x 4¾. N.Y., L.C., B.P., U.W. (243)

—— ——, a Christmas, New Year and birthday gift. NewYork, Leavitt & Allen, n. d., **c. 1855.** 5–264 p., 7 pl., 7¼ x 4⅞. "The carpenter's daughter." B.P. (244)

Also issued as "Gem annual," n. d., "Friendship's gift," n. d., and "Lady's annual," n. d., but pl. vary.

**Friendship's token.** See "**Friendship.**"

—— ——. New York, Leavitt & Allen, **n. d.** [1853, 54, or 55]. 2 p. l., 9–260 p., 5 pl., 7¼ x 5. C.U. (245)

Really "The magnolia," 1836, with different pl., and p. 261–300 omitted.
See also "The coral," "Gift of affection," n. d., "Morning glory," n. d., "Memory," c. 1854, "Snow flake," n.d., "Aloe," 1854.

—— —— and lover's gift. Buffalo, Geo. H. Derby & Co., 32mo. * (246)

**Gallery of mezzotints, The,** an annual for **1849.** New York, M. H. Newman & Co., 1849. 224 p. [?], 21 pl., 8¼ x 5½. "To Lamartine." F. (247)

**Garland, The,** New York, Leavitt & Allen, **n. d.** See 1855. N. Y. (247a)

—— ——, for **1830,** designed as a Christmas and New-Year's present. New York, Josiah Drake, 1830, c. 1829. viii, 9–324 p., 12 pl., 5⅝ x 3⅝. N.Y. (248)

"Consists of choicest pieces which have appeared in 'The token' and 'Legendary.'"
Issued also for 1831, New York, C. H. Peabody, 1831, c. 1829. F. (248a)
Issued again 1839 with added p. and different pl. See below.

—— —— for **1839.** A Christmas, New Year and birthday present. Boston, Julius A. Noble, 1839. viii, 9–10, 1 l., 11–116, 1 l., 117–264, 1 l., 265–294, 1 l., 295–331 p., 1 p., [8 pl.,] 6¼ x 4. N.Y., L.C., B.A. (249)

Same as 1830 with p. 325–31 added and 4 l. text inserted, unpaged, in body of vol., each to go with pl. inserted. All the pl. are different.

—— —— for **1840,** a Christmas, New Year and birthday present. Boston, Julius A. Noble, 1840. viii, 9–331 p., [7 pl.,] 6½ x 3¾. N.Y., L.C., C.U., B.P. (250)

This is same as 1830 with p. 325–31 added, but has 3 of the pl. of 1839, and 4 of the pl. of 1830.

**Garland, The,** or token of friendship, a Christmas and New Year's gift for **1848,** ed. by Emily Percival. [v.1.] Boston, D. P. King, 1848, c. 1847. viii p., 1 l., 11–324 p., [7 pl.,] 7½ x 4¾. "The garland." N.Y., B.P., L.C., U.W. (251)

Also edition with imprint "Z. & B. F. Pratt," and "John Philbrick." Some copies have plate at p. 17 omitted. Really "Amaranth," 1847, with first article changed and engr. t. changed to illum. t. and one pl. substituted. See also "Keepsake of friendship," 1849, which is same with another substitution in 1st article. See also "Ladies' [or Lady's] gift," 1850, 1851, "Gift of affection," n. d.

—— ——, or token of friendship. a Christmas and New Year's gift for **1849,** ed. by Emily Percival. [v. 2.] Boston, David P. King, 1849, c.1848. vi p., 1 l., 9–288 p., 5 pl., 7¼ x 4¾. "The garland." C.U., B.P., L.C. (252)

Also edition with imprint "Charles Burnett, Providence."
This is really "Amaranth," 1848, with change in first article. See also "Keepsake of friendship," 1850, which is same except still another first article.

—— —— or token of friendship, a Christmas and New Year's gift for **1850**, ed. by Emily Percival. [v. 3.] Boston, Phillips, Sampson & Co., 1850, c. 1849. vi p., 1 l., 9–322 p., 6 pl., 7½ x 4¾. "Song." N.Y., B.P., L.C., U.W. (253)

This is "Amaranth," 1849, except first 3 p. of text, different front. and illum. t.
Also issued as "Casket," [1853], with still another different first article — "The quiet eye" — and as "Keepsake of friendship," Worcester, 1851, with change in first text pages. A col. presentation pl. and col. t. in place of front. and engr. t.
Also issued as "Memory's gift," N. Y., 1869, as "Token of friendship," Boston, 1852, and "Magnolia," 1852.

—— ——, or token of friendship, a Christmas and New Year's gift for **1851,** ed. by Emily Percival. [v. 4.] Boston, Phillips, Sampson & Co., 1851, c. 1850. 288 p., 6 pl., 7¼ x 4¾. "Zelica." L.C., N.Y., B.P. (254)

Really "Amaranth, "1850, with first article changed and col. t. and col. front. substituted.
See also "Magnolia" [1853].

—— —— or token of friendship, a Christmas and New Year's gift for **1852,** ed. by Emily Percival. [v. 5.] Boston, Phillips, Sampson & Co., 1852, c. 1851. 5 p. l., 276 p., 6 pl., 7¼ x 4¾. "Humility." N.Y., L.C., B.P., U.W. (255)

This is "Wreath of wild flowers,"1846, with unpaged l. preceding p. 1, preface changed, and pl. added. It was issued also as "Amaranth," 1851, with a variation in text of the unpaged preliminary l., as "Keepsake of friendship, ed. by G. S. Monroe," 1853, as "Magnolia" [pref. d. 1853], as "Token of friendship," Bost. [1854], and N. Y., n. d.

**Garland, The,** or token of friendship, a Christmas and New Year's gift for **1853,** ed. by Emily Percival. [v. 6.] Boston, Phillips, Sampson & Co., 1853, c. 1852. 288 p., 7 pl., 7¼ x 4¾. "The heather bell."
C.U. (256)

Really "Amaranth," 1852.
Also see "Keepsake of friendship," 1854, and "Magnolia," 1855, which are same except first article.

—— —— or token of friendship, a Christmas and New Year's gift for **1854,** ed. by Emily Percival. [v. 7.] Boston, Phillips, Sampson & Co., 1854, c. 1853. 288 p., 7 pl., 7¼ x 4¾. "Use of flowers."
L.C., C.U., B.P., U.W. (257)

Really "Amaranth," 1853, with first article changed.
See also "Keepsake of friendship," 1855, same except first article.

—— ——, or token of friendship, a Christmas and New Year's gift for **1855,** ed. by Emily Percival. [v. 8.] Boston, Phillips, Sampson & Co., 1855, c. 1854. 288 p., 7 pl., 7¼ x 4¾. "Daughter of the bardi."
B.P., U.W., P.M. (258)

Also issued without date, c. 1854. H.U. N.Y.
Also issued Leavitt & Allen, N. Y., n. d.
Also pub. by Geo. A. Leavitt, N. Y., 1869, omitting all pl. but engr. t., and omitting p. 7–8 ["list of illus."]. This is really "Amaranth," 1854, with engr. t. added

—— —— or token of friendship, a Christmas and New Year's gift, ed. by Emily Percival. [v. 8.] New York, Geo. A. Leavitt, **1869.** 1–6, 9–288 p., engr. t., 7 x 4½.
P.M. (259)

This is same as 1855, with list of plates [p. 7–8] and all plates but engr. t. omitted.

**Gathered leaves,** or miscellaneous papers by Miss Hannah F. Gould. Boston, Wm. J. Reynolds, **1846,** c. 1845. 304 p., front., 6¾ x 4¼.
N.Y. (260)

**Gem, The,** a Christmas and New Year's present for **1840.** [v. 1.] Philadelphia, Henry F. Anners, c. 1839. viii p., 1 l., 17–287 p., 7 pl., 6 x 4.
N.Y., B.P., U.W. (261)

—— ——, a Christmas and New Year's present for **1842.** [v. 2.] Philadelphia, Henry F. Anners, c. 1841. vi, 7–288 p., 7 pl., 6¼ x 4.
B.P., C.U. (262)

—— ——, a Christmas and New Year's present for **1844.** Philadelphia, John Robinson. vi, 7–288 p., [6 pl.,] 6¼ x 4.
U.W. (263)

Same as 1842 as to text.

—— —— for **1848,** ed. by Father Frank. New York, E. Kearney, c. 1848. iv p., 1 l., 7–284 p.
B.P., P.M. (264)

Same as "Juvenile gem," 1846.
Issued 1852, omitting 8 of the 11 articles on p. 232–84, and repaged, ending p. 252.

**Gem, The,** for **1849.** New York, Edward Kearney. 252 p., 8 pl., 6 x 3⅝. B.P. (265)

Also issued with imprint Henry F. Anners, 1854.
Same as "American juvenile keepsake," 1834, with 1 pl. omitted.
See also "Youth's keepsake," N. Y., n. d., "The gift," 1847, which omit list of pl. and most of the pl.

—— ——, a present for all seasons, ed. by Father Frank. Philadelphia, Henry F. Anners, **1852.** iv p., 1 l., 7–252 p. C.U. (266)

Same as 1848, except 32 p. [8 articles] omitted.

Also issued with imprint date 1853. F. (267)
Also issued with imprint date 1855. N.Y. (268)

—— ——, a token of affection for **1854.** Philadelphia, Henry L. Anners, 1854. 252 p., [4 pl.,] 5⅞ x 3¾. F. (269)

Same as 1849.

—— ——, a token of affection for all seasons. Philadelphia, Henry F. Anners, **1855.** iv p., 1 l., 7–252 p., [4 pl.,] 5¾ x 3¾. N.Y. (270)

Same as 1848, except 32 p. are omitted.

**Gem annual, The,** a Christmas and New Year gift. New York, Leavitt & Allen, **n. d.** [1856 or after]. 3 p. l., 11–264 p., 6 pl., 7¼ x 4¾. "The carpenter's daughter." C.U. (271)

This is "Friendship's offering", c. 1855.
See also "Friendship's gift," n. d., and "Lady's annual," n. d., which have different plates, and no list of pl.

—— ——, a Christmas and New Year gift. New York, Leavitt & Allen, **n. d.**, 8, 11–264 p., [5 pl.,] 7¼ x 4¾. "The seaman's wife." B.A. (271a)

This is "Forget-me-not," c. 1855, with different pl.
See also "Philopœna," n. d.

—— ——, a Christmas, New Year and birth-day present for **1854.** Philadelphia, E. H. Butler & Co., 1854, c. 1853. 9–328 p., 8 pl., 7¼ x 4¾. N.Y., B.P., L.C. (272)

—— —— a Christmas, New-Year and birthday gift for **1855.** Philadelphia, E. H. Butler & Co., 1855, c. 1854. x p., 1 l., 13–328 p., 8 pl., 7⅛ x 4¾. N.Y., L.C., B.P., U.W. (273)

**Gem of the season, The,** with ten fine illustrations. New York, Leavitt & Allen, **n. d.**, [1856 or after]. 3 p. l., 9–288 p., 10 pl., 9¼ x 6½. "The new year." U.W. (274)

—— ——, with twenty plates by Sartain, ed. by John Holmes Agnew. [v. 1.] New York, Leavitt, Trow & Co., **1846,** c. 1845. viii, 1–60 p., 20 pl., 9½ x 6¼. N.Y., B.P., C.U. (275)

—— —— for **1848,** with 20 splendid engravings. New York, Leavitt, Trow & Co., 1848, c. 1847. 224 p., 20 pl., 8¼ x 5¾. "Time's far flight." C U., U.W. (276)

**Gem of the season, The,** for **1849,** with 20 splendid engravings. New York, Leavitt, Trow & Co. 224 p., 20 pl., 9½ x 7¼. "To a lady."
N.Y., C.U., B.A., L.C. (277)

—— —— for **1850,** ed. by N. Parker Willis. New York, Leavitt & Co., 1850, c. 1849. 5–222 p., 1 l., 16 pl., 9½ x 6¾. N.Y., U.W. B.A. (278)

—— —— for **1851,** Elegantly illustrated. New York, Leavitt & Co., 1851. 236 p., 10 pl., 9¼ x 6¾.
N.Y., C.U. (279)

—— ——, a souvenir for **1852.** New York, Leavitt & Co., 1852. 2 p. l., 9–244 p., 12 pl., 9 x 7. L.C. (280)

—— —— a souvenir for **1853,** elegantly illustrated. New York, Leavitt & Allen, 1853. 1 p. l., 9–228 p., 12 pl., 9¼ x 6½. N.Y. (281)

Reissued for 1854.

—— ——, a souvenir for **1854.** N.Y. (282)

Exactly like 1853.

—— ——, with 10 beautiful illustrations. New York, Leavitt & Allen, c. **1856.** xiv p., 1 l., 17–264 p., 10 pl., 9¼ x 6½. N.Y., C.U., U.W. (283)

**Gem of the western world, The,** for **1851,** ed. by Mary E. Hewitt. New York, Cornish, Lamport & Co., c. 1851. vi p., 1 l., 9–320 p., 9 pl., 7¾ x 5½.
B.P., B.A., U.W. (284)

**Gems for the fireside,** comprising moral tales, essays, biography and poetry. New York, John F. Scovill, **n. d.** [circa 1855]. 9–430 p., 6 engravings, and 6 colored pl., 8¾ x 5¾. "Song of the sea" [music].
B.A. (285)

This is probably a magazine.

**Gems for you,** from New Hampshire authors, ed. by F. A. Moore. Manchester, N. H., William H. Fisk, **1850,** c. 1850. x, 11–312 p., 7¼ x 4½. C.U. (286)

Also issued with sub-title, "A gift for all seasons." Reissued in 1851. Reprinted in 1854 with plates added and called "Book of gems."

**Gems from American female poets,** ed. by R. W. Griswold. Philadelphia, H. Hooker, 1842. x, 11–92 p., 32 mo. L.C. (287)

**Gems from American poets.** New York, D. Appleton & Co. [**1842**]. Engr. front. * (288)

**Gems from the sacred mine,** or holy thoughts upon sacred subjects, by clergymen of the Episcopal Church, ed. by Thomas Wyatt. Philadelphia, Lippincott, Grambo & Co., **1851,** c. 1850. vi p., 1 l., 13–236 p., 7 pl., 6¾ x 4⅜. B.P. (289)

**Gems of beauty,** or literary gift for 1849, ed. by Emily Percival. [v. 1.] Boston, Phillips & Sampson, **1849,** c. 1848. 3 p. l., 15–296 p., 8 pl., 9¼ x 6¼. L.C. (290)

**Gems of beauty,** or literary gift for **1850,** ed. by Emily Percival. [v. 2.] Boston, Phillips, Sampson & Co., 1850, c. 1849. 3 p. l., 15–296 p, 8 pl., 9¼ x 6¼. B.P., L.C. (291)

—— ——, or literary gift for **1851,** ed. by Emily Percival. [v. 3.] Boston, Phillips, Sampson & Co., 1851, c. 1850. 3 p. l., 15–296 p., 8 pl., 9¼ x 6¼. N.Y. (292)

—— ——, or literary gift for **1852,** ed. by Emily Percival. [v. 4.] Boston, Phillips, Sampson & Co., 1852. 3 p. l., 9–288 p., 8 pl. [and illum. list of pl.], 9¼ x 6¼. U.W. (293)

—— ——, or literary gift for **1853,** ed. by Emily Percival [v. 5.] Boston, Phillips, Sampson & Co., 1853, c. 1852. 3 p. l., 11–288 p., 8 pl. [and illum. list of pl.], 9¼ x 6¼. N.Y., L.C. (294)

—— ——, or literary gift for **1854,** ed. by Emily Percival. [v. 6.] Boston, Phillips, Sampson & Co., 1854, c. 1853. 3 p. l., 11–290 p., 9 pl., 9¼ x 6½. B.A. (295)

—— ——, or literary gift for **1855,** ed. by Emily Percival. [v. 7.] Boston, Phillips, Sampson, & Co. 1855, c. 1854. viii, 9–288 p., 9 pl., 9¼ x 6½. N.Y. (296)

**Gift, The,** Philadelphia, Carey & Hart, **n.d.** vi p., 1 l., 17–328 p., 8 pl. [7 pl. in reality, vig. t. being omitted], 7⅜ x 4¾. "The brook." N.Y.S., U.W. (297)

Same as 1843, with vig. t. and dates omitted.

—— ——, a Christmas, New Year and birthday present. Philadelphia, Carey & Hart, **n. d.** iv, 7–300 p., [13 pl.]. 8¾ x 5½. "A gleam of sunshine." N.Y. (298)

Reissue of 1845, changing front. and engr. t., and adding 5 Cheney pl.

—— ——, a Christmas and New Year's present, ed. by N. P. Willis. Boston, **1829.** x, 348 p., 3¾ x 6. F. (299)

—— ——, a poetical remembrancer selected from the work of native and foreign authors. Concord, N. H., Currier & Hall and Asa McFarland, **1835.** 322 p., front., 4⅞ x 3. B.P (300)

—— ——, a Christmas and New Year's present for **1836,** ed. by Miss Leslie. [v. 1.] Philadelphia, E. L. Carey & A. Hart. xii, 17–292 p., 9 pl., 6¼ x 4. N.Y., L.C., B.P. (301)

—— ——, a Christmas and New Year's present for **1837,** ed. by Miss Leslie. [v. 2.] Philadelphia, E. L. Carey & A. Hart, c. 1836. vi p., 1 l., 17–325 p, 10 pl., 6¼ x 4. L.C., B.A., U.W. (302)

A few copies were issued in 7½ x 4½ size with proof plates. N. Y.

—— ——, a Christmas, New Year and birthday present for **1839,** ed. by Miss Leslie. [v. 3.] Philadelphia, E. L. Carey & A. Hart, c. 1838. iv p., 1 l., 17–328 p., 9 pl., 6½ x 4¼. N.Y., L.C., B.P.L. (303)

**Gift, The,** a Christmas and New Year's present for **1840,** ed. by Miss Leslie. [v. 4.] Philadelphia, Carey & Hart, c. 1839. viii, 17–328 p., 9 pl., 7¼ x 4¾. N.Y., B.P., L.C., U.W. (304)

There is an edition with n. d. on title, and no preface, but c. 1839. P.M. (305)

—— ——, a Christmas and New Year's present for **1842.** Philadelphia, Carey & Hart, c. 1841. viii, 17–322 p., 8 pl, 7¼ x 4¾. N.Y., L.C., B.P., U.W. (306)

Said to have been issued also in large paper size.

—— ——, a Christmas and New Year's present, **1843.** Philadelphia, Carey & Hart, c. 1842. vi p., 1 l., 17–328 p., 8 pl., 7¼ x 4¾. N.Y., L.C. (307)

Also issued in large paper, 9¼ x 6. 2 p. l., vii–viii p., 1 l., 17–328 p. C.U.
Also issued without date, omitting the vig. title. N.Y., U.W. (307a)

—— ——, a Christmas and New Year's present, **1844.** Philadelphia, Carey & Hart, 1844, c. 1843. iv p., 1 l. 7–296 p., 8 pl., 8⅝ x 5½. N.Y., L.C., B.A., U.W (308)

—— ——, a Christmas, New Year and birthday present, **1845.** Philadelphia, Carey & Hart, 1845, c. 1844. iv p., 1 l., 7–300 p., 8 pl., 8⅝ x 5½. N.Y., L.C., B.P., U.W. (309)

This was reissued without date with engr. front. and engr t. different, and 5 Cheney pl. added.

—— ——, for **1847.** New York, Edward Kearny. 252 p., [4 pl.,] 5¾ x 3¾. N.Y. (310)

A reprint, with new t. and 2 articles omitted, and articles rearranged of "American juvenile keepsake," 1834, omitting list of pl. and several pl. See also "Youth's keepsake," N. Y., n. d., and "Gem," 1849.

—— ——, **1851.** viii, 13–304 p., 8 pl., 7¼ x 4¾. "Crevice in the tower." C.U. (311)

Note: This copy without title in C. U. has 1851 on cloth back, and in preface refers to "Gift for 1851."

**Gift book for young ladies,** or familiar letters on their acquaintances, male and female, employments, friendships, etc., by Dr. Wm. A. Alcott. Auburn, [N. Y.,] Derby & Miller, **1853,** c. 1852. xvi, 13–307 p., front., 7 x 4½. U.W. (312)

**Gift book of gems, The.** A literary offering for all seasons, illustrated with fine mezzotint engravings, ed. by Emily Percival. Boston, Phillips, Sampson & Co., **1853,** c. 1852. 288 p., 8 pl., 9⅛ x 6½. B.A. (313)

—— —— illustrated. Bangor, [Me.,] David Bugbee & Co., **c. 1856.** xii, 312 p., [6 pl.,] 8¼ x 6. L.C., C.U. (314)

Last p. misnumbered 324.

**Gift for all seasons,** a juvenile annual. Philadelphia, Henry F. Anners, **1844.** vi, 7–216 p., front., 6 x 3¾. N.Y. (315)

**Gift for all seasons,** illustrated with steel engravings. New York, D. Appleton & Co., **1853.** 288 p., 9 pl., 6½ x 4¼. H.U., N.Y. (316)

Has title "The gift" on back.

**Gift for the holidays.** Philadelphia, American Sunday School Union. 9 pl * (317)

**Gift for you, A,** of prose and poetic gems, by Eugene Sinclair. Boston, G. W. Cottrell, **1857,** c. 1855. x, 11–312 p., 7½ x 4½. P.M. (318)

Also reissued in 1858, with illuminated title, "Gem of prose and poetry," and colored front., back of cover reading, "Gift of prose and poetic gems," 6¾ x 4¼. F. (319)

Reissued in 1859 with engr. front., 6¾ x 4½. B.P. (320)

——— ———, as a remembrancer, a present for all seasons, by Gertrude Radcliffe Whedon. Albany, 1865. 4to. * (321)

**Gift from fairyland, A.** New York, D. Appleton & Co. **c. 1838.** vi p., 1 l., 174 p., illus., illum. t., 7⅛ x 4½. F. (322)

**Gift leaves of American peotry,** ed. by Rufus W. Griswold. New York, J. C. Riker, **c. 1849.** x p., 1 l., 13–288 p., 7 pl., 8¾ x 5¾. F. (323)

**Gift of affection.** Title on back of **Affection's gift.** New York, n. d.

**Gift of affection, The,** a Christmas and New-Year's present. New York, Leavitt & Allen, 379 Broadway, **n. d.** [1856 or after]. 3 p. l., 9–260 p., 6 pl., 7 x 4¾. "The magnolia, 'not in the autumn.'" B.P. (324)

This is "Magnolia," 1836, with pp. 261–300 omitted and different plates. See also "Coral" and "Friendship's token," n. d., "Morning glory," n. d., "Memory," c. 1854, "Snow flake," n. d., "Aloe," 1854.

——— ———, a Christmas and New-Year's present. New York, Leavitt & Allen, 379 Broadway, **n. d.** [1856 or after]. viii, 9–264 p., 6 pl., 7¼ x 4¾. "The student's dream." B.P., C.U. (325)

Also issued with street address of pub. omitted. N.Y. (325a)

——— ———, a Christmas and New Year's present. New York, Leavitt & Allen, **n. d.** viii, 11–324 p., ||6 pl.,] 7¼ x 5. "The gift. Friendship." P.M. (326).

Also issued by Geo. A. Leavitt [5 pl.] B.A. (326a)

This is "Amaranth," 1847, with change in first article, and different pl. See also "Ladies' [Lady's] gift," 1850, 1851, "Garland," 1848, "Keepsake of friendship," 1849.

**Gift of affection.** New York, Leavitt & Allen, 47 Dey St., **n. d.** [1855 ?]. x, 11–260 p., 8 pl., 7¼ x 5. "Poetry of the affections." F. (327)

——— ———, a souvenir for **1852.** New York, Leavitt, & Co., 1852. x p., 1 l., 11–288 p., 7 pl. U.W. (328)

**Gift of affection.** A souvenir for **1853,** ed. by Rufus W. Griswold. New York, Leavitt & Allen, 1853 * (329)

—— ——. New York, **1869.** * (330)

**Gift of flowers,** or love's wreath. New York, Leavitt & Allen, **n. d.** [1853, 54 or 55]. 262 p., 8 pl. "Hymn to the flowers." U.W. (331)

—— ——, or love's wreath for **1853,** ed. by Rufus W. Griswold. New York, Leavitt & Allen, 1853. 287 p., [6 pl.,] 6¾ x 4⅜. N.Y., L.C. (332)

Reissued for 1854.

—— ——, love's wreath for **1854.** Same as 1853 except color of the border design around each page. N.Y. (333)

**Gift of friendship, The,** a token of remembrance for **1847.** [v. 1.] Philadelphia, Henry F. Anners, 252 p., [6 pl.,] 6 x 3¾. B.A., U.W. (334)

**Gift of Friendship, The,** a token of remembrance for **1848.** [v. 2.] Philadelphia, Henry F. Anners, c. 1847. 252 p., 6 pl., 6½ x 4. (335)

—— ——, or token of remembrance for **1848;** Dew drops of the nineteenth century, ed. by Seba Smith. New York, John Levison, pref. d. 1845. viii, 9–216 p., [6 pl.,] 7½ x 4¼. U.W. (336)

This has no connection with the Phila. publication of same name.

A reissue of "Dew-Drops of the nineteenth century," 1847–8, omitting the col. pl., and substituting 6 engr.

—— ——, a token of remembrance for **1849.** [v. 3.] Philadelphia, Henry F. Anners, c. 1848. 256 p., 6 pl., 6½ x 4. B.P., B.A. (337)

—— ——, a token of remembrance for **1850.** [v. 4.] Philadelphia, Henry F. Anners, c. 1849. 252 p., 6 pl., 6½ x 4. L.C. (338)

—— ——, a token of remembrance for **1851.** [v. 5.] Philadelphia, Henry F. Anners, c. 1850. viii, 244 p., 6 pl., 6⅝ x 4. L.C., U.W. (339)

—— ——, a token of remembrance for **1852.** [v. 6.] Philadelphia, Henry F. Anners, c. 1851. vi, 7–252 p., 6 pl., 6½ x 4. L.C. (340)

—— ——, a token of remembrance for **1853.** [v. 7.] Philadelphia, Henry F. Anners, c. 1852. 252 p., 6 pl., 6½ x 4. L.C., B.P., C.U. (341)

—— ——, a token of remembrance for **1854.** [v. 8.] Philadelphia, Henry F. Anners, c. 1853. 252 p., 6 pl., 6½ x 4. L.C., C.U., U.W. (342)

—— ——, a token of remembrance for **1855.** [v. 9.] [Pref. calls it 10th vol.] Philadelphia, Henry F. Anners, c. 1854. 252 p., 5 pl., 6½ x 4¼. N.Y., L.C., B.A. (343)

**Gift of love, A.** Boston, G. W. Cottrell, **n. d.** 128 p. 9–128 p., col. t., 5¼ x 3¾. N.Y. (344)

Half-t. to second group of paging, "The memento."

**Gift of love,** a token of friendship for **1853,** ed. by Rufus W. Griswold. New York, Leavitt & Allen, 1853. xiv, 15–288 p. [6 pl.,] 6¾ x 4⅝. F. (344a)

Illuminated t. p. reads "Gift of love, a souvenir for 1853."

Also issued with date 1854.

—— ——, a token of friendship for **1854,** ed. by Rufus W. Griswold. New York, Leavitt & Allen, 1854. xiv, 15–288 p., [6 pl.,] B.A. (344b)

Same as 1853.

**Gift of sentiment.** Friendship's gift. New York, Leavitt & Allen, **n. d.** [1853, '54 or '55]. viii, 11–264 p., 8 pl., 7¼ x 5. "Poetry of the sentiments." F. (345)

Same as 1853 with p. 265–320 omitted, and floral border in various colors instead of all in green.

—— ——. A souvenir for **1853,** ed. by Rufus W. Griswold. Illustrated. New York, Leavitt & Allen, 1853. ix, 11–320 p., [6 pl., ] 6¾ x 4½. N.Y., B.P. (346)

All pages have floral border in green.
Also issued without date, with p. 265–320 omitted and borders in different colors. See above.

Also issued 1854, with p. 289–320 omitted. See below.

—— ——, a souvenir for **1854,** ed. by Rufus W. Griswold. Illustrated. New York, Leavitt & Allen, 1854. viii, 11–288 p., 6 pl. B.A. (346a)

Same as No. 345 above with p. 289-320 omitted.

**Gifts of genius,** a miscellany of prose and poetry by American authors. New York, C. A. Davenport, **c. 1859.** xii, 13–264 p., 7¾ x 5. F. (347)

**Girls' gem.** Title on back of **Holiday gem for girls.**

**Girls' scrap book, 1839.** [Philadelphia ] American Sunday School Union. vii p., 1 p., 1 l., 11-238 p., [5 pl., ] 6½ x 5¼. N.Y. (348)

**Golden chalice, The,** or mental draughts from many fountains. Boston, J. W. Hubbard, [ date erased ]. 7–392 p., [plates, ] 9 x 5¾. C.U. (349)

Probably "Ladies' companion" was issued as an annual under this name.

**Golden gift, The,** a token for all seasons, ed. by J. M. Fletcher. Boston, J. Buffum, **c. 1846.** viii, 9–128 p., front., 4½ x 2¾. N.Y. (350)

Also issued with imprint of G. W Cottrell, Boston. F. (350a)

Also at Nashua, N. H. J. Buffum, 1847, c. 1846. F. (350b)

Also at Nashua, N. H. J. Buffum, **1848,** c 1846, and **1850,** c 1846, front., presentation pl., F. (350c)

Also Boston, J. Buffum, 1851. F. (350d)

**Golden gift, 1849.** Date on illuminated title of 1850.

—— ——, a wreath of gems from the prose and poetical writers of England and America. Prepared especially as a gift book for all seasons. By Emily Percival. Boston, Phillips, Sampson & Co., **1850,** c. 1849. 2 p. l., 7–252 p., illum. t. (dated 1849), 7¾ x 5½. B.P., B.A., U.W. (351)

Reissued in 1853 with additional pages. See below.

—— ——, a token for all seasons, ed. by J. M. Fletcher. Boston, J. Buffum, **1851.** viii, 9–128 p., 2 col. t., 4½ x 3¾. F. (352)

Same as c. 1846 copy.

—— ——, a wreath of gems from the prose and poetical writers of England and America Prepared especially as a gift book for all seasons By Emily Percival Boston, Phillips Sampson & Co., **c. 1853.** 2 p 1, 7–288 p., [6 pl.,] 7⅝ x 5⅝. N.Y., B.P U W (353)

Same as 1850, with p. 253–288 added.

**Golden keepsake, The,** or ladies' wreath. A gift for all seasons, ed. by Mrs. S. T. Martyn. New York, J. M. Fletcher & Co., **n. d.** vi p., 1 1., 418 p., 1 1., 24 pl., 8½ x 5½. N.Y. (354)

**Golden leaflets,** a selection of poetry designed as a present for all seasons, ed. by J. M. Fletcher Boston, J. Buffum, **c. 1848.** 128 p., 5¼ x 3½. U.W. (355)

Also issued **1852,** c. 1848. F. (355a)

**Golden present, The,** a gift for all seasons, ed. by Mrs. J. Thayer. Boston, J. Buffum, **c 1848.** 128 p., 5¼ x 3⅜ B.P. (356)

In 1849 this same book was issued with imprint Worcester, J. Buffum, 1849, 4½ x 2¾. P.M. (356a)
Also issued in Nashua, N. H., J. Buffum, 1849, 4½ x 2¾. N.Y. (356b)

In 1850 this same book was issued with imprint, Nashua, J. Buffum, 4½ x 2⅞, but without the illum. t. F. (356c)
Also in 1850 at Worcester, S. A. Howland. F. (356d)
In 1851 it was issued at Worcester, S. A. Howland. U.W. (356e)

**Golden vase, The,** a gift for the young, by Hannah F. Gould. Boston, **1843** (?) * (356f)

—— ——, a gift for the young, by Hannah F. Gould. 2d ed. Boston, Benjamin B. Mussey, **1844,** c. 1842. viii, 9–224 p., [4 pl.,] 6⅜ x 4¼. F. (356g)

Same as 1843.

**Golden wreath, The,** a Christmas and New Year's present, elegantly illustrated. New York, D. Appleton & Co., **n. d.** [185–?]. 288 p., 10 pl., 9¼ x 6½. B.P. (357)

**Good girls' annual,** a Christmas and New Year's gift by Frances Broderip. N. Y., Leavitt & Allen Bros., **n. d.** [circa 1857]. 2 p.l., 11–292 p., [2 pl.,] 6¾ x 4¼. "Wee Maggie." N.Y. (358)

**Harbinger, The,** a May-gift. Boston, Carter, Hendee & Co., **1833.** vi p , 1 l., 96 p., 8⅛ x 4⅞. F. (359)

**Hare-bell, The,** a token of friendship, ed. by Rev. C. W. Everest. New York, J. Winchester, **1844,** c. 1843. viii, 9–192 p., front., 4⅝ x 2¾. F. (360)

—— ——, a token of friendship, ed. by Rev. C. W. Everest. Hartford, 2d ed., Henry S. Parsons, **1844,** c. 1843. viii, 9–192 p., front., 4⅝ x 2¾. N.Y. (361)

The 10th ed. was dated 1849. F. (361a)
Same except front. is different.

—— ——, a token of friendship, ed. by C. W. Everest. Hartford, W. Jas. Hamersley, **1852,** c. 1843. viii, 9–128 p., 4⅝ x 2¾. F. (362)

Same as 1844 with 15 articles omitted, 1 transferred, front. omitted, and whole re-paged.

**Hawthorn, The,** a Christmas and New Year's present, **1845.** New York, J. C. Riker, 1845. iv p., 2 l., 9–208 p., 6½ x 4¼. L.C., B.P., C.U., U.W. (363)

**Holiday gem for girls, The,** embellished with fine engravings. Philadelphia, American Sunday School Union, **c. 1843.** 3 p. l., 9–184 p., [4 pl.,] 5⅞ x 3¾. F. (364)

**Holiday gift,** Philadelphia, **1849.** 10 pl., 12mo. * (365)

—— ——, **1851,** 9 pl. * (366)

**Home annual, The,** a token for **1854,** ed. by J. T. Headley. New York, Leavitt & Allen. 304 p., 16 pl., 10½ x 7⅝. F. (367)

—— ——, a token for **1855,** ed. by J. T. Headley. New York, Leavitt & Allen, 1855. v, 5–304 p., 16 pl., [and illum. t.,] 9¼ x 6½. B.P. (368)

**Home recreation,** a collection of tales of peril and adventure, voyages and travels. A new gift book for young readers, by Grandfather Merryman. New York, D. Appleton & Co., **1850,** c. 1849. 5–238 p., 1 l., [10 pl.,] 6½ x 4⅝. F. (369)

**Honeysuckle, The,** for **1848.** New York, Nafis & Cornish, 1848. viii, 9–304 p., [6 pl. and illum. t. List of pl is that of "Token," 1840, but none of them are present,] 7 x 4¼. L.C., U.W. (370)

This is "Token and Atlantic souvenir," 1840, with different pl. and illum. t. L.C.
See also "Atlantic souvenir," n. d., "Token of friendship," n. d., "Friendship's gift," n. d., "Moss rose," 1846.

**Housekeepers' annual** and lady's register, **1844.** Boston, Redding & Co., c. 1843. 11–96 p., col. front., 7 x 4½ B.P. (371)

Not a true gift book.
Also issued for **1845,** T. H. Carter & Co. B.P. (371a)

**Humming bird, The,** a Christmas, and New-Year's gift, ed. by Ida Maitland. New York, Leavitt & Allen, 379 Broadway, **n. d.** [1856 or after]. 5–254 p., 6 pl., 6⅛ x 4¼. "Children at play." B.A., P.M. (372)

Also issued by Leavitt & Allen, no street, n. d., and 2 pl. changed. L.C. (372a)
Issued later, 1869, Geo. A. Leavitt, list of pl. omitted, and pl. changed. F. (372b)
Also issued Geo. A. Leavitt, n. d., and no street. F. (372c)

**Hyacinth, The.** New York, J. C. Riker, **1831.** 240 p., engr. front., engr. t., 16mo. * (373)

**Hyacinth, The,** or affection's gift, a Christmas, New-Year's and birth-day present for **1845.** [v. 1.] Philadelphia, Henry F. Anners, c. 1844. vi, 7–216 p., [4 pl.,] 6 x 3¾. N.Y., L.C. (374)

This was issued later with a leaf design printed over the "for 1845" on title. Otherwise the same. F. (374a)

—— ——, or affection's gift, a Christmas, New-Year's and birth-day present for **1846.** [v. 2.] Philadelphia, Henry F. Anners, c. 1845. 216 p., [6 pl.,] 6 x 3⅞. L.C., U.W. (375)

—— ——, or affection's gift, a Christmas, New-Year's and birth-day present for **1847.** [v. 3.] Philadelphia, Henry F. Anners, c. 1846 216 p., [5 pl.,] 6 x 3¾. N.Y., C.U. (376)

—— ——, or affection's gift, a Christmas, New-Year's and birth-day present for **1848.** [v. 4.] Philadelphia, Henry F. Anners, c. 1847. 216 p., [5 pl.,] 6 x 3¾. N.Y., L.C., U.W. (377)

—— ——, or affection's gift, a Christmas, New-Year and birth-day present. [v. 5.] Philadelphia, Henry F. Anners, **1849,** c. 1848. 220 p., 5 pl., 6 x 3¾. N.Y., C.U., B.P. (378)

—— ——, or affection's gift. A Christmas, New Year and birth-day present for **1850.** [v. 6.] Philadelphia, Henry F. Anners, 1850, c. 1849. 216 p., 5 pl., 6 x 3¾. N.Y., L.C. (379)

—— ——, or affection's gift, a Christmas, New Year and birth-day present for **1851.** [v. 7.] Philadelphia, Henry F. Anners. 216 p., 5 pl., 6 x 3¾. B.P., L.C. (380)

—— ——, or affection's gift, a Christmas, New Year and birth-day present for **1852.** [v. 8.] Philadelphia Henry F. Anners. 216 p., 5 pl., 6 x 4. N.Y., L.C. (381)

—— ——, or affection's gift, a Christmas, New Year and birth-day present for **1853.** [v. 9.] Philadelphia, Henry F. Anners, c. 1852. 216 p., 5 pl., 6 x 4. N.Y., L.C., U.W. (382)

—— ——, or affection's gift, a Christmas, New-Year and birth-day present for **1854.** [v. 10.] Philadelphia, Henry F. Anners, c.1853. 216 p., 5 pl., 6 x 3¾. L.C., B.P., C.U. (383)

**Hyacinth, The,** or affection's gift, a Christmas, New Year and birth-day present for **1855.** [v. 11.] Philadelphia, Henry F. Anners, c.1854. 216 p., 5 pl., 6 x 3⅞. F. (384)

**Illustrated ladies' keepsake,** ed. by A. Abbott. New York, John S. Taylor, **1852.** vi, 384 p., 13 pl., 9¼ x 6¼. * (385)

**Illustrated souvenir.** A gift book for the holidays for 1852, ed. by the author of the "Glory and downfall of Edom." Boston, Stone & Pratt, **c. 1852.** 3 p. l., 1–190, 1–190 p., 42 pl., 8¾ x 5½. B.P. (386)

**Infant's annual, The.** New York, C. Wells, **1839.** 1–28, 1–29 p., illus., 4½ x 3¾. C.U., U.W. (387)

**Iris, The,** or annual visitor for **1844,** ed. by Daniel Mallory. New York, Robert P. Bixby & Co. x, 11–220 p., [6 pl.,] 5⅝ x 3¾. N.Y., L.C. (388)

**Iris, The,** an illuminated souvenir for **1851,** ed. by John S. Hart. [v. 1.] Philadelphia, Lippincott, Grambo & Co., 1851, c. 1850. xii p., 1 l., 19–312 p., 12 pl., 9 x 6¼. N.Y., L.C., C.U., U.W. (389)

—— ——, an illuminated souvenir for **1852,** ed. by John S. Hart. [v. 2.] Philadelphia, Lippincott, Grambo & Co., 1852, c. 1851. xvi, 19–298 p., 12 pl., 9 x 6⅛. L.C. (390)

—— ——, an illuminated souvenir for **1853,** ed. by John S. Hart. [v. 3.] Philadelphia, Lippincott, Grambo & Co., 1853, c 1852. xiv p., 1 l., 17–314 p., 12 pl., 9⅛ x 6¼ N.Y., B.A., P.M. (391)

**Irving offering, The,** a token of affection for **1851.** New York, Leavitt & Co., 1851, c. 1850. viii p., 2 l., 13–276 p., 6 pl., 7½ x 4¾. N.Y., P.M. (392)

—— ——, a token of affection for **1852.** New York. Leavitt & Co., 1852. 4 p. l., 13–312 p., 7 pl., 7½ x 4¾. U.W. (393)

**Jackson wreath, The,** or national souvenir, by Robert Walsh, with continuation by James McHenry. Philadelphia, Jacob Maas, **1829.** viii, 9–88 p., 3 l., 8 pl., 8¼ x 5. F. (394)

**Jewel, The,** a token of friendship for **1839.** New York. pl., 16mo. * (395)

—— ——, or token of friendship, an annual for **1843.** New York, R. P. Bixby, 1843. 248 p., 5 pl., 6 x 3¾. N.Y. (396)

Reissued in 1844.
Also issued as "Juvenile forget-me-not," N. Y., n. d., with pl. different.

—— ——, or token of friendship, an annual for **1844.** New York, R. P. Bixby & Co., 1844. viii, 9–248 p., 5 pl., 6 x 3¾. C U., U.W. (397)

Same as 1843.

**Jewel, The,** a holiday gift for boys and girls, ed. by Emma F. Allston. New York, J. Winchester, **1844.** vi, 7–160 p., 10 pl., 5¼ x 4¼. F. (398)

—— ——, or token of friendship. New York, Ansel Edwards, **1846.** 248 p., [6 pl., 5 pl. on list,] 5¾ x 3¾ F. (399)

Same as 1843, with 1 pl. added

—— ——, or token of friendship, a Christmas or New-Year's present. Hartford, S. Andrus & Son **1847** c 1846. 248 p., 5 pl., 5¾ x 3¾. U.W. (400)

Same as 1843.

**Josephine gallery, The,** ed. by Alice and Phœbe Cary. New York, Derby & Jackson, **1859**, c. 1858. viii, 9–287 p., [8 pl.,] 9¼ x 6⅞. U.M. (401)

**Juvenile annual, The,** or holiday melodies, by Mrs. M. H. Maxwell. Boston, Stone & Pratt, **1852,** c. 1852. iv p., 1 l., 7–101 p., front., 4½ x 2¾. N.Y. (402)

**Juvenile forget-me-not, The,** a Christmas and New Year's present. New York, Leavitt & Allen, **n. d.** [1856 or after]. 248 p., [6 pl.,] 6¼ x 4¼. P.M. (403)

This is "Jewel," 1843, with different pl.
Also issued N. Y., Geo. A. Leavitt, n. d., with different pl. except front. U. W. (403a)
Also N. Y., 1869, with all pl. different except front. U.W.

**Juvenile forget me not.** A Christmas, New Year's and Birth Day present for **1839.** [v. 1.] Philadelphia, Thomas T. Ash & Henry F. Anners, c. 1838. 180 p., 6 pl., 6¼ x 4. N.Y., B.P. (404)

—— ——, a Christmas, New Year's and Birth Day present for **1841.** Philadelphia, Henry F. Anners, c. 1840. 180 p., [4 pl.,] 6 x 3¾. L.C. (405)

—— ——, a Christmas and New Year's present. New York, George A. Leavitt, **1869.** 248 p., [6 pl.,] 6¼ x 4¼. C.U. (406)

Same as N. Y., n. d. issue. Really "Jewel," 1843. Pl. vary.

**Juvenile gem, The,** for **1846,** ed. by Father Frank. New York, E. Kearny, c. 1845. iv p., 1 l., 7–284 p., [4 pl. and illum. t., illus.,] 5¾ x 3¾. B.P., C.U., U.W. (407)

Also issued without date, c.1845. F. (407a)
The same was issued as "Gem," 1848. See also "Gem," 1852, 1855.

**Juvenile keepsake, The,** a gift book for young people, ed. by Clara Arnold. Boston, Phillips, Sampson & Co., **c. 1851.** xii, 13–148 p., 8 pl., 7 x 5½. N.Y., H.U. (408)

**Juvenile scrap-book** and youth's annual. Providence, S. R. Weeden, **n. d.** 180 p., 8 woodcuts, 5½ x 3⅝. B.P. (409)

Title "Youth's Annual," on back of cover.

—— —— and youth's annual. Providence, **1845.** * (410)

**Juvenile scrap book** for **1849**, a Christmas and New Year's present for young people. New York. viii, 9–144 p., 28 pl., 5⅞ x 3¾. F. (411)

**Juvenile sketch-book,** a token for New Year. Boston N. S. Simpkins & Co., 1828. 3 p. l., 9–211 p., front., 5¾ x 3⅜. H.U. (412)

**Juvenile souvenir, The,** by the ed. of the "Juvenile miscellany," **1828.** Boston, Marsh & Capen and John Putnam, c. 1827. 184 p., [3 pl.,] 5½ x 3½. B.P., B.A. (413)

**Keepsake, The,** ed. by J. T. Headley. New York, Leavitt & Allen, 379 Broadway, **n. d.** [1856 or after]. v, 5–304 p., 9¾ x 7½. "John Morley." U.W. (414)

Also issued without street and number on imprint. F. (414a)

—— ——, a Christmas, New Year's and birthday present for **1845.** New York, D. Appleton & Co., 1845, c. 1844. 288 p.,10 pl., 6½ x 4¼. N.Y., U.W. (415)

—— ——, or token of remembrance for **1848.** Dew drops of the nineteenth century, ed. by Seba Smith. New York, John Levison. viii, 9–216 p., [5 (?) engr. pl., and 5 (?) flower pl.,] 7½ x 4½. F. (416)

This is the same as "Dewdrops of the nineteenth century," 1846–7, except pl. See also "Gift of friendship," 1848.

—— ——, a gift for the holidays, with illustrations by artists of eminence. [v. 7.] New York, J. C. Riker, **1851.** 288 p., 9 pl., 9¼ x 7. B.A. (417)

The successor of "Opal," v. 1–6.

—— ——, a gift for the holidays, with illustrations by artists of eminence. [v. 8.] New York, John C. Riker, **1852.** 304 p., 10 pl., 9¼ x 6¾. F. (418)

—— ——, a gift for the holidays, with illustrations. [v. 9.] New York, **1853.** B.M. (419)

Compiled from the English "Keepsake" and other sources, by W. T.

**Keepsake Americaine.** New York, [in French and printed in Paris,] **1831.** * (420)

Has pl. of "Atlantic souvenir," 1830.

—— ——. N. Y. [et Philadelphie, **1832,** all in French]. xii, 362 p., [12 pl.,] 6½ x 4. F. (421)

**Keepsake of friendship,** a Christmas and New Year's annual for **1849,** ed. by G. S. Monroe. [v. 1.] Worcester, Tucker & Ruggles, 1849. viii p., 1 l., 11–324 p., 6 pl., 7¼ x 4¾. "Friendship." C.U. (422)

Really "Amaranth," 1847, with first article changed. See also "Garland," 1848, which is same except first article.

**Keepsake of friendship,** a Christmas and New Year's annual for **1850**, ed. by G. S. Monroe. [v. 2.] Worcester, E. N. Tucker, 1850. vi p., 1 l., 9–288 p., 6 pl., 7¼ x 4¾ "Friendship." B.P., B.A., U.W. (423)

Really "Amaranth," 1848, with first article changed. See also "Garland," 1849, which is the same except first article.

—— ——, a Christmas and New Year's annual for **1851,** ed. by G. S. Monroe. [v. 3.] Worcester, E. N. Tucker, 1851. 322 p., 6 pl., 7¼ x 4¾. "Friendship." B.A. (424)

Really "Amaranth," 1849, with p. 9–11 replaced by two poems, and front. and engr. t. replaced by col. presentation pl., and col. t. See also "Garland," 1850, "Casket," 1853, "Memory's gift," n. d., and 1869, "Token of friendship" [1852], "Magnolia," 1852.

—— ——, **1852.** ? * (425)

"Amaranth," 1850, was probably reissued as "Keepsake of friendship," 1852.

—— ——, a Christmas and New Year's annual for **1853,** ed. by G. S. Monroe. [v. 5.] Boston, Phillips, Sampson & Co., 1853. 5 p. l., 276 p., 6 pl., 7¼ x 4¾. "Humility." N.Y., B.P., U.W. (426)

This is "Wreath of wild flowers," 1846, with unpaged p. l. added, and plates added. It was first reissued as "Amaranth," 1851, in the same fashion with different article on the unpaged leaf, then as "Garland," 1852, with still another change in unpaged p. l. See also "Magnolia" [pref. d. 1853], "Token of friendship," N. Y., n. d., which are same except unpaged l. and pl.

—— ——, a Christmas and New Year's annual for **1854,** ed. by G. S. Monroe. [v. 6.] Boston, Phillips, Sampson & Co., 1854, c. 1853. 3 p.l., 5–288 p., 7 pl., 7¼ x 4¾, "Friendship." B.P. (427)

This is really "Amaranth," 1852, with first article changed. See also "Garland," 1853, "Magnolia," 1855.

—— ——, a Christmas and New Year's annual for **1855,** ed. by G. S. Monroe. [v. 7.] Boston, Phillips, Sampson & Co., 1855, c. 1854. 1 p.l., 3–288 p., 7 pl., 7¼ x 4¾, "Use of flowers." N.Y., C.U., B.P. (428)

Also issued omitting all dates on title, c. 1854. U.W. (428*a*)

Also issued with imprint, New York, Leavitt & Allen, c. 1854. This is identical except different pl. and list of pl. omitted [p. 3–4]. N.Y., U.W. (428*b*)

Later reissued by Leavitt & Allen, with only 1 pl., similar to those in former issue by same firm. N.Y. (428*c*)

Reissued by George A Leavitt, **1869** [5 pl.] F. (428d)

Really "Amaranth," 1853, with first article changed. See "Garland," 1854, same except first article.

**Lady's album, The.** New York, Nafis and Cornish, **n. d.** [circa 1845]. xii, 348 p., 21 pl., 7⅛ x 4¼. "The kelp gatherer." B.P. (429)

Title on engr. t. p., "Album."

Also issued with 13 pl. F. (429*a*)

Also issued Nafis and Cornish, n. d., but with 1848 on back of book. (429*b*)

Also issued as "Moss rose," n. d. [c. 1845] and 1854.

Really "Lady's cabinet album," 1832, et seq.

**Ladies' and gentlemen's pocket annual** for **1834,** an illuminated pocket-book. * (430)

**Lady's annual, The,** a Christmas and New Year gift. New York, Leavitt & Allen, **n. d.** [1856 or after]. 1 p. l., 7–264 p., 6 pl., 7⅞ x 5¾. H.U., U.W. (431)

Also copies with "Ladies' annual" on cover.
Really "Friendship's offering," c. 1855, with different pl.
Issued as "Friendship's gift," n. d.
Issued as "Gem annual," n. d., but with different pl. and a list of pl.

—— ——, a souvenir of friendship for **1849,** ed. by Emily Percival. N. Y., D. Appleton & Co., 1849. 216 p., 26 pl., 6¾ x 4½. N.Y., B.P., C.U. (432)

**Lady's annual register** and housewife's memorandum book for 1838–1843. Boston. 7¾ x 4¾. B.P.

These are not true gift books.

**Lady's book, The,** of flowers and poetry, to which are added a botanical introduction and a complete floral dictionary, and a chapter on plants in rooms, ed. by Lucy Hooper. New York, J. C. Riker, **1842,** c. 1841. 11–263 p., [col. pl. of flowers,] 7¼ x 4½. C.U. (433)
This is also issued, 1843, c. 1841, p. [3]–275. F. (434)

**Lady's cabinet.** Title on back of **"Young lady's cabinet of gems."**

**Lady's cabinet album, The.** New York, pub. for the booksellers, **n. d.** xii, 348 p., 21 pl., 6¾ x 4¼. "Kelp-gatherer." B.P., U.W. (435)

Engr. t., "Album."
This is same as 1832, except has col. presentation pl. and different front., and vig. t., which do not agree with list of pl.

—— ——. New York, Peabody & Co., **1832.** xii, 348 p., 21 pl., 6½ x 4⅛. B.P. (436)
Reissued exactly identical, Peabody & Co., **1834.** B.P. (436*a*)
Reissued exactly identical, E. Sands, **1835.** N.Y. (436*b*)
An edition by E. Sands, **1837.** B.A. (436*c*)
See "Lady's album," n. d., "Moss rose," n. d.

**Ladies' casket, The,** and friendship's offering. New York, Burdick, Reed and Roberts, **n. d.** [circa 1850]. 8½ x 5½. N.Y. (437)

Really vol. 9 of a magazine.

—— ——. Lowell. 32mo. * (438)

**Ladies' choice.** See **"Young ladies' choice."**

**Ladies' companion,** or sketches of life, manners and morals at the present day, ed. by a lady. Philadelphia, H. C. Peck & Theo. Bliss, **1851,** c. 1851. 288 p., illum. t., 7¼ x 4¾. N.Y.S. (439)

Illum. t. reads, "Young lady's companion."

**Ladies' diadem, The,** a token of friendship for **1848, 1853** ed. by Edward A. Rice. New York. 8½ x 5½. B.P., U.W.

These are really magazines.

**Ladies' gems, 1849.** * (440)

**Ladies' gift, The,** a souvenir of friendship. Boston, Phillips, Sampson & Co., **n. d.** viii, 11–324 p., [2 pl. and illum. t.,] 7¼ x 4¾. "Friendship." L.C., B.A., U.W. (441)

Also issued as "**Lady's gift.** U. W. (442)
Same as 1850, which see for note.

—— ——, a souvenir for all seasons, ed. by Walter Percival. Nashua [N. H.], Charles T. Gill, **1849.** vi p., 1 l., 13–312 p., 10 pl., 7½ x 4¾. C.U. (443)

This is "Friendship's gift," 1848.

—— ——, or souvenir of friendship, illustrated. Boston. David P. King, **1850.** viii, 11–324 p., [2 pl. and col. front.,] 7¼ x 4¾. U.W. (444)

This is "Amaranth," 1847, with first article changed, all but 2 pl. omitted.
See also "Gift of affection," n. d., "Garland." 1849, "Keepsake of friendship," 1849.

**Ladies' gift, The,** or souvenir of friendship, illustrated. Boston. David P. King, **1851.** N.Y., B.P. (445)

Same as 1850, which see for note.

**Ladies' illustrated keepsake, The,** ed. by Asahel Abbott. [v. 1.] New York, John S. Taylor, **1852,** c. 1851. vi p., 1 l., 9–384 p., 12 pl. [really 13 pl.], 8¾ x 5¾. N.Y. (446)

—— ——. **1853.** * (447)

**Ladies' keepsake,** a gift for all seasons. Highly embellished. New York, John F. Scovill, **n. d.** [circa 1862]. 208 p., [6 pl.,] 8½ x 5½. N.Y.S. (448)

**Ladies' keepsake and home library.** New York. 9⅛ x 6¼

This is a magazine.

**Lady's manual, The,** of moral and intellectual culture by Rev. Hubbard Winslow and Mrs. John Sanford. New York, Leavitt & Allen, **1854,** c. 1853. viii p., 1 l., 9–81, 5–175 p., 8 pl., 6½ x 4½. "The appropriate sphere of woman." B.P. (449)

Called "Benison" on back of cover.
Also issued as "Affection's gift," n. d., "Token and Atlantic souvenir," n. d., and "Memory's gift," n. d.

**Ladies' parlor companion, The.** New York, **1852.** [v. 8]. 8¾ x 5½.

Really a magazine, "Baptist memorial."

**Ladies' scrap-book, The,** a New Year and Christmas gift. New York, Leavitt & Allen, **n. d.** [1856 or after]. iv, 7–268 p., [6 pl.,] 7¼ x 4¾. C.U. (450)

Same as 1845, except pl. vary and last p. are omitted.

—— ——. Hartford, S. Andrus & Son, **1845,** c. 65th year of U. S. independence. iv p., 1 l., 7–336 p., 10 pl., 6¾ x 4¼. P.M. (451)

This is also issued, Hartford, S. Andrus & Son, **n. d.,** c. 65th year of U. S. independence, and with col. flower pl. in place of front. called for. B.P. (452)
Also issued **1850.** F. (452*a*)
Also issued, Hartford, S. Andrus & Son, **1854,** omitting last two pl. F. (452*b*)

**Ladies' souvenir, The,** ed. by N. Parker Willis. New York, Leavitt & Allen, **c. 1853.** 5–224 p., 12 pl., 9¼ x 6¾. U.W. (453)

**Lady's token, The,** a gift of friendship, ed. by Coatesworth Pinckney. Nashua, N. H., J. Buffum, **1848,** c. 1848. 128 p., col. t., 4½ x 2¾. C.U. (454)

Same, Boston, G. W. Cottrell, c. 1848, col. t. F. (454*a*)

**Ladies' vase, The,** or polite manual for young ladies. Original and selected. By an American lady. 3d ed. Hartford, Henry S. Parson, **1847,** c. 1847. vi, 7–139 p , front., 4⅜ x 2¾. F. (454b)

**Ladies' vase of wild flowers, The,** a collection of gems from the best authors, by Miss Colman. Auburn, Alden Beardsley & Co., **1852,** c. 1846. viii, 9–126 p , col. front.. 4½ x 2¾. F. (454c)

**Ladies' wreath, The,** a selection from the female poetic writers of England and America, a gift book for all seasons, by Mrs. Hale. Boston, Marsh, Capen & Lyon, **1837,** c. 1836. 408 p., [engr. front., and vig. t.,] 7⅛ x 4½. N.Y., B.P. (455)

—— ——, 2d edition, improved and enlarged. **1839.** 436 p. B.P. (456)

**Ladies' wreath,** an illustrated annual. New York, 1847. v. 1,+ 8½ x 5½.

This is a magazine.

**Ladies' wreath, The,** a souvenir for all seasons, illustrated. Boston, Phillips, Sampson & Co., **1855.** 288 p., 6 pl., 7¼ x 4¾. F. (457)

Also issued without date. B.P. (457*a*)

**Laurel, The,** a gift for all seasons, being a collection of poems by American authors. Boston, Edward R. Broaders, **1836**, c 1835. 252 p., 6 x 3½. F. (458)

Same as the following.

—— ——, a gift for all seasons, being a collection of poems by American authors. Baltimore, Bayly & Burns, **1837,** c. n. d. 252 p., 5¾ x 3¾. F. (459)

**Laurel leaves,** original poems, stories and essays by Longfellow, Whittier, Holmes, Bryant, Lowell. Boston, Wm. F. Gill & Co., **1876,** c. 1875. xvi p., 2 l., 21-446 p., 8½ x 6¾. B.A. (460)

—— ——, a chaplet woven by the friends of the late Mrs. Osgood, ed. by Mary E. Hewitt. New York, Lamport, Blakeman & Law, **1854.** 8–347 p., front., col. t., 9 x 5¾. F. (461)

This was first published as "The Memorial," 1851.

**Laurel wreath, The,** a Christmas, and New Year's gift ed. by Rev. S. D. Burchard. New York, Leavitt & Allen, 379 Broadway, **n. d.** [1856 or after]. viii, 9–263 p., 6 pl., 7¼ x 4¾. "Annuals." N.Y., B.P. (462)

This is the 1846 issue with p. 264–364 omitted, and sonnet p. 70 replaced by "Sea gull"; plates are different.

**Laurel Wreath, The,** ed. by Rev. S. D. Burchard. Hartford, S. Andrus & Son, **c. 1845.** 2 p. l., vii-viii, 9–364 p., 7 pl. [and col. front.], 7⅜ x 4½. "Annuals." H.U., B.A. (463)

Same as 1846, except that "Sonnet" p. 70 and "Sea gull" p. 364 are transposed, 3 pl. omitted, list of pl. revised to agree, preface omitted, and col. front added. B.A.

Another issue of this, with 10 pl. [and col. front.]. F. (464)

—— ——, ed. by Rev. S. D. Burchard. Hartford, S. Andrus & Son, **1846,** c. 1845. viii, 9–364 p., 10 pl., 6¾ x 4¼. "Annuals." N.Y., B.P., B.A. (465)

Also issued for 1847, with no date on title page, c. 1845) and **1847** on back of book. U.W. (465*a*)
Also issued without date, c. 1845. [See 7 pl. edition above, and also the N. Y. n. d. issue with p. 9–263 and different pl.].

**Leaflets of memory,** compiled by the ed. of the "Oriental Annual." New York, Leavitt & Allen, **n. d.** [1856 or after]. xii p., 2 l., 17–224 p., 12 col. pl., 9¼ x 6¾. "Wild flowers." N.Y. (466)

—— ——, an annual for **1845,** ed. by Reynell Coates. [v. 1.] Philadelphia, Butler & Williams, c. 1844. x p., 1 l., 13–328 p., 12 pl., 9⅛ x 6¼. N.Y.,B.A. (467)

—— ——, an annual for **1846,** ed. by Reynell Coates. [v. 2.] Philadelphia, E. H. Butler & Co., 1846, c. 1845. viii, 15–306 p., 12 pl., 9⅛ x 6¼. N.Y., L.C., B.P. (468)

—— ——, an illuminated annual for **1847,** ed. by Reynell Coates. [v. 3.] Philadelphia, E. H. Butler & Co., 1847, c. 1846. viii, 15–306 p., 12 pl., 9⅛ x 6¼. L.C., B.P. (469)

—— ——, an illuminated annual for **1848,** ed. by Reynell Coates. [v. 4.] Philadelphia, E. H. Butler & Co., 1848, c. 1847. viii, 17–312 p., 12 pl., 9⅛ x 6¼. N Y., L.C., C.U. (470)

—— ——, an illuminated annual for **1849.** [v. 5.] Philadelphia, E. H. Butler & Co., 1849, c. 1848. xvi. 17–312 p., 12 pl., 9⅛ x 6¼. L.C., C.U. (471)

—— ——, an illuminated annual for **1850,** ed. by Reynell Coates. [v. 6.] Philadelphia, E. H. Butler & Co., 1850, c. 1849. xvi, 17–312 p., 12 pl., 9 x 6. N.Y., L.C., P.M. (472)

—— ——, an illuminated annual for **1851,** ed. by Reynell Coates. [v. 7.] Philadelphia, E. H. Butler & Co., 1851, c. 1850. xvi, 17–312 p., 12 pl., 9⅛ x 6⅛. L.C., H.U. (473)

—— ——, an illuminated annual for **1852,** ed. by Reynell Coates. [v. 8.] Philadelphia, E. H. Butler & Co., 1852, c. 1851. xvi, 17–312 p., 12 pl., 9⅛ x 6⅛. L.C., B.P. (474)

**Leaflets of memory,** an illuminated annual for **1854.** [v. 9.] Philadelphia, E. H. Butler & Co., 1854, c. 1853. xvi, 17–314 p., 11 pl., 9⅛ x 6⅛. L.C., P.M. (475)

—— ——, an illuminated annual for **1855.** [v. 10.] Philadelphia, E. H. Butler & Co., 1855, c. 1854. xvi, 17–314 p., 11 pl., 9 x 6. L.C., P.M. (476)

—— ——, an illuminated annual New York, Leavitt & Allen, c. 1855 [**1856** on cover]. 4 p. l., 17–308 p., 10 pl., 9 x 6⅛. C.U., B.P. (477)

—— ——, with ten beautiful illustrations. New York, Leavitt & Allen, n. d., **c. 1856.** 4 p. l., 17–264 p., 9½ x 6¾. N.Y., C.U. (478)

**Legendary, The,** consisting of original pieces principally illustrative of American history, scenery and manners, ed. by N. P. Willis. Boston, S. G. Goodrich, **1328,** c. 1828. v. 1–2 together: v. 1, vi. p., 1 l., 1–286 p.; v. 2, viii, 1–278 p., 7⅞ x 4¾. F. (479)

Probably originally issued in 2 vols. separately.

**Liberty bell, The,** by friends of freedom, **1839.** [v. 1.] Boston, American anti-slavery society, 1839, c. 1839. viii, 104 p., engr. front., 6¾ x 4. N.Y., L.C. (480)

Also with imprint Boston for the Mass. anti-slavery fair. N.Y., U.W. (480*a*)

—— ——, by friends of freedom, **1841.** [v. 2.] Boston, Mass. anti-slavery fair, 1841. 3 p. l., 144 p., 6¼ x 4⅛. F. (481)

—— ——, by friends of freedom, **1842.** [v. 3.] Boston, Mass. anti-slavery fair, 1842. vi, 204 p., engr. front., 6¼ x 4. N.Y., L.C. (482)

—— ——, by friends of freedom, **1843.** [v. 4.] Boston Mass. anti-slavery fair, 1843. viii, 208 p., front., 7½ x 4½. L.C., U.W. (483)

—— ——, by friends of freedom **1844.** [v. 5.] Boston, Mass. anti-slavery fair, 1844. vi–viii, 232 p., front., 7½ x 4½. L.C. (484)

—— ——, by friends of freedom, **1845.** [v. 6.] Boston, Mass. anti-slavery fair, 1845. vi p., 1 l., 356 p., front., 7½ x 4½. N.Y., L.C. (485)

—— ——, by friends of freedom, **1846.** [v. 7.] Boston, Mass. anti-slavery fair, 1846. vi p., 1 l., 268 p., front., 7¼ x 4¾. N.Y., L.C. (486)

A few issued on large paper, 8¼ x 4¾.

—— ——, by friends of freedom, **1847.** [v. 8.] Boston, National anti-slavery bazaar, 1847. viii, 304 p., engr. t., 7½ x 4½. N.Y. (487)

Also on large paper, 8¼ x 5.

—— ——, by friends of freedom **1848.** [v 9.] Boston, National anti-slavery bazaar, 1848. viii, 292 p.. engr. t., 7¼ x 4¾. N.Y., L.C. (488)

Also in large paper, 8¼ x 5.

**Liberty bell, The,** by friends of freedom, **1849.** [v. 10.] Boston, National anti-slavery bazaar, 1849. viii, 292 p., front. and engr. t., 7 x 4½. N.Y., L.C. (489)

—— ——, by friends of freedom, **1851.** [v. 11.] Boston, National anti-slavery bazaar, 1851. viii, 304 p., engr. t., 7¼ x 4½. N.Y. (490)

—— ——, by friends of freedom, **1852.** [v. 12.] Boston, National anti-slavery bazaar, 1852 viii, 304 p., engr. t., 7½ x 4½. N.Y., L.C. (491)

—— ——, by friends of freedom, **1853.** [v 13.] Boston, Mass. anti-slavery fair, 1853. viii, 208 p., engr. t., 7½ x 5¾. N.Y., L.C. (492)

—— ——, by friends of freedom, **1856.** [v. 14.] Boston, Mass. anti-slavery bazaar, 1856. viii, 200 p., engr. t., 7¼ x 4½. N.Y., L.C. (493)

—— ——, by friends of freedom, **1858.** [v. 15.] Boston National anti-slavery bazaar, 1858. viii, 328 p., 7¼ x 4¾. (494)

—— ——, by William R. Wallace. N. Y. 1862.

This is not an annual.

**Lilies and violets,** or thoughts in prose and verse on the graces of maidenhood, by Rosalie Bell. New York, **1855.** * (495)

**Lily, The,** a holiday present with steel embellishments. New York, E. Sands, **c. 1830.** vi, 7–232 p., [10 pl.] 5¾ x 3¾. "Young Tyrolese." B.P., U.W. (496)

Also issued for 1839 [date on back only].

Also issued as "Forget me not," n. d., Nafis & Cornish, without presentation pl., plates vary.

—— ——, a colored annual for **1831.** New York, R. Schoyer, 1831, c. 1830. vi, 7–232 p., [7 pl. colored by hand,] 5¾ x 3½. N.Y. (497)

Same as 1830.

—— ——, a colored annual for **1832.** New York, Charles Wells, c. 1830. vi, 7–232 p., 10 pl., 6½ x 4. N.Y. (498)

Same as 1830. Pl. same, but on yellow paper and uncolored; has wider margins.

—— ——, a colored annual for **1834.** New York, Charles Wells, c. 1830. vi, 7–232 p., [10 pl.,] 6¼ x 4. N.Y., L.C. (499)

Same as 1830.

—— ——, a colored annual for **1835.** New York, E. Sands, 1835, c. 1830. vi, 7–232 p., [7 pl.,] 6¼ x 4. N.Y., L.C. (500)

Same as 1830, except pl. vary and are in black, on yellow paper.

—— ——, a holiday present with steel embellishment. New York, E. Sands, [**1839** on back of cover,], c. 1830. vi, 7–232 p., [10 pl.,] 5¾ x 3¾. F. (500*a*)

Same as 1830.

**Lily of the valley, The,** a gift for all seasons, with illustrations. Boston, James M. Usher, **n. d.** 4 p. l., 13–236 p., 6 pl., 7¼ x 4¾. F. (501)

—— —— for **1851,** ed. by Mrs. M. A. Livermore. [v. 1.] Boston, James M. Usher, c. 1850. 320 p., 7 pl., 6¾ x 4½. L.C., B.P., U.W. (502)

Also issued as "Friendship's gift," n. d. and 1852.

"Mignonette," 1856, is same up to p. 258 except poem, "The lost jewel," p. 31–4, is substituted for "The angel guest."

—— —— for **1852,** ed. by Mrs. M. A. Livermore. [v. 2.] Boston. James M. Usher, c. 1851. viii, 11–307 p., 6 pl., 6¾ x 4½. B.P., B.A. (503)

Also issued as "Mayflower," Lowell, 1853.

—— —— for **1853,** ed. by Elizabeth Doten. [v. 3.] Boston, James M. Usher, 1853, c. 1852. vi p., 1 l., 11–306 p., 6 pl., 6¾ x 4½. L.C., B.P. (504)

Issued as "Mayflower," 1854.

—— —— for **1854,** ed. by Elizabeth Doten. [v. 4.] Boston, James M. Usher, 1854, c. 1853. vi p., 1 l., 11–314 p., 7 pl., 7 x 4½. B.P., H.U. (505)

Issued as "Mayflower," 1855.

—— —— for **1855,** ed. by Elizabeth Doten. [v. 5.] Boston, James M. Usher, 1855, c. 1854, viii p., 1 l., 11–303 p., 7 pl., 6⅞ x 4⅝. N Y., B.P., L.C., U.W. (506)

Probably reissued as "Mayflower," 1856.

—— —— for **1856,** with illustrations. [v. 6.] Boston, James M. Usher, 1856, c. 1855. iv p., 1 l., 13–256 p., 6 pl., 7 x 4¾. N.Y., C.U., U.W. (507)

Issued as "Mayflower," 1857.

—— —— for **1857,** with illustrations. [v. 7.] Boston, James M. Usher, 1857, c. 1856. iv p., 1 l., 13–356 p., 6 pl., 7 x 4¾. N.Y., L.C., B.P. (508)

—— —— for **1858,** with illustrations. [v. 8.] Boston, James M. Usher, 1858, c. 1857. 4 p. l., 13–243 p., 6 pl., 7 x 4¾. N.Y., U.W. (509)

Also issued as "Mayflower," Lynn, n. d.

—— —— for **1859,** with illustrations. [v. 9.] Boston, James M. Usher, 1859. 4 p. l., 13–236 p., 6 pl., 7 x 4¾. U.W. (510)

**Literary amaranth, The,** or prose and poetry by Nathan C. Brooks. Philadelphia, Kay & Brother, **1840.** viii p, 1 l., 11–264 p., 8 pl., 7 x 4½. N.Y., U.W. (511)

Second ed. Kay & Brother, **1845.** F. (512)

Engr. t. reads "Amaranth"; also back has "Amaranth," both editions.

**Literary casket,** a gift for all seasons. New York, **n. d.** B.P., U.W.

Really a monthly magazine, issued as an annual.

**Literary souvenir,** a Christmas and New Year's present ed. by Wm. E. Burton. Philadelphia, E. L. Care and A. Hart, **1838,** c. 1838. 2 p. l., 17–212 p., 16 pl., 8 x 5¼. L.C., N.Y., P M. (513)

—— ——, a Christmas and New Year's present for **1840,** ed. by Wm. E. Burton. Philadelphia, E. L. Carey and A. Hart, 1840, c. 1839. 2 p. l., 17–226 p., 13 pl., 8 x 5⅛. N.Y., L.C., B.P., U.W. (514)

—— ——, a Christmas and New Year's present for **1844,** with 10 engravings. Philadelphia, Carey and Hart. vi p., 1 l., 9–252 p., 10 pl., 6 x 3¾. N.Y., C.U., B.P. (515)

—— ——, a Christmas and New Year's present for **1845,** with 10 engravings. Philadelphia, Carey and Hart, 1845, c. 1844. vi p., 1 l., 13–252 p., 10 pl., 6¼ x 4⅛. L.C. (516)

**Little gem, The,** a Christmas, New Year's and birthday present. Hartford, Silas Andrus & Son, **1847.** vi, 7–144 p., front. and col. t., 3⅞ x 2¾. F. (517)

**Little gift.** Boston, **1844.** * (518)

—— ——. Boston, T. H. Carter & Co., **1845.** * (519)

**Little keepsake, The,** selected from the writings of J. C. Lavater. New York, S. Colman, **1843.** 96 p., 5 pl., 4⅜ x 3⅝. F. (520)

—— ——, **1844.** * (521)

—— ——. Boston, T. H. Carter & Co., **1845.** * (522)

**Little republic, The,** original articles by various hands, ed. by Mrs. T. S. Smith. New York, Wiley & Putnam, 1848. 1 p. l., vi, 228 p., front., 5¾ x 4¾. F. (523)

**Love gift, A,** for **1845.** Boston, Saxton, Peirce & Co., 1845. xiv, 15–144 p. ,illum. t., 5¾ x 3½. N.Y. (524)

**Lyric gems,** a collection and select sacred poetry, ed. by Rev. S. F. Smith. Boston, Gould, Kendall & Lincoln, **c. 1844.** viii, 9–128 p., 4⅜ x 2¾. F. (524a)

**Magnolia, The,** or gift book of friendship, ed. by Clara Arnold. New York, Leavitt & Allen, **n. d.** 288 p., [6 pl.,] 7½ x 5. N.Y. (525)
This is 1855 with nearly all pl. different.

—— —— for **1836,** ed. by Henry W. Herbert. [v. 1.] New York, Monson, Bancroft, c. 1835. vi p., 1 l., 9–300 p., 13 pl., 7½ x 4¾. "The Magnolia 'Not in the autumn.'" P.M., N.Y., U.W. (526)

Reprinted in 1839, omitting preface.
Reprinted in 1841, New York, A. & C. B. Edwards, c. 1835, with first line of "advertisement" altered.
Issued in 1842, New York, S. E. S. Brown, c. 1835, 12 pl.
Issued in 1843, New York, Robt. P. Bixby & Co., 12 pl.
Issued without date in 1844 [1844 on back of vol.], New York, Robt. P. Bixby & Co., v, 9–300 p., 7 pl. Has only part of the plates of 1836 and a different frontispiece.

**Magnolia, The**—(*continued*).

issued as "Morning glory," n. d. with different pl.

Issued as "Coral," n. d., with different pl.; as "Friendship's token," N. Y., n. d., omitting p. 261–300; as "Memory", c. 1854, with less and different pl., omittin p. 261–300; as "Gift of affection," n. d.; as "Snow flake", n. d., omitting p. 261–300, and different pl., and as "Aloe," 1854, different pl. and omitting p. 265–300.

—— ——, for **1837,** ed. by Henry William Herbert. [v. 2.] New York, Bancroft & Holley, c. 1836. v. p., 1 l., 9–352 p., 15 pl., 7½ x 4¾.
—— N.Y., L.C., B.P. (527)

—— ——, **1839,** with 13 fine engravings. 7¼ x 4¾. L.C. (528)

Same as 1836, with preface omitted.

—— ——, **1841.** New York, A. & C. B. Edwards, c. 1835. N.Y. (529)

Same as 1836, first line of "advertisement" changed.

—— ——, **1842.** New York, S. E. S. Brown, c. 1835. 12 pl., 7¼ x 4⅝. N.Y., U. M. (530)

Same as 1836, except pl. vary.

—— ——, **1843.** New York, Robt. P. Bixby & Co. 12 pl. C.U., L.C. (531)

Same as 1836, except variation in pl.

This was also issued in 1844 without date [**1844**] on back of cover. N.Y. (531*a*)

—— ——, Friendship's gift of moral and entertaining literature, ed. by Mrs. M. O. Stevens. Boston, Jordan & Wiley, **1847.** 8 x 5¼. B.P.

This is a magazine [v. 1–2 bound as 1 vol.].

—— ——, or gift book of friendship, ed. by Clara Arnold Boston, Phillips, Sampson & Co., n. d. [pref. dated Aug., 1851, **1852** on back of cover]. vi p., 1 l., 9–322 p., 6 pl., 7½ x 4¾. "Love of nature."
N.Y., U.W., B.P. (532)

This is "Amaranth," 1849, with articles on p. 9–11 changed from "Medora" to "Love of nature."

See also "Casket" Boston [1853], and N. Y., n. d., "Garland," 1850; "Memory's gift," N. Y., 1869; and N. Y., n. d.; "Token of friendship" [1852], "Keepsake of friendship," 1851.

—— ——, or gift book of friendship, ed. by Clara Arnold. Boston, Phillips, Sampson & Co., n. d. [**1853** on back, pref. dated Aug. 1852]. 288 p., 6 pl., 7¼ x 4¾. "The village home." L.C. (533)

This is "Amaranth," 1850, with first article changed, and all pl. but 2 different.

See also "Garland," 1851, "Keepsake of friendship," 1852.

—— ——, or gift book of friendship. Boston, Phillips, Sampson & Co., n.d. [pref d. Aug. 1853]. 2 p. l., vi, 276 p., 6 pl., 7¼ x 5. "Who are the happy?" U.M. (534)

This is "Wreath of wild flowers," 1846, with pl. and unpaged p. l. added, and preface changed.

See also "Amaranth," 1851, "Garland," 1852, "Keepsake of friendship," 1853, "Token of friendship" [1854], all of which are the same with variations in first unpaged article, and in pl. and preface.

**Magnolia, The,** or gift book of friendship, ed. by Clara Arnold. Boston, Phillips, Sampson & Co., **1855,** c. 1854. 288 p., 7 pl., 7½ x 4¾. "Friendship." N.Y.,C.U., B.P. (534*a*)

Also issued without date, except c. 1854. N.Y. (534*b*)
An edition by Leavitt & Allen, N. Y., n. d., with pl. different. N.Y. (534*c*)
Reissued by Geo. A. Leavitt, New York, **1869** [with 4 pl.]. F. (535)

This is "Amaranth," 1852, with "Heather bell" changed to "Friendship," rest the same, and with engr. t. and engr. front. changed to col. t. and col. front.
See also "Garland" 1853," "Keepsake of friendship," 1854.

**Maple leaf, The,** or Canadian annual. Toronto, **1849.** * (536)

**Marriage offering, The,** a compilation of prose and poetry. Boston, Wm. Crosby & H. P. Nichols, **1848,** c. 1848. viii, 207 p., engr. t., 6⅞ x 4⅜. F. (537)

Reissued with imprint date, **1849.** U.W. (537*a*)
Reissued with imprint date, **1851.** B.A. (537*b*)
Reissued with imprint date, **1852.** B.P. (537*c*)
Reissued with imprint date, **1859.** C.U. (537*d*)

**Marriage ring, The,** or how to make home happy, from the writings of John Angell James. 30th thousand. Boston, Gould, Kendall & Lincoln, **c. 1842.** vi, 7–128 p., 4¼ x 2¾. F. (537e)

This with "Family circle" added, and a t. and preface prefixed, was issued as "Wedding gift."

**Masonic offering, The,** for **1852,** ed. by John Perry and Paschal Donaldson. New York, Cornish Lamport & Co. c. 1881. viii, 9–320 p., 8 pl., 8 x 5½. F. (538)

Also issued in **1854.** * (538*a*)

**Masonic token, The,** a gift book, ed. by William T. Anderson. New York Masonic Publishing and Furnishing Co. 1878, c. 1868, 290 p., 4 pl., and illus. in text, 9 x 5⅞. F. (539)

**Mayflower, The,** a gift for all seasons, ed. by Emma Florence. Lynn [Mass.], Thomas Herbert, **n. d.** 3 p. l., 13–243 p., 6 pl., 7 x 4¾. N.Y., B.A. (540)

This is "Lily of the valley," 1858.

—— ——, for 1846, ed. by Robert Hamilton. [v. 1.– Boston, Saxton & Kelt, **1846,** c. 1845. vi p., 1 l., 11.] 354 p., 7 pl., 6¾ x 4½. N.Y., L.C., B.P. (541)

—— ——, for **1847,** ed. by Mrs. E. Oakes Smith. [v. 2.] Boston, Saxton & Kelt, 1847, c. 1846. xv p., 1 l., 17–304 p., 9 pl., 6¾ x 4½. N.Y., L.C., B.P. (542)

—— ——, for **1848,** ed. by Mrs. E. Oakes Smith. [v. 3.] Boston, Saxton & Kelt, 1848, c. 1847. xvi, 17–304 p,, 9 pl., 6¾ x 4½. N.Y., B.P., U.W. (543)

—— ——, a gift for all seasons, ed. by Emma Florence. Lowell. John Philbrick, **1853.** viii, 11–307 p., 6 pl., 7⅛ x 4½. B.P. (544)

This is "Lily of the valley," 1852.

**Mayflower, The,** a gift for all seasons, ed. by Emma Florence. Boston, John Philbrick, **1854,** c. 1852. vi p., 1 l.,11–306 p., 6 pl., 6⅞ x 4½.
B.P., U.W. (545)

Also issued with imprint Lowell, John Philbrick. F. (545*a*)
This is "Lily of the valley," 1853.

—— ——, a gift for all seasons, ed. by Emma Florence, Boston, John Philbrick, **1855.** vi p., 1 l., 11–314 p., 7 pl., 7¼ x 4½. N.Y., B.P. (546)

Also issued with imprint Lowell, John Philbrick. F. (546*a*)
This is "Lily of the Valley," 1854.

—— ——, **1856.** * (547)

Probably "Lily of the valley," 1855, was reissued as "Mayflower," 1856.

**May-flower, The,** for 1857, with illustrations. Lynn Thomas Herbert, **1857.** iv p., 1 l., 13–256 p., 6 pl., 7x4¾
L.C. (548)

This is "Lily of the valley," 1856.

**Memento, The,** a gift of friendship, ed. by C. W. Everest. New York, Buckland & Sumner, **1847,** c. 1844. [2d ed.] x, 11–292 p., [4 pl.,] 6⅞ x 4¼.
B.A., U.W. (549)

Preface says "has been before the public under another name." Several pages have been added.
Also issued in **1848,** with 288 p. U.W. (549*a*)
Also issued in **1849,** with 288 p. F. (549*b*)
Also issued in **1850,** with 288 p. F. (549*c*)

**Memento of friendship,** a gift of affection, ed. by C. W. Everest. Hartford [Conn.], Brockett & Hutchinson **c. 1851.** x, 11–288 p., 6 pl., 7⅜ x 4½.
N.Y., U.W. (550)

Also issued with [5 pl.] and imprint Brockett & Hutchinson. F. (550*a*)
Same as "Memento," 1847, except preface has new date, Aug. 27, 1851, and has additional pl. and less p.

**Memorial, The,** a Christmas and New Year's offering, ed. by F. S. H[ill]. [v. 1.] Boston, True & Greene, n. d. [**1827** on back label, pref. d. Nov. 1826]. viii, 9–268 p., [4 pl.,] 6½ x 4. N.Y., B.P., L.C. (551)

—— ——, a Christmas, New Year's and Easter offering for **1828,** ed. by Frederic S. Hill. [v. 2.] Boston, True & Greene. x p., 1 l., 13–407 p., 12 pl., 6¼ x 4.
B.P., B.A. (552)

—— ——, written by friends of the late Mrs. Osgood, and ed. by Mary E. Hewitt. New York, George P. Putnam, **1851,** c. 1850. vi, 7–346 p., 10 pl., 9 x 6.
F. (553)

Also issued as "Lauer

**Memories of home, The,** an illustrated annual for all seasons. New York, **1860.** iv, 5–428 p., [7 pl.,] 8½ x 5¾.
F. (554)

**Memory.** New York, Leavitt & Allen, **c. 1854.** 4 p l., 11–260 p., [8 pl.,] 6¾ x 4½. "Magnolia, 'not in the autumn.' " P.M. (555)

Illuminated title reads, "Memory, a souvenir." Back of book has "Memory's gift."
This is "Magnolia," 1836, with different and less pl., and p. 261–300 omitted. See also "Friendship's token," N. Y., n. d., "Coral," n. d., "Morning glory," n. d., "Gift of affection," n. d., "Snow flake," n. d., "Aloe," 1854.

**Memory and hope.** Boston, Ticknor, Reed & Fields, **1851**, c. 1850. xii, 244 p., 8 x 5¼. F. (555*a*)

**Memory's gift.** New York, Leavitt & Allen, **n. d.** vi p., 1 l., 9–322 p., [4 pl.?] 7 x 5. "The quiet eye." P.M. (556)

Also issued by Geo. A. Leavitt, **1869.**
This is "Amaranth," 1849, with first article changed and different pl.
The "Casket," N. Y., n. d., and Boston [1853] are also same.
See also "Garland," 1850, "Token of friendship, [1852]," "Keepsake of friendship," 1851, "Magnolia," 1852.

—— ——. New York, Leavitt & Allen, **n. d.** [1853, '54 or '55]. vi, 9–264 p., [6 pl.,] 7¼ x 5. "The portrait." N.Y., U.W. (557)

Also issued as "Friendship's offering," N. Y., n. d. "Moss rose," N. Y., c. 1854, and "Philopœna," n. d., with variation in pl.

—— ——. New York, Leavitt & Allen, **n. d.** [1856 or after]. 3 p. l., vii, 9–81p., 1 l., 5–175 p., 6 pl., 7¼ x 4¾. "Appropriate sphere of woman." U.W. (558)

This is "Lady's manual," 1854.
Also issued as "Affection's gift," N. Y., n. d., and "Token and Atlantic souvenir," N. Y., n. d.

—— ——. New York, George A. Leavitt, 1869. vi, 9–322 p., [6 pl.,] 7 x 5. N. Y., C. U. (558*a*)

Same as No. 556 above.

**Merry's [Robert] annual for all seasons,** [by S. G. Goodrich]. New York, Samuel Colman, **1840,** c. 1839. x, 11–200 p., front. and illum. t., 5½ x 4¼. B.P. (559)

**Mignonette, The,** or the graces of the mind. New York, D. Appleton & Co.,. **1842.** 1 p. l., 6–192 p., [8 pl.,] 4⅜ x 2¾. H.U. (560)

**Mignonette The,** a gift for all seasons. New York, D. Appleton & Co., **c. 1856.** 288 p., 9 pl., 7⅝ x 5¼. N.Y., B.P. (561)

—— ——, a gift for all seasons, by Bell Hawthorn. Boston, Shepard, Clark & Co., **1856.** 258 p., [5 pl.,] 6⅞ x 4⅝. "Gaspar Poussin. L.C. (562)

This is "Lily of the valley," 1851, with p. 259–320 omitted; p. 31–4, a different poem substituted, and pl. are same except engr. t. and one other are omitted.
See also "Friendship's gift," 1852.

**Mirror of life, The,** ed. by Mrs. L. C. Tuthill. Philadelphia, Lindsay & Blakiston, **1848,** c. 1847. xii, 13–240 p., 11 pl., 9 x 5¾. U.W. (563)

Also issued without date, c. 1847. B.A. (563*a*)

**Miscellanies first published under the name of the Talisman,** by G. C. Verplanck, W. C. Bryant, Robt. C. Sands, in 3 vols., illustrated with fine engravings. New York, **1833.** N.Y. (564)

These 3 vols. are same as Talisman, N. Y., 1828–30.

**Missionary memorial, The,** a literary and religious souvenir. New York, E. Walker, **1846,** c. 1845. xii, 372 p., col. front., col. t., 7½ x 4⅝. B.A. (565)

Re-issued with added pl. as " Christ's messengers," 1848; "Christian souvenir and missionary memorial," 1851.
Also issued as "The Evergreen," New York, n. d., with p. 253–372 omitted, and proem added. pl. vary.

**Mrs. Gilman's gift book.** Title on back, on an eng. t. of "Gift book of stories and poems." (See addenda.)

**Moral and religious souvenir.** Boston, N. S. Simpkins & Co., **1828,** c. 1827. 288 p., 3 pl., 5½ x 3½. [In slip case.] N.Y., U.W. (566)

**Morning glory, The,** a gift for all seasons, by H. W. Herbert. New York, Cornish, Lamport & Co., **n. d.** [circa 1851]. vi, 9–300 p., [7 pl.,] 7¼ x 4½. B.P. (567)

This is "Magnolia," 1836, with variation in plates. See also "Coral," n. d., "Friendship's token," N. Y., n. d., "Memory," c. 1854, "Gift of affection," n. d., "Snow flake," n. d., "Aloe," 1854.

**Moss rose, The.** New York, Leavitt & Allen, **n. d.** vi p., 1 l., 9–264 p., [6 pl.,] 7¼ x 4¾. "The baron's vow." B.A., B.P., U.W. (568)

Also issued by George A. Leavitt, n. d. [circa 1869]. P. M. (568*a*)

Also pub. as "Snow flake," c. 1855.

—— ——. New York, Leavitt & Allen, **n. d.** [1853, 54, or 55]. 2 p. l., vii–viii, 9–264 p., [6 pl.,] 7¼ x 5. "Cecelia." U.W. (569)

Also issued as "Passion flower," n. d., "Friendship," c. 1854, "Friendship's offering, N. Y., n. d., 'Cecelia' "; pl. vary.

**Moss-rose, The,** by C. W. Everest. [1st ed.] * (570)

—— ——, for a friend, ed. by C. W Everest. Hartford, Brown & Parsons, **1843,** c. 1842. 2d ed. x, 11–192 p., front., 4⅛ x 2½. (F. 571)

Same as 1st ed., except some of former articles are omitted and new ones substituted, and engr. front. added.

**Moss rose, The,** or an annual gift. New York, Nafis & Cornish, n. d. [**1845** on back]. xii, 348 p., 21 pl., [really only 10 pl.,] 7 x 4½. "Kelp gatherer." N.Y., C.U., U.W. (572)

An issue 1854 omitted p. 251–348, and had 7 pl. This is "Lady's cabinet album," 1832, with variation in pl. See also "Lady's album," n. d.

—— ——, a gift for all seasons, ed. by S. G. Goodrich. New York, Nafis & Cornish, **1846.** vii–viii, 9–304 p., [11 pl.,] 7⅛ x 4½. "Rainbow bridge." B.P., B.A., U.W. (573)

Also issued, N. Y., n. d., [1846 on back,] [9 pl.]. B.A. (573*a*)

This is "Token and Atlantic souvenir," 1840, with plates changed. See also "Atlantic souvenir," n. d., "Honeysuckle," 1848, "Friendship's gift," n. d., "Token of friendship," n. d.

—— ——, a Christmas and New Year's present, ed. by S. G. Goodrich. New York, Nafis & Cornish, **1847.** 2 p. l., 9–272 p., [4 pl.,] 7 x 4¼. "The stranger's nephew." N.Y., B.P. (574)

This is "Token and Atlantic souvenir," 1841, with pl. changed, and the article "Ireland and the Irish," p. 65–180, replaced by 12 short pieces.

—— ——, ed. by Alfred A. Phillips. New York, Nafis & Cornish, **n. d.** [pref. dated 1847]. viii, 9–311 p. 8 pl., 7⅜ x 4½. "The early settler" B.P., L.C. (575)

**Moss-rose, The,** for **1850,** ed. by Mrs. Emeline P. Howard. New York, Nafis & Cornish, c. 1849. viii, 9–312 p., 10 pl., 7¼ x 4¾. "Harry Lincoln." N.Y., C.U. (576)

Also issued without date and sub-title "for all seasons" [pref. dated 1849]. N.Y. (576*a*)

**Moss rose, The,** for all seasons, ed. by Mrs. Emeline P. Howard. New York, Cornish, Lamport & Co., c. **1851.** vi p., 1 l., 9–344 p., 7 pl., 7¼ x 4⅞. "Isabel." B.P. (577)

—— ——, a gift for all seasons. New York, Lamport. Blakeman & Law, **1854.** xii, 250 p., [7 pl.,] 7¼ x 4¾, "Kelp gatherer." F. (578)

This is the [1845] issue with p. 251–348 omitted; really the "Lady's cabinet album," 1832, with p. 251–348 omitted.

—— ——, New York, Leavitt & Allen, **c. 1854.** vi, 9–264 p., 8 pl., 7¼ x 5. "The portrait." F. (579)

Also an edition n. d. [1856 or after]. F. (579*a*)
Also issued as "Memory's gift," n. d., "Friendship's offering," n. d., and "Philopœna," n. d., with variation in pl.

**Mother's and young lady's annual,** a gift book for the holidays, with 42 engravings and flowers. Boston, Cyrus Stone, c. **1853.** vi, 3–200, 5–202 p., 42 pl. B.P., U.W. (580)

**Mother's present, The,** a holiday gift for the young; original and selected, by Mrs. Colman. Boston, S. Colman, **1847,** c. 1846 viii, 9–222 p., [5 pl.,] 6⅛ x 3⅞. L.C. (581)

**Mourner's chaplet,** an offering of sympathy for bereaved friends, by John Keese. Boston, Gould, Kendall & Lincoln, **1844,** c. 1844. vii p., 1 l., 9–128 p., 4½ x 2¾. L.C. (582)

**Mourner's friend, The,** or sighs of sympathy for those who sorrow, ed. by J. B. Syme. Worcester, S. A. Howland, 1852, c. 1852. 180 p., front., 6⅛ x 3¾. F. (583)

**Mourner's gift,** ed. by Mrs. M. A. Patrick. New York, Charles S. Francis, **1841.** * (584)

**My holiday annual,** a Christmas and New Year's gift, by V. T., illustrated. New York, Allen Bros., **n. d.** 278 p., 6½ x 4¼. F. (585)

See also "My new annual."

**My new annual,** a Christmas and New Year's gift by V. T. New York, Allen Bros., **n. d.,** 242 p., illus., 6½ x 4½. F. (586)

See also "My holiday annual."

**My teacher's new year's present,** or select biography of the young, by F. T. Gray. Boston, Benj. H. Greene, **1847,** c. 1846. viii, 9–96 p., front., illus. 4¾ x 3¼. F. (586*a*)

—— ——, for the year **1848,** by F. T. Gray. Boston, Benj. H. Greene, 1848. viii, 9–128 p., front., 4½ x 2¾. F. (587)

**My teacher's new year's present,** for the year **1850,** by F. T. Gray. Boston, Benj. H. Greene, 1850. viii, 9–64 p., front., 4¾ x 3. F. (588)

**National temperance offering, The,** and sons and daughters of temperance gift, ed. by S. F. Cary. New York, R. Vandien, **c. 1850.** x, 11–320 p., 16 pl., 9 x 5¾. U.W. (589)

**New Hampshire book, The,** being specimens of the literature of the Granite State. Nashua, David Marshall, **1842,** c. 1841. x p., 1 l., 13–391 p., 7½ x 4¾. F. (590)

Also issued in 1844 by Chas. T. Gill, Nashville [N. H.] N.Y.S. (590*a*)

**New Orleans book, The,** ed. by Robt. Gibbes Barnwell. New Orleans, **1851,** c. 1850. xii, 384 p., 7½ x 4½. B.A., P.M. (591)

**New York illustrated magazine annual.** New York, 1847.

This is a magazine.

**Newest keepsake for 1840.** Norwich, M. B. Young, **1840.** xix, 21–207 p., 5¾ x 3¾. B.P. (592)

Not a true annual.

**North star, The.** The poetry of freedom by her friends. Philadelphia, Merrihew & Thompson, **1840,** [ed. by Whittier]. 16mo. (593)

Not a true gift book.

**Oasis, The,** ed. by Mrs. Child. Boston, **1828.** illus. 12mo. * (594)

—— ——, ed. by Mrs. Child. Boston, Allen and Ticknor, **1834,** c. 1834. xvi, 1–276 p., 14 pl., 6¼ x 4¼. F. (595)

—— ——, or golden leaves of friendship, ed. by N. L. Ferguson. Boston, Dayton & Wentworth, **1854,** c. 1850. 272 p., front., 6¾ x 4½. F. (596)

—— ——, or golden leaves of friendship, ed. by N. L) Ferguson. New York, Dayton & Wentworth, **1855,** c. 1854. 252 p., front., 6¾ x 4½. N.Y., L.C., C.U. (597)

This is the same as 1854 with p. 253–72 omitted.

—— ——, or golden leaves of friendship, ed. by M. J. Percival. Boston, Wentworth & Co., **1856,** c. 1856. 252 p., front., 6¾ x 4½. U.W. (598)

Same as 1854 with p. 253–72 omitted.
Also issued with pages 253–72 restored, but not called for in contents. F. (598*a*)
Also issued, Boston, Thayer & Eldridge, 1860, 252 p. L.C. (599)

**Odd fellows gem.** Springfield, **1845.** * (599*a*)

—— ——, containing sentiments of "friendship, love and truth," ed. by a lady. Nashua [N. H.] Chas. T. Gill, **1846,** c.1844. 156 p., illum. t., 4¼ x 2¾. N.Y. (600)

**Odd-fellows keepsake,** a concise history of odd-fellowship in the U. S. New York, **1850,** c. 1850. vi p., 1 l., 334 p., 7¼ x 4¾. U.W.

Not a literary gift book.

**Odd-fellows offering, The,** for **1843,** ed. by Paschal Donaldson. [v. 1.] New York, Samuel A. House & Co., c. 1842. iv p., 1 l., 7–272 p., [5 pl.,] 6½ x 3½. L.C. (601)

—— ——, for **1844,** ed. by Paschal Donaldson. [v. 2.] New York, Henry D Loomis, 1844, c. 1843. 288 p., 11 pl., 6¼ x 4⅛. H.U. (602)

—— ——, for **1845,** ed by Paschal Donaldson. [v. 3.] New York, McGowan & Treadwell, 1845, c. 1844. 288 p., 9 pl., 7½ x 4½. N.Y., C.U. (603)

—— ——, for **1846,** ed. by Paschal Donaldson. [v. 4.] New York, McGowan & Treadwell, 1846, c. 1845. 300 p., 8 pl., 8½ x 5¼. N.Y., U.W. (604)

—— ——, for **1847,** ed. by Paschal Donaldson. [v. 5.] New York, John G. Treadwell, 1847, c. 1846. 288 p., 11 pl., 8½ x 5¼. N.Y., L.C., U.W. (605)

—— ——, for **1848,** ed. by James L. Ridgely & Paschal Donaldson. [v. 6.] New York, Edward Walker, 1848, c. 1847. 288 p., 12 pl., 8½ x 5½. N.Y., L.C., U.W. (606)

—— ——, for **1849,** ed. by Paschal Donaldson. [v. 7.] New York, Edward Walker, 1849, c. 1848. 320 p., 12 pl., 8½ x 5½. N.Y., L.C., U.W. (607)

—— ——, for **1850.** [v. 8.] New York, Edward Walker, 1850, c. 1849. 298 p , 11 pl., 8¾ x 5½. N.Y., L.C., U.W. (608)

—— ——, for **1851.** [v. 9.] New York, Edward Walker, 1851, c. 1850. 294 p., 11 pl., 8½ x 5½. N.Y., U.W. (609)

—— ——, for **1852.** [v. 10.] New York, Edward Walker, 1852, c. 1851. 320 p., 11 pl., 8½ x 5½. N.Y., B.A., U.W. (610)

—— ——, for **1853.** [v. 11.] New York, Edward Walker, 1853, c. 1852. 288 p., 11 pl., 8½ x 5½ C.U., U.W. (611)

Also issued as "Odd-fellows perpetual offering," n. d.

—— ——, for **1854.** [v. 12.] New York, Edward Walker, 1854, c. 1853. 320 p., 10 pl., 8½ x 5½. C.U. (612)

**Odd-fellows perpetual offering,** comprising gems of American literature. New York, Edward Walker, **n. d.** 288 p., 11 pl., 8½ x 5½. L.C. (613)

Same as "Odd-fellows offering" for 1853.

**Odd-fellows token, The,** devoted to friendship, love and truth. Ed. by Kate Barclay. Geneva [N. Y.], **1846,** c. 1846. 124 p., illum. t., 4½ x 2⅞. F. (613*a*)

**Odd volume, The,** a collection of odds and ends in prose and verse, collected and arranged by an odd fellow. New York, Peabody & Co., **1832.** viii, 9–144 p., front., 6⅝ x 3¾. L.C. (614)

**Odd volume, The,** a collection of odds and ends in prose and verse, collected and arranged by an odd fellow, second series. New York, Peabody & Co., **1833.** 288 p., 4 pl., 5¾ x 3½. L.C. (615)

Also issued by E. Sands, New York, **1835.** F. (615*a*)

**Offering, The,** for **1829.** Cambridge, Hilliard & Brown, 1829, c. 1828. ix p., 1 l., 252 p., 4 pl., 5½ x 3½. N.Y., B.P., H.U. (616)

—— ——, a Christmas and New Year's present. Philadelphia, Thomas T. Ash, **1834,** c. n. d. 288 p., 11 pl., 6 x 3¾. L.C., B.P. (617)

"Old plates poorly reproduced in mezzotint."

**Offering of beauty, The,** a present for all seasons, embellished with eleven colored engravings, ed. by Amelia W. Lawrence. Philadelphia, Carey & Hart, **1848,** c. 1847. viii, 13–320 p., 10 pl., 9 x 6. N.Y., L.C. (618)

Also issued as "The offering to beauty," but with only 8 pl. Philadelphia, Carey & Hart, **1849.** F. (618*a*)

**Offering to beauty, An,** composed of the choicest descriptions of female loveliness, virtues, accomplishments, attractions, and charms, comprising the poetry of woman, by J. W. Hanson. Lowell, Merrill & Straw, **1853.** 324 p., [5 pl.,] 7½ x 4½. N.Y. (619)

**Opal, The,** a pure gift for the holy days, ed. by N. P. Willis. [v. 1.] New York, John C. Riker, **1844,** c. n. d. x p., 2 l., 13–264 p., 9 pl., 7¼ x 5. N.Y., L.C., B.P., U.W. (620)

—— ——, a pure gift for the holy days, **1845,** ed. by Mrs. Sarah J. Hale. [v. 2.] New York, J. C. Riker, 1845, c. n. d. x p., 1 l., 13–264 p., 8 pl., 7¼ x 4½. N.Y., L.C., B.P., U.W. (621)

—— —— a pure gift for the holy days, **1846,** ed. by John Keese. [v. 3.] New York, J. C. Riker, 1846, c. n. d. viii p., 1 l., 11–304 p., 9 pl., 8 x 5½. N.Y., B.P., L.C., U.W. (622)

—— —— a pure gift for the holy days, **1847,** ed. by John Keese. [v. 4.] New York, J. C. Riker, 1847, c. n. d. viii p., 1 l., 11–304 p., 9 pl., 8¾ x 5¾. N.Y., L.C., U.W. (623)

Some engravings hand-colored in some copies.

—— —— a pure gift for the holy days, **1848,** ed. by Mrs. Sarah J. Hale. [v. 5.] New York, J. C. Riker, 1848, c. n. d. viii p., 1 l., 19–320 p., 9 pl., 5¾ x 8¾. N.Y., L.C., B.A., U.W. (624)

—— —— a pure gift for all seasons, ed. by Mrs. Sarah Josepha Hale. [v. 6.] New York, J. C. Riker, **1849,** c. n. d. viii, 9–304 p., 7¾ x 5½. N.Y., B.A. (625)

Succeeded by "Keepsake," v. 7+.

**Oriental annual, The,** ed. by James P. Walker. New York, Leavitt & Allen, **n. d.** 4 p.l., 17–264 p., 10 pl., 9¼ x 6¾. "The salaam." P M., U W (626)

**Our country,** or the American parlor keepsake, ed. by Wm. H. Ryder. Boston, J. M. Usher, **c. 1854.** x p., 1 l., 13–252 p., 4 pl., 6¾ x 4½. H.U. (627)

**Our day,** a gift for the times, ed. by J. G. Adams. Boston, B. B. Mussey & Co., **1848.** 288 p., illum. t., 6½ x 4¼. F. (628)

**Our gift.** Boston, Abel & Tompkins, **1851,** c. 1850. 144 p., 6⅛ x 3¾. * (629)

**Parents' present, The,** ed. by author of Peter Parley's tales. Boston, Light & Horton; Wm. Pierce, **1835,** c. 1834. 232 p., front. and wood cuts in text, 5½ x 3¾. F. (629*a*)

Consists of selections from "Father's present," Dublin [Ire.], 1833, with additions chiefly American.

**Parlor annual and Christian family casket.** New York, **1846.** L.C., B.P. (630)

The "Family circle," a magazine, was issued as an annual, under above title. See "Family circle and parlor annual." Also "Youth's parlor annual."

**Parlour book, The.** New York, Charles S. Francis, **1838.** viii, 9–334 p., front., 6 x 3¾. F.

This is one of a series of works, each with different title. Not a true annual.

The others were "Young men's evening book," "The winter evening book," "The summer day book," "The leisure hour book."

**Parlour scrap book, The,** ed. by Willis Gaylord Clark. Philadelphia, Carey, Lea & Blanchard, **1836,** c. 1836. 72 p., 16 pl., 10¾ x 8¾. B.P. (631)

Some copies have **1837** on front cover.

**Passion flower, The,** a Christmas and New Year's gift. New York, Leavitt & Allen, n. d., **c. 1854.** 3 p.l., 7–260 p., 6 pl., 7¼ x 4¾. "Prior of St. Michael." B.P. (632)

This is "Pearl," Phila. 1853, with variation in pl. and p. 261–70 omitted.

See also "Forget-me-not," N. Y., n. d., "Pearl gift," N. Y., n. d., and "Philopœna," N. Y., n. d.

—— ——, a Christmas and New Year's gift. New York, Leavitt & Allen, **n. d.** [1856 or after]. 1 p.l., 5–6, vii–viii, 9–264 p., 6 pl., 7¼ x 4¾. "Cecelia." L.C., B.A., U.W. (633)

Also issued as "Moss Rose," N. Y., n. d., "Friendship," c. 1854, "Friendship's offering, N. Y., n. d., 'Cecelia' "; pl. vary.

—— ——, by Miss Anna J. Reid.

A mo. magazine, not a true annual.

**Pastor's gift** to the pupils of the Bulfinch St. Sunday school. Boston, Benj. H. Greene, **1847,** c. 1846. vi p, 1 l., 9–96 p., 5 x 3⅛. * (634)

—— —— to the pupils of the Bulfinch St. Sunday school, Jan. 1, **1849.** Boston, Benjamin H. Greene, 1849. viii, 9–64, 1–16 p., front., 4⅝ x 3. F. (635)

**Pearl, The,** or affection's gift, a Christmas and New Year's present. [v. 1.] Philadelphia, Thomas T. Ash, **1829,** c.1828. 252 p., 6 pl., 5¾ x 3¼. N.Y., L.C., B.P. (636)

**Pearl, The,** or affection's gift, a Christmas and New Year's present. [v. 2.] Philadelphia, Thomas T. Ash, **1830.** 4 p. l., 15–220 p., 9 pl., 6⅛ x 4. N.Y., B.P. (637)

—— ——, or affection's gift, a Christmas and New Year's present. [v. 3.] Philadelphia, Thomas T. Ash, **1831.** x p., 2 l., iv–xvi, 17–222 p., 8 pl., 6 x 6¾. N.Y., U.W., P.M. (638)

—— ——, or affection's gift, a Christmas and New Year's present. [v. 4.] Philadelphia, Thomas T. Ash, **1832,** c. 1831. 223 p., 10 pl., 6⅛ x 3⅞. N.Y., L.C., U.W. (639)

—— ——, or affection's gift, a Christmas and New Year's present. [v. 5.] Philadelphia, Thomas T. Ash, **1833,** c. 1832. viii, 9–216 p., 9 pl., 6 x 3⅞. N.Y., B.P., U.W. (640)

—— ——, or affection's gift, a Christmas and New Year's present. [v. 6.] Philadelphia, Thomas T. Ash, **1834,** c. n.d. 208 p., 8 pl., 6 x 3⅞. N.Y., B.P. (641)

—— ——, or affection's gift, a Christmas and New Year's present. [v. 7.] Philadelphia, Thomas T. Ash, c. 1835 [**1836** on back]. 7 pl., 6 x 4. N.Y., L.C., U.W. (642)

—— ——, or affection's gift for **1837,** a Christmas and New Year's present. [v. 8.] Philadelphia, Thomas T. Ash and Henry F. Anners. iv p., 1 l., 7–224 p., 7 pl., 6¼ x 4. N.Y., B.P., U.W. (643)

This is called 6th vol. in preface, really it is v. 8.

—— ——, or affection's gift for **1840.** A Christmas and New Year's present. Philadelphia, Henry F. Anners, c. 1839. xii, 13–222 p., 6 pl., 6¼ x 4. N.Y., L.C., B.P. (644)

—— ——, a Christmas, New Year and birthday present for **1849.** [v. 1.] Philadelphia, Henry F. Anners, 1849, c.1848. 6 pl., 6 x 3¾. B.P., U.W. (645)

—— ——, a gift of friendship for all seasons. Philadelphia, J. & J. L. Gihon, c. 1851 [engr. t. has **1853**]. 2 p.l., 7–270 p., 9 pl., 6¾ x 4¾. "The prior of St. Michael." L.C., U.W. (646)

Issued as "Pearl gift," omitting p. 264–70, and as "Forget-me-not," n. d., "Philopœna," n. d., and "Passion flower," c. 1854, with p. 261–70 omitted, and variation in plates.

**Pearl gift, The,** Pensez-à-moi. New York, Leavitt & Allen, **n. d.** [1853, 54, or 55]. 2 p. l., 7–263 p., 9 pl., 7¼ x 4⅞. F. (647)

This is "Pearl," 1853, with p. 264–70 omitted. See also "Forget-me-not," n. d., "Philopœna," n. d., and "Passion flower," c. 1854.

**Pearl offering, The,** a compendium of religious, literary and philosophical knowledge. New York, **n. d.** 378 p., 14 pl., 8¾ x 5½. B.P. (648)

Also issued with London imprint.

**Pet annual, The,** or gift for all seasons, ed. by Edward B. Fellows. New York, Leavitt & Allen, **n. d.** [circa 1856]. x p., 1 l., 13–251 p., 6 pl., 6¼ x 4⅛. N.Y., L.C., B.P., U.W. (649)

Also issued by Geo. A. Leavitt, n. d. [circa 1869]. 6½ x 4½. C.U. (650)

**Peter Parley's annual,** a Christmas and New Year's present for young people. New York, Evans & Dickerson, **1855.** viii, 264 p., front. C.U. (651)

**Peter Parley's gift for 1839.** New York, S. Colman. 2 p.l., 168 p., front., 5¾ x 4¼. B.P. (652)

**Philadelphia book, The,** or specimen of metropolitan literature. Philadelphia, Kay & Biddle, **1836.** iv, 13–380 p., 7½ x 4½. L.C. (653)

**Philipena, The,** by Mrs. Lunt. Lowell, 1847. (654)

Title on back of cover of "Forget-me-not," Lowell, 1847.

*

—— ——, or friendship's token, a present for all seasons. Worcester, S. A. Howland, **1848,** c.1846. 126 p., illum. t., 4⅜ x 2⅞. F. (654*a*)

Also issued Boston, G. W. Cottrell & Co. 4½ x 3. P. M. (655)

**Philopœna, The,** a gift for all seasons. New York, Leavitt & Allen, 379 Broadway, **n. d.** [1856 or after]. 2 p.l., 7–260 p., [5 pl. and illum. presentation pl.,] 7 x 4½. "Handel." C.U., H.U. (656)

—— ——, a gift for all seasons. New York, Leavitt & Allen, **n. d.** 7–8, 11–264 p., [6 pl.,] 7⅜ x 4⅞. "The seaman's wife." B.A. (657)

Same as "Forget-me-not," c. 1855, and "Glen annual," n. d., with plates varying.

—— ——, a gift for all seasons. New York, Leavitt & Allen, **n. d.** [1856 or after]. vi, 9–264 p., 6 pl., 7 x 4¾. "The portrait." B.P. (658)

Same as "Friendship's offering," N. Y., n. d., "Memory's gift," n. d., "Moss rose," n. d.

—— ——, a gift for all seasons. New York, Leavitt & Allen, **n. d.** [1853, 54, or 55]. 2 p.l., 7–260 p., [5 pl.,] 6¾ x 4¾. "Prior of St. Michael." B.P. (659)

This is "The pearl" [1853], with p. 261–70 omitted and variation in pl.

See also "Pearl gift," "Forget-me-not," n. d., "Passion flower," c. 1854.

—— ——, a perennial gift, with steel embellishments, ed. by Paschal Donaldson. New York, E. Sands, **c. 1844.** (1845 on back.) 2 p.l., 7–144 p., 18 pl., 7 x 4¾. N.Y., U.W. (660)

Also issued in [1851], [1852], and [1854] exactly the same, but with p. 145–201 added, and pl. changed.

—— —— or friendship's offering for **1847,** ed. by a lady. New York, John Levison. 96 p., [10 pl.,] 9 x 6¼. U.W. (661)

—— —— or friendship's offering, a gift for all seasons, ed. by a lady. New York, John Levison [**1851** on back]. 2 p.l., 7–201 p., 12 pl., 7¼ x 5. U.W. (662)

Also issued in **1852** and **1854** [date on back only]. This is same as c. 1844, except p. 145–201 added.

**Pictorial family annual,** ed. by Robert Sears. New York, Robert Sears, **1849,** c.1848. 368 p., [2 pl.,] illus. 8¾ x 5¾. B.P. (663)

**Poetic wreath, The,** for **1840.** New York, Charles Wells, 1840. xxiii, 1, 25–395 p., [12 pl.,] 7 x 4⅜. F. (664)

**Poetry of love, The,** ed. by Rufus W. Griswold. New York, Leavitt, Trow & Co., **1848,** c.1844. viii, 9–128 p., 4⅜ x 3. F. (665)

**Poetry of the seasons, The.** Boston, A. Tompkins & B. B. Mussey, **1842,** c.1841. 3 p.l., 9–136 p., 6¼ x 3¾ F.

Not a true token.

**Poet's gift, The,** illustrated by one of her painters, ed. by John Keese. Boston, T. H. Carter & Co., **1845,** c. 1841. 320 p., [2 pl., illus.,] 7¼ x 4½. L.C., U.W. (666)

Called "American poet's gift" on cover.

This is the 2d vol. of "Poets of America," 2 v., arranged as a distinct work.

**Poet's offering, The,** for **1850,** ed. by Sarah Josepha Hale. Philadelphia, Grigg, Elliot & Co., 1850. 576 p., 14 pl., 9¾ x 7. U.M. (667)

**Portfolio of entertainment and instruction.** Philadelphia, Presbyterian Board of Publication, **c. 1855.** 256 p., illus., 9¼ x 7½. P.M. (668)

**Portfolio for youth, A,** by Robert Ramble. Philadelphia, J. Crissy, **1835,** c. 1835. xvi, 17–352 p., front., illus., 6⅛ x 4½. F. (669)

Called "Youth's portfolio" on back.

**Premium, The,** a present for all seasons consisting of elegant selections from British and American writers of the 19th century. Philadelphia, Carey, Lea & Blanchard, **1833,** c.1833. viii, 310 p., 5 x 3½. H.U., C.U. (670)

Also issued in **1835.** L.C. (671)

Also issued in **1836.** L.C. (672)

**Primrose The,** a gift of friendship, ed. by Rev. C. W. Everest. Hartford, Henry S. Parsons, **1848,** c. 1848 viii, 9–128 p., front., 4⅜ x 2¾. F. (673)
Also issued in **1850.** N.Y. (674)
Also issued in **1852,** W. J. Hamersley. F. (675)

**Rainbow, The, 1847,** ed. by A. J. McDonald. Albany, A. L. Harrison, c. secured. viii, 9–272 p., 10 pl., 7½ x 4¾. F. (676)
Also issued in **1848.** N.Y., L.C. (677)

**Religious keepsake, The,** ed. by Mrs. Sigourney. Hartford, S. Andrus & Son, **n. d.** 288 p., 10 pl., 6¼ x 4. "The infant St. John." F. (678)
It was also issued in **1846.** F. (679)
This is "Religious souvenir," 1839.

**Religious offering, 1839.** Philadelphia. * (679*a*)

—— ——, **1840.** ed. by Miss Catharine H. Waterman, Philadelphia, Wm. Marshall & Co., c. 1839. vi p., 1 l., 9–288 p., 10 pl., 6¼ x 4¼. N.Y., B.P., U W. (680)

**Religious souvenir, The,** for Christmas and New-Year's presents, ed. by Mrs. L. H. Sigourney. Hartford, S. Andrus & Son, **n. d.** 288 p., 10 pl., 6⅝ x 4¼. "The patroon." C.U. (681)

This is really a reissue of 1840 [in 1845], with front. omitted.

Also issued by Leavitt & Allen, N. Y., n. d. [1856 or after], omitting p. 263–288, and with a variation in pl., 7¼ x 4¼. U.W. (682)

See also 1845, 1846, which have same text, but vary in pl.

—— ——, a Christmas, New Year's and birthday present for **1833,** ed. by G. T. Bedell. [v. 1.] Philadelphia, Key, Mielke & Biddle, c.1832. 287 p., 9 pl., 5⅞ x 3¾. N.Y., U.W., B.P. (683)

—— ——, a Christmas, New Year's and birthday present for **1834,** ed. by G. T. Bedell. [v. 2.] Philadelphia, Key & Biddle, 1834, c.1833. vi p., 1 l., 9–288 p., 8 pl., 6 x 3¾. L.C., B.P., U.W. (684)

—— ——, a Christmas, New Year's and birthday present for 1835, ed. by G. T. Bedell. [v. 3.] Phildelphia, Key & Biddle, **1835,** c. 1834. vi p., 1 l., 9–272 p., 8 pl., 6 x 3¾. N.Y., B.P., U.W. (685

—— ——, a Christmas, New Year's and birthday present for **1836,** ed. by Chauncy Colton. [v. 4.] Philadelphia, Key & Biddle, 1836, c. 1835. viii, 9–284 p., 8 pl., 6 x 3¾. L.C., N.Y., U.W. (686)

—— —— for **1837,** ed. by Chauncy Colton. [v. 5.] New York, Hall & Voorhies, 1837, c.1835. viii, 9–288 p., 8 pl., 6¼ x 3¾. N.Y., L.C., B.P. (687)

—— —— for **1839,** ed. by Mrs. L. H. Sigourney. [v. 6.] New York, Schofield & Voorhies, c.1838. 288 p., 8 pl., 6 x 3¾. "Infant St. John." N.Y., L.C., C.U., U.W. (688)

This was reprinted in 1845 with variation in pl.
Reissued as "Religious Keepsake," n. d.
Reissued as "Christian keepsake," N. Y., n. d., with different pl., and omitting p. 263–288.

—— —— for **1840,** ed. by Mrs. L. H. Sigourney. [v. 7.] New York, Schofield & Voorhies, c. 1839. 288 p., 8 pl., 6⅝ x 4½. C.U., B.P., U.W., B.A. (689)

This was reissued in Hartford 1845 and in 1846, with changes in pl., also an edition Hartford n. d., and New York, Leavitt & Allen [1856?].

—— —— for 1839 republished for **1845.** Hartford, S. Andrus & Son, 1845, c. 1838. 288 p., 10 pl., 6⅜ x 4. "Infant St. John." C.U., U.W. (690)

Has a "new frontispiece, and several other improvements in embellishments," otherwise same as 1839. See following for a different issue in same year.

**Religious souvenir, The,** for 1840, republished for **1845,** ed. by Mrs. L. H. Sigourney. Hartford, S. Andrus & Son, 1845, c. 1839. 288 p., 11 pl., 6⅝ x 4½. "The patroon." B.P., C.U., U.W. (691)

Has "8 new engravings, and several [all but 3] of old ones are removed." Otherwise same as 1840.
Also issued without date (see 681).

**Religious souvenir, The,** for Christmas and New Year's presents, ed. by Mrs. L. H. Sigourney. Hartford, S. Andrus & Son, **1846.** 288 p., 11 pl., 6⅝ x 4⅜. "The patroon." N.Y., L.C., U.W. (692)

Identical with 1845.

Really 1840 with variation in pl.

**Remember!** A keepsake, ed. by Richard and Elizabeth Stoddard. New York, Leavitt & Allen, **n. d.** [1868 ?]. 312 p., [7 pl.,] 7½ x 5. P.M. (693)

Also an edition, Geo. A. Leavitt, n. d. [1869 or after]. F. (693*a*)

**Remember me, The,** a religious and literary miscellany, intended as a Christmas and New Year's present. Philadelphia, E. Littell, **1829,** c. 1828. xii, 13–306 p., 8 pl., 5½ x 3½. C.U. (694)

Also issued n. d., c. 53d year of U. S. Independence. N.Y. (695)

—— ——, a token of love for **1851.** [v. 1.] Philadelphia, Henry F. Anners, c. 1850. viii, 280 p., 6 pl., 7⅜ x 4⅞. L.C., C.U., U.W. (696)

—— ——, a token of love for **1852.** [v. 2.] Philadelphia, Henry F. Anners, c. 1851. 2 p. l., 7–288 p., 6 pl., 7¼ x 5. C.U., B.P. (697)

—— ——, a token of love for **1853.** [v. 3.] Philadelphia, Henry F. Anners, c. 1852. 288 p., 5 pl., 6¾ x 4½. L.C., P.M. (698)

—— ——, a token of love for **1854.** [v. 4.] Philadelphia, Henry F. Anners, c. 1853. 252 p., 6 pl., 6½ x 4⅛. L.C. (699)

—— ——, a token of love for **1855.** [v. 5.] Philadelphia, Henry F. Anners, c. 1854. 252 p., 5 pl., 6¼ x 4. P.M. (700)

**Remembrancer, The,** for **1841.** Philadelphia, T. E. Chapman; Marshall, William & Butler. viii, 26 p., 6⅜ x 4. F. (701)

**Rhode Island book, The,** selections in prose and verse from writings of Rhode Island citizens, by Anne C. Lynch. Providence, H. Fuller, **1841.** viii, 352 p., front., 7 x 4⅜. N.Y.S. (702)

**Rosary, The,** of illustrations of the Bible, ed. by Rev. Edward Everett Hale, Boston, Phillips & Sampson, **1849,** c. 1848. 293 p., pl., 9½ x 6¼. F. (702*a*)

**Rose, The,** or affection's gift for 1842, ed. by Emily Marshall. [v. 1.] New York, D. Appleton & Co., **1842,** c. 1841. 216 p., 10 pl., 6¼ x 3¾. N.Y., L.C., U.W. (703)

—— ——, or affection's gift for **1843,** ed. by Emily Marshall. [v. 2.] New York, D. Appleton & Co., 1843, c. 1842. vi p., 1 l., 9–216 p., 10 pl., 6 x 3¾ C.U., U.W. (704)

—— ——, or affection's gift for **1844,** ed. by Emily Marshall. [v. 3.] New York, D. Appleton & Co., 1844, c. 1843. vi p., 1 l., 9–256 p., 10 pl., 5¾ x 3½. N.Y., P.M. (705)

—— ——, or affection's gift for **1845,** ed. by Emily Marshall. [v. 4.] New York, D. Appleton & Co., 1845, c. 1844. 252 p., 10 pl., 6¼ x 4⅛. N.Y., L.C., U.W. (706)

**Rose, The,** or affection's gift for **1846,** ed. by Emily Marshall. [v. 5.] New York, D. Appleton & Co., 1846, c. 1845. 252 p., 10 pl., $6\frac{1}{8}$ x 4.
N.Y., L.C., B.P., U.W. (707)

—— ——, or affection's gift for **1847,** ed. by Emily Marshall. [v. 6.] New York, D. Appleton & Co., 1847, c. 1846. vi p., 1 l., 9–252 p., 10 pl., 6 x $3\frac{3}{4}$.
C.U., U.W. (708)

—— ——, or affection's gift for **1848,** ed. by Emily Marshall. [v. 7.] New York, D. Appleton & Co., 1848, c. 1847. 312 p., 10 pl., $6\frac{3}{4}$ x $4\frac{1}{4}$.
N.Y., B.P., U.W. (709)

**Rose of Sharon, The,** a religious souvenir for **1840,** ed. by Miss Sarah C. Edgarton. [v. 1.] Boston, A. Tompkins & B. B. Mussey, 1840, c. 1839. 352 p., 4 pl., $6\frac{1}{8}$ x $4\frac{1}{4}$. L.C., B.P., U.W. (710)

—— ——, a religious souvenir for **1841,** ed. by Miss Sarah C. Edgarton. [v. 2.] Boston, A. Tompkins & B. B. Mussey, 1841, c. 1840. 304 p., 4 pl., $6\frac{7}{8}$ x $4\frac{3}{8}$.
L.C., C.U., B.P., U.W. (711)

—— ——, a religious souvenir for **1842,** ed. by Miss Sarah C. Edgarton. [v. 3.] Boston, A. Tompkins & B. B. Mussey, 1842, c. 1841. iv p., 1 l., 7–302 p., 5 pl., $6\frac{7}{8}$ x $4\frac{3}{8}$. N.Y., L.C., B.P., U.W. (712)

—— ——, a religious souvenir for **1843,** ed. by Miss Sarah C. Edgarton. [v. 4.] Boston, A. Tompkins & B. B. Mussey, 1843, c. 1842. iv p., 2 l., 9–312 p., 5 pl., $6\frac{7}{8}$ x $4\frac{3}{8}$. N.Y., B.P., U.W. (713)

—— ——, a religious souvenir for **1844,** ed. by Miss Sarah C. Edgarton. [v. 5.] Boston, A. Tompkins & B. B. Mussey, 1844, c. 1843. vi p., 1 l., 9–304 p., 5 pl., $6\frac{7}{8}$ x $4\frac{3}{8}$. N.Y., B.P., U.W. (714)

—— ——, a religious souvenir for **1845,** ed. by Miss S. C. Edgarton. [v. 6.] Boston, A. Tompkins & B. B. Mussey, 1845, c. 1844. vi p., 1 l., 9–304 p., 7 pl., $6\frac{3}{4}$ x $4\frac{3}{8}$. N.Y., L.C., B.P., U.W. (715)

—— ——, a religious souvenir for **1846,** ed. by Miss S. C. Edgarton. [v. 7.] Boston, A. Tompkins & B. B. Mussey, 1846, c. 1844. vi p., 1 l., 9–304 p., 7 pl., $6\frac{3}{4}$ x $4\frac{1}{2}$. N.Y., L.C., B.P., U.W. (716)

—— ——, a religious souvenir for **1847,** ed. by Miss S. C. Edgarton. [v. 8.] Boston, A. Tompkins & B. B. Mussey, 1847, c 1846. vi p., 1 l., 9–304 p., 7 pl., $6\frac{7}{8}$ x $4\frac{3}{8}$ N.Y., L.C., B.P., U.W. (717)

—— ——, a religious souvenir for **1848,** ed. by Mrs. S. C. Edgarton Mayo. [v. 9.] Boston, A. Tompkins & B. B. Mussey & Co., 1848, c. 1847. vi p., 1 l., 9–304 p., 7 pl., $6\frac{7}{8}$ x $4\frac{1}{2}$. N.Y., B.P., U.W. (718)

—— ——, a religious souvenir for **1849,** ed. by Mrs. S. C. Edgarton Mayo. [v. 10.] Boston, A. Tompkins & B. B. Mussey & Co., 1849, c. 1848. 304 p., 7 pl., $6\frac{3}{4}$ x $4\frac{1}{2}$. N.Y., L.C., B.P., U.W. (719)

**Rose of Sharon, The,** or gems of sacred poetry, 6th edition, Auburn, [N. Y.] Derby, Miller & Co., **1849,** 128 p., illum. t., 4⅜ x 2¾. F. (719*a*)
This has no connection with series of same name published in Boston.

—— ——, a religious souvenir for **1850,** ed. by Mrs. C. M. Sawyer. [v. 11.] Boston, A. Tompkins & B. B. Mussey & Co., 1849, c. 1849. 304 p., 7 pl., 6¾ x 4⅜. N.Y., L.C., B.P., U.W. (720)

—— ——, a religious souvenir for **1851,** ed. by Mrs. C. M. Sawyer. [v. 12.] Boston, A. Tompkins & B. B. Mussey & Co., 1851, c. 1850. vi p., 1 l., 9–303 p., 7 pl., 6¾ x 4½. N.Y., L.C., B.P., U.W. (721)

—— ——, a religious souvenir for **1852,** ed. by Mrs. C. M. Sawyer. [v. 13.] Boston, A. Tompkins & B. B. Mussey & Co., 1852, c. 1851. vi p., 1 l., 9–303 p., 7 pl., 6¾ x 4½. N.Y., L.C., B.P., U.W. (722)

—— ——, a religious souvenir for **1853,** ed. by Mrs. C. M. Sawyer [v. 14.] Boston, A. Tompkins & B. B. Mussey & Co., 1853, c. 1852. vi p., 1 l., 9–304 p., 7 pl., 6⅞ x 4½. N.Y., L.C., B.P., U.W. (723)

—— ——, a religious offering for **1854,** ed. by Mrs. C. M. Sawyer. [v. 15.] Boston, A. Tompkins & B. B. Mussey & Co., 1854, c. 1853. vi p., 1 l., 9–303 p., 7 pl. 6⅞ x 4½. L.C., C.U., B.P., U.W. (724)

—— ——, a religious souvenir for **1855,** ed. by Mrs. C. M. Sawyer. [v. 16.] Boston, A. Tompkins & B. B. Mussey & Co., 1855, c. 1854. vi p., 1 l., 9–304 p.,7 pl., 6⅞ x 4¼. N.Y., L.C., B P., U.W. (725)
[Called 17th issue in preface.]

—— ——. a religious souvenir for **1856,** ed. by Mrs. C. M. Sawyer. [v. 17.] Boston, Abel Tompkins, 1856, c. 1855. vi p., 1 l., 9–304 p., 7 pl., 6⅞ x 4½. N.Y., B.P., U.W. (726)
[Called 18th issue in preface.]

—— ——, a religious souvenir for **1857,** ed. by Mrs. C. M. Sawyer. [v. 18.] Boston, Abel Tompkins, 1857, c. 1856. vi p., 1 l., 9–304 p., 7 pl., 6⅞ x 4½. N.Y., L. C., B.P., U.W. (727)

**Rosebud, The,** illustrated with numerous engravings. New York, Leavitt & Allen, **n. d.** [1853 or after]. 4 p. l., 15–258 p., 6 pl., 6¼ x 4¼. N.Y., L.C., U.W. (728)

**Rosette, The, a** juvenile annual for 1846. Boston, Waite, Peirce & Co., **1846,** c.1845. viii, 9–176 p., 6 pl., 6 x 3¾. B.P. (729)
Also issued by Binney, Otheman & Co., **1848.** [4 pl.] N.Y. (730)

**Rough and ready annual,** or military souvenir. New York, D. Appleton & Co., **1848,** c.1847. 262 p., 20 pl., 7½ x 4½. B.P. (731)
Preface calls it "American gift book."

**Ruby, The,** a token of friendship for **1849.** [v. 1.] Philadelphia, Carey & Hart, 1849, c. 1848. viii, 13–304 p., 11 pl., 7⅛ x 4¾. F. (732)
Has same pl. as "Gift."

—— ——, a token of friendship for **1850.** [v. 2.] Philadelphia, Carey & Hart, 1850, c. 1848. viii, 13–304 p., 11 pl., 7 x 4¾. B.A., U.W. (733)

**Rural annual and year-book of the country,** beautifully illustrated, by Thomas Miller. New York, Leavitt & Allen, **n. d.** [1856 or after]. iv, 283 p., [8 pl.,] 6½ x 4. B.P. (734)

**Sabbath bells,** chimed by the poets, elegantly illustrated. Philadelphia, Hubbard Bros., **1873,** c. 1873. xvi, 17–112 p., [2 pl.]. F. (735)

**Sabbath school annual, The,** ed. by Mrs. M. H Adams. Boston, James M. Usher, **1847,** c. 1846. x, 11–172 p., 7 pl., and illus., 6½ x 4¼. B.P. (736)

**Sacred annual, The,** a gift for all seasons, ed. by Rev. H. Hastings Weld. Philadelphia, T. K. Collins, Jr., **1850.** 200 p., 11 pl., 10½ x 7¼. U.W. (737)

—— ——, a gift for all seasons, ed. by H. H. Weld. Philadelphia, T. K. Collins, Jr., **1851.** 200 p., 9 pl., 10½ x 7¼. F. (737*a*)
Same as 1850.

**Sacred flora, The,** or flowers from the grave of a child. By Henry Bacon. Boston, A. Tompkins & B. B. Mussey, **1848,** c. 1844. viii, 9–160 p., illum. t., 4¼ x 2¾. F. (737*b*)

**Sacred gift of devout and useful sayings.** Boston, G. W. Cottrell, **c. 1851.** iv, 5–96 p., 3 x 2¼. F. (738)

**Sacred offering, The,** or tableaux of remarkable incidents in the old and new Testament. Boston, Whittemore, Niles & Hall, **n. d.** x, 314 p., [6 pl.,] 7¼ x 5. F. (739)
This is really "Sacred tableaux," 1848, with less no. of pl.

—— —— [v. i.] Boston, Joseph Dowe, 1836 c. 1835. viii, 9–216 p. 6⅛ x 4⅛. F. (739*a*)
Selected poems from "The Sacred Offering" series published in London.

—— —— a poetical gift [v. 2]. Boston, Joseph Dowe, 1839, c. 1837. 216 p. 6⅛ x 3¾. F. (739*b*)

**Sacred tableaux, The,** or remarkable incidents in the old and new Testament. ed. by Thomas Wyatt. Boston, John M Whittemore, **1848,** c. 1847. x, 314 p., 40 pl., 7¼ x 5. C.U., U.W. (740)
Also issued as "Sacred offering," with most of the pl. omitted.

**Sacred wreath.** Philadelphia, Orrin Rogers, **1839.** 24 pl. * (741)

**Saint Nicholas annual, The,** a Christmas and New Year's gift made expressly under the direction of Saint Nicholas for all good little girls and boys. Boston, B. H. Greene, **1843.** xi, 7–112 p., [5 pl.,] 4¼ x 3⅛. B.P. (742)

—— —— **1843,** 284 p., 5⅞ x 3¾. * (742*a*)

**Saint Nicholas gift.** Boston, T. H. Carter & Co., **1844.** * (743)

—— ——. T. H. Carter & Co., **1845.** * (744)

**Sapphire, The,** a collection of graphic and entertaining tales, brilliant poems, and essays. Boston, John L. Shorey, **1867,** c. 1866. vi, 7–319 p., 7 x 4½. P.M. (745)

This is vol. 2 of "Gem" series.

**Scenes in the lives of the Apostles,** ed. by H. Hastings Weld. Philadelphia, Lindsay & Blakiston, **c. 1846.** xii, 13–239 p., 8 pl., 9 x 6. F. (746)

**Scenes in the life of the Savior,** by poets and painters, ed. by Rufus W. Griswold. Philadelphia, Lindsay & Blakiston, **1846,** c. 1845. x p., 1 l., 13–240 p., 8 pl., 9 x 6. F. (747)

This was reissued without date. C.U. (747*a*)

**Scrap book, The,** a selection of humorous stories, interesting fables and authentic anecdotes. New York, pub. for the booksellers, **n. d.** 2 p. l., 5–288 p., [15 pl.,] and illus., 4¾ x 3½. F. (748)

This book also issued with a title-page "The scrap book or humorous annual," with date 1840 on back of cover.

**Scrap table, The,** for **1831.** Boston, Carter, Hendee & Babcock, **1830.** 4 p. l., 9–184 p., 7¾ x 4¾. N.Y.S. (749)

**Scripture gift book, The,** ed. by Edward E. Hale. New York, W. H. Appleton [**pref. d. 1848**]. vi, 13–291 p., 6 pl., 8⅜ x 6⅜. F. (750)

Also issued by Geo. A. Leavitt, n. d. [1869 or after]. U.W. (750*a*)

**Snow drop, The,** ed. by Rev. C. W. Everest. New York, J. S. Redfield. * (750*b*)

**Snow flake, The,** a Christmas, New Year and birthday gift. New York, Leavitt & Allen, **n. d.** [1856 or after]. 4 p. l., 11–260 p., 6 pl., 7¼ x 4¾. "Magnolia. 'Not in the autumn.' " L.C. (751)

This is "Magnolia," 1836, with p. 261–300 omitted and less and different pl.

See also "Coral," n. d., "Friendship's token," N. Y., n. d., "Memory," 1854, "Gift of affection," n. d., "Morning glory," n. d., "Aloe," 1854.

—— ——, a gift for innocence and beauty, ed. by T. S. Arthur, **1846.** Philadelphia, E. Ferrett & Co., **1846,** c. 1845. iv p., 1 l., 9–284 p., 10 pl., 8¾ x 5½. C.U., U.W. (752)

—— ——, a holiday gift for **1849.** Philadelphia, E. H. Butler & Co., 1849, c. 1848. vi p., 1 l., 13–330 p., 10 pl. 7⅞ x 4¾. N.Y., L.C., U.W. (753)

—— ——, a holiday gift for **1850.** Philadelphia, E. H. Butler & Co., 1850, c. 1849. vi p., 1 l., 13–330 p., 9 pl., 7⅛ x 4¾. N.Y., L.C., U.W. (754)

—— ——, a Christmas, New Year and birthday gift for **1851.** Philadelphia, E. H. Butler & Co., 1851, c. 1850. x p., 1 l., 13–330 p., 9 pl., 7¼ x 4¾. L.C., P.M. (755)

**Snow flake, The,** a Christmas, New-Year and birthday gift for **1852.** Philadelphia, E. H. Butler & Co., 1852, c. 1851. xp., 1 l., 13–330 p., 9 pl., 7¼ x 4¾. N.Y., L.C., U.W. (756)

—— ——, a Christmas, New-Year and birthday gift for **1854.** Philadelphia, E. H. Butler & Co., 1854, c. 1853. xp., 1 l., 13–328 p., 8 pl., 7¼ x 4¾. L.C., C.U. (757)

—— ——, a Christmas, New-Year and birthday present for **1855.** Philadelphia, E. H. Butler & Co., 1855, c. 1854. xp., 1 l., 13–328 p., 8 pl., 7⅛ x 4¾. L.C., C.U. (758)

—— ——, a Christmas, New Year and birthday gift. New York, Leavitt & Allen, n. d., **c. 1855.** vi p., 1 l., 9–264 p., 6 pl., 7¼ x 5. "The baron's vow." F. (759)
This is same as "Moss rose," n. d.

**Snow flakes,** a chapter from the book of nature. Boston, American Tract Society, **c. 1863.** 146 p., 13 pl. [paged in], 9 x 6¾. B.A. (760)

**Songs of the flowers,** with their language, by Fannie Frisbie. Boston, G. W. Cottrell, **c. 1855.** 96 p., 3 x 2. F. (760*a*)

**Sons of temperance offering,** for **1850,** ed. by T S. Arthur. [v. 1.] New York, Nafis & Cornish, c. 1849. viii, 9–320 p., 10 pl., 8 x 5½. N.Y., L.C., C.U. (761)

—— —— for **1851,** ed. by T. S. Arthur. [v. 2.] New York, Cornish, Lamport & Co., c. 1850. viii, 9–320 p., 10 pl., 8 x 5½. L.C. (762)

**Souvenir, The,** or picturesque pocket diary, for **1826** Philadelphia, 1826. 16mo., pl. * (763)

**Souvenir annual, The,** New York, George A. Leavitt, **n. d.** [circa 1869]. 3 p.l., 17–294 p., [2 pl.,] 8¼ x 6¼. P.M. (764)

This is "Souvenir gallery," 1850, omitting last 2 p. and with different pl.

**Souvenir gallery,** an illustrated gift book for all seasons, ed. by Emily Percival. Boston, Phillips, Sampson & Co., **1850,** c. 1849. 3 p. l., 15–296 p., [7 pl.,] 9¾ x 7¾. "Count Voisin's only daughter." F. (765)

Also issued Boston, Phillips & Sampson, **c. 1853.** 3 p. l., 15–294 p., 13 pl., last 2 p. omitted, otherwise same. U. W. (766)

Also issued as "Souvenir annual " n. d., omitting last 2 p., and pl. different.
Also issued as "Annual Souvenir Gallery," 1852, with last 2 p. omitted.

**Souvenir of friendship, The,** a Christmas and New-Year's present, elegantly illustrated. New York, D. Appleton & Co., **1857.** 288 p., 10 pl., 9½ x 6½. F. (767)

**Spirit of the annuals,** for **1831.** Philadelphia, E. Littell, 1831. xp., 1 l., 13–467 p., front., 5⅜ x 3¼. "Containing all the best pieces in Literary souvenir, Keepsake, Forget-me-not, Iris, Amulet, etc., etc." F. (768)

**Stranger's gift, The,** a Christmas and New Year's present, ed. by Hermann Bokum. Boston, Light & Horton, **1836,** c. 1835. 3 p. l., 9–103 p., front., 7⅜ x 4½. B.A. (769)

**String of diamonds, The,** gathered from many mines by a gem fancier. New edition revised and enlarged. Hartford, Wm. James Hamersby, **c. 1857.** vii, 9–296 p., front., 7¼ x 5. F. (769*a*)

**Sunday school gift, 1842.** * (770)

**Tablet, The.** Original prose and verse by New Haven writers. New Haven, 1831. * (771)

**Talisman, The,** for **1828** [ed. by Francis Herbert, *i. e.* Bryant] [v. 1.] New York, Elam Bliss, 1827, c. 1827. xp., 1 l., 288 p., 7 pl., and 2 autograph pl., 5⅜ x 3½. N.Y., B.A., B.P. (772)

See "Miscellanies," name of reissue of this series.

—— —— for **1829.** [Francis Herbert.] [v. 2.] New York, Elam Bliss, 1828, c. 1828. xp., 1 l., 342 p., 6 pl., 5½ x 3½. N.Y., B.A. (773)

—— —— for **1830.** [v. 3.] New York, 3d edition, Elam Bliss, 1829, c.1829. xii, 358 p., 12 pl., 5¾ x 3⅝. N.Y., B.P. (774)

Third edition probably means vol. 3, as all issues seem to have it.

**Talisman, The,** an offering of friendship with oil colored illuminations, ed. by Henry D. Moore. Philadelphia, Hogan & Thompson, **1852,** c. 1851. viii p., 1 l, 13–262 p., 12 pl., 9 x 5⅞. L.C., B.P. (775)

**Temperance gift, The,** ed. by T. S. Arthur. New York, Leavitt & Allen, **n. d.** [1853, 54 or 55]. viii, 264 p., 8 pl., 7¼ x 4⅞. F. (776)

**Temperance keepsake, The,** an offering for all seasons, ed. by T. S. Arthur. New York, Lamport, Blakeman & Law, **1854.** viii, 9–287 p., 7⅜ x 5. F. (776*a*)

**Temperance offering,** for **1851,** ed. by T. S. Arthur. New York, Cornish, Lamport & Co. viii, 320 p., 10 pl., 8 x 5⅞. * (777)

—— ——, for **1853,** ed. by T. S. Arthur. New York, Cornish, Lamport & Co., c. 1853. vi p., 1 l., 9–264 p., 7 pl., 7¼ x 5. N.Y. (778)

—— ——, for all seasons, ed. by T. S. Arthur. New York, Lamport, Blakeman & Law, **1854.** N.Y. (779)

Identical with 1853, except a slight change in introduction wording.

**Temperance token, The,** or crystal drops from the old oaken bucket, ed. by Kate Barclay. Auburn, N. Y., **1848.** 128 p., illum. t. F. (780)

**Thought-blossom,** a memento, ed. by N. Parker Willis. New York, Leavitt & Allen, 1854, c. 1853. 224 p., 16 pl., 9¼ x 6½. U.W. (781)
Also issued **n. d.,** c. 1853. U.W. (782)
Also issued **1855,** c. 1853. L.C. (783)

**Token, The,** and Atlantic Souvenir, a Christmas and New Year's gift. New York, Leavitt & Allen, **n. d.** [1856 or after]. viii, 9–81 p., 1 l., 5–175 p., 6 pl., 7¼ x 5. "The appropriate sphere of woman."
N.Y., L.C. (784)

This is a stolen name and cheap makeup, being really "Lady's manual," 1854.
Also issued as "Affection's gift," n. d., "Memory's gift," n. d.

—— ——, or affection's gift, a Christmas and New-Year's present, ed. by S. G. Goodrich. New York, Ansel Edwards, **n. d.** [circa 1846]. 1 p. l., vii–viii, 9–312 p., 6 pl., 7⅜ x 4½. "The wonders of the deep."
N. Y., L.C. (785)

This is "Token," 1838, reprinted, and with different pl. It was again reprinted in Hartford, see below.

—— ——, or affection's gift, a Christmas and New-Year's present, ed. by S. G. Goodrich. Hartford, S. Andrus & Son, **n. d.** 1 p. l., vii–viii, 9–312 p., [6 pl.,] 7¼ x 4½. "The wonders of the deep." N.Y. (786)

Has illum. t., "The token, a gift book for all seasons."
This is "Token," 1838, reprinted and with different pl. It was also reprinted in New York. See above.

—— ——, or affection's gift, a Christmas and New Year's present, ed. by S. G. Goodrich. New York, Leavitt & Allen, no street address given, **n. d.** [1853 or after]. 1 p. l., vii–viii, 9–262 p., [5 pl. and presentation pl.,] 7⅞ x 5⅞. "The wonders of the deep."
N.Y., U.W. (787)

This is "Token," 1838, with pages 263–312 omitted, and different pl., and fancy borders around the pages.
There are two editions, Leavitt & Allen, 379 Broadway, n. d. [1856 or after], which are like this, but each with different plates. One edition omits the presentation pl. One has red borders to all pages, the other is without borders and 7⅛ x 4⅞. U.W., F. (788)

—— ——, a Christmas and New Year's present. [v. 1.] Boston, S. G. Goodrich, **1828,** c. 1827. viii, 9–368 p., 12 pl., 5½ x 3½. N.Y., B.P. (789)

—— ——, a Christmas and New Year's present, ed. by N. P. Willis. [v. 2.] Boston, S. G. Goodrich, **1829,** c. 1828. x, 348 p., 15 pl., 5¾ x 3⅝.
L.C., B.P., B.A. (790)

Also issued in large paper. 6¾ x 4½. N.Y.

—— ——, a Christmas and New Year's present, ed. by S. G. Goodrich. [v. 3.] Boston, Carter & Hendee, **1830,** c. 1829. xii, 13–340 p., 13 pl., 5⅝ x 3⅝.
N.Y., L.C., B.P., B.A. (791)

—— ——, a Christmas and New Year's present, ed. by S. G. Goodrich. [v. 4.] Boston, Gray & Bowen, **1831,** c.1830. vi p., 1 l., 9–320 p., 11 pl., 6 x 4.
N.Y., L.C., B.P., B.A. (792)

**Token, The,** a Christmas and New Year's present, ed. by S. G. Goodrich. [v. 5.] Boston, Gray & Bowen, **1832,** c.1831. iv, 5–392 p., 20 pl., 6½ x 4⅜.
N.Y., L.C., B.P., B.A., U.W. (793)

—— ——, and Atlantic souvenir, a Christmas and New Year's present, ed. by S. G. Goodrich. [v. 6.] Boston, Gray & Bowen, **1833,** c.1832. xii, 13–354 p., 20 pl., 6½ x 4¼.
N.Y., L.C., B.P., B.A., U.W. (794)

With this issue "The token" absorbed "Atlantic souvenir."

—— —— and Atlantic souvenir, a Christmas and New Year's present, ed. by S. G. Goodrich. [v. 7.] Boston, Charles Bowen, **1834,** c. 1833. viii, 9–352 p., 14 pl., 6½ x 4½. N.Y., L.C., B.P., B.A. (795)

—— —— and Atlantic souvenir, a Christmas and New Year's present, ed. by S. G. Goodrich. [v. 8.] Boston, Charles Bowen, **1835,** c.1834. 376 p., 13 pl., 6¼ x 4⅛.
N.Y., L.C., B.P., U.W. (796)

—— —— and Atlantic souvenir, a Christmas and New Year's present, ed. by S. G. Goodrich. [v. 9.] Boston, Charles Bowen, **1836,** c.1835. viii, 9–360 p. 12 pl., 7 x 4½. N.Y., L.C., B.P., B.A. (797)

—— —— and Atlantic souvenir, a Christmas and New Year's present, ed. by S. G. Goodrich. [v. 10.] Boston, Charles Bowen, **1837,** c.1836. viii, 9–348 p., 12 pl., 7⅛ x 4½.
N.Y., L.C., B.P., B.A., U.W. (798)

—— —— and Atlantic souvenir, a Christmas and New Year's present, ed. by S. G. Goodrich. [v. 11.] Boston, American Stationers Co., **1838,** c.1837. viii, 9–312 p., 10 pl., 7¾ x 5. "The wonders of the deep."
N.Y. L.C., B.P., B.A., U.W. (799)

This was enlarged in size of page.
This was reprinted and at least 2 ed. issued [1842, 1844] by A. & C. B. Edwards, N. Y., plates vary, and there were at least two editions issued as "Token or affection's gift," New York, A. Edwards, n. d. [circa 1846]. It was again reprinted as "Token or affection's gift," Hartford, S. Andrus & Son, and had several editions n. d., 1846, 1847, 1850. All these spurious ed. had different pl.

This was again issued as "Token or affection's gift," New York, Leavitt & Allen, n. d. [1853 and after], with p. 263–312 omitted, plates changed and a fancy border about each page. At least 3 editions of this shortened "Token" were issued, each varying in the plates from the others and from the original. In 1842 [date only on back of vol.] this was republished in New York by A. & C. B. Edwards, while a "Token" of the regular series [the last issued] was pub. the same year in Boston.

—— —— and Atlantic souvenir, a Christmas and New Year's present, ed. by S. G. Goodrich. [v. 12.] Boston, Otis Broaders & Co., **1839,** c.1838. viii, 296 p., 9 pl., 6¾ x 4½. N.Y., L.C., B.P. (800)

Restored to early size of page.

**Token, The,** and Atlantic souvenir, a Christmas and New Year's present, ed. by S. G. Goodrich. [v. 13.] Boston, Otis Broaders & Co., **1840,** c.1839. viii, 9–304 p., 10 pl., 6⅞ x 4½. "Rainbow bridge."
N.Y., L.C., B.P., B.A., U.W. (801)
Some copies have "The token," on back, others "Token and affection's gift."
This was issued as "Friendship's gift," n. d., as "Token of friendship," n. d., and as "Atlantic souvenir," n. d., all with p. 265–304 omitted and pl. changed; as "Moss rose," 1846, and "Honeysuckle," 1848, with different pl. and illum. t.

—— —— and Atlantic souvenir, a Christmas and New Year's present, ed. by S. G. Goodrich. [v. 14.] Boston, W. D. Ticknor, **1841,** c.1840. 272 p., 12 pl., 6¾ x 4½ "The stranger's nephew." N.Y., B.P., B.A. (802)
This was issued as "Moss rose," 1847, with different pl. and p. 65–180 different.

—— —— and Atlantic souvenir, an offering for Christmas and the new year. [v. 15.] Boston, David H. Williams, **1842,** c.1841. viii, 9–320 p., 10 pl., 6¾ x 4½. "The lesson of a moment."
N.Y., L.C., B.P., B.A. (803)
This was the final issue of the series. Goodrich had trouble financially and with his printers and writers, which accounts for the issue also in 1842 in New York of a reprint of 1838. See below.

—— ——, or affection's gift, a Christmas and New Year's present, ed. by S. G. Goodrich. New York, A. & C. B. Edwards, n.d. [**1842** on back]. viii, 9–312 p., [6 pl.,] 7¼ x 4½. "The wonders of the deep."
N.Y., B.P. (804)
This is "Token," 1838. See also the n. d. editions also issued by same firm; plates are different.
Also issued in **1844** [date on back only] with less plates [8 pl.] and 3 of them different, list of pl. being omitted.
L.C. (804*a*)

—— ——, or affection's gift, a Christmas and New Year's present, ed. by S. G. Goodrich. Hartford, S. Andrus & Son, **1846.** viii, 9–312 p., 5 pl. [with titles erased], 7¾ x 4½. "The wonders of the deep." (805)
This is "Token," 1838, with pl. changed.
Also issued S. Andrus & Son, **1847,** identical except col. t. added. F. (806)
Also issued S. Andrus & Son, **1850,** same as 1846 except front. is replaced by col. flower pl., and pl. vary. See also n. d. issues by this firm.
L. C. (807)

—— ——, a gift for all seasons. New York, D. Appleton & Co., **1857,** c. 1856. 288 p., 9 pl., 7¼ x 4¾.
L.C. (808)
Mostly made up of German annuals' articles.
Also an edition n. d., c. **1856.** N.Y., B.P., U.W. (809)

**Token of friendship, A.** Boston, G. W. Cottrell, **n. d.** 128 p., 1 l., 5¼ x 3¾. "Home." N.Y. (810)

—— ——, a new edition, ed. by author of "Affection's Keepsake," New York, D. Appleton & Co., **n. d.** x, 11–128 p., engr. front, 4 x 2¾. "The praise of a true *frende.*" F. (811)

**Token of friendship, The.** New York, Leavitt & Allen **n. d.** viii, 9-264 p., 6 pl., 7¼ x 5. "Rainbow bridge." C.U., P.M. (812)

This is "Token," 1840, with different pl. See also "Friendship's gift," n. d., and "Atlantic souvenir," n. d. Also "Moss rose," 1846, and "Honeysuckle," 1848.

—— ——, an offering for all seasons; illustrated. Boston, Phillips, Sampson & Co., **n. d.** 5 p. l., 276 p., 6 pl., 7¼ x 4¾. "Who are the happy?" N.Y., B.A., U.W. (813)

Also an edition with pref. d. 1854.
Also an edition Leavitt & Allen, n. d., with varying pl.
This is "Wreath of wild flowers," 1846, with pl. and preliminary unpaged l. added.
See also "Amaranth," 1851, with unpaged l., containing "Forest maid," also "Garland," 1852, "Keepsake of friendship," Boston, 1853, "Magnolia," [1853].

—— ——, a gift book for the holidays for **1851,** ed. by Bradford K. Peirce. Boston, Charles H. Peirce, c. 1850. viii p., 2 l., 13–324 p., 7 pl., 7½ x 4¾. "Home habits." N.Y., B.P., P.M. (814)
Also an edition **1852** exactly similar. F. (815)

—— ——, an offering for all seasons, illustrated. Boston, Phillips Sampson & Co., n. d. [**pref. d. Ag. 1852**]. vi p., 1 l., 9–322 p., 6 pl., 7¼ x 4¾. "The new year." N.Y. (816)

This is "Amaranth," 1849, with first article changed, and col. t. and col. front. substituted.
See also "Casket," Boston [1853], and N. Y., n. d., and "Garland," Boston, 1850, "Memory's gift," N. Y., 1869, and n. d., 'Keepsake of friendship," 1851, and "Ma-3 nolia," 1852.

—— ——, an offering for all seasons, illustrated. Boston, Phillips, Sampson & Co., n. d. [**pref. d. Ag. 1854**]. 5 p. l., 276 p., 6 pl., 7¼ x 4¾. "Who are the happy?" F. (817)

Also an edition without date, otherwise same, and an edition New York, Leavitt & Allen, n. d., with varying pl.
This is "Wreath of wild flowers," 1846, with pl. and unpaged p. leaf added.
Also issued as "Amaranth," 1851, "Garland," 1852, "Keepsake of friendship" Boston, 1853, and "Magnolia" [1853].

**Token of love,** ed. by a lady [E. M. M.]. New York, D. Appleton & Co., **n. d.** viii, 9–126 p., engr. front., 4 x 2½. "The annoyer.' C.U. (818)

**Token of remembrance, A,** a new edition, ed. by author of "Affection's Keepsake," New York. D. Appleton & Co. **n. d.** x, 11–128 p., front 4 x 2½. "Stanzas." F. (818*a*)

**Union annual, The, 1837.** Philadelphia, American Sunday school union, 1837, c.1836. vi p., 1 l., 9–269 p., 7 pl., 5⅞ x 3¾. N.Y., L.C., U.W. (819)

**Unique, The,** a biography of many distinguished characters, with fine portraits. Boston, J. P. Peaslee, **1829.** 253 p. [8 pl.], 4¾ x 3. F. (820)
This is not a true Annual.
Also Hingham, **1834.** 4th ed. * (820*a*)

**Violet, The,** a Christmas and New Year's gift. New York, Leavitt & Allen, **n. d.** [1853, 54 or 55]. 3 p. l., 7–250 p., [6 pl.,] 6¾ x 4½. "The lighthouse."
N.Y., U.W. (821)
An edition by George A. Leavitt, n. d.
Also issued 1869, same except pl. vary.

—— ——, a Christmas and New Year's gift or birthday present, **1837,** ed. by Miss Leslie. [v. 1.] Philadelphia, E. L. Carey & A. Hart, c.1836. 4 p. l., 17–212 p., 6 pl., 5⅞ x 3¾. N.Y., B.P., U.W. (822)

—— ——, a Christmas and New Year's gift or birthday present, **1839,** ed. by Miss Leslie. [v. 2.] Philadelphia, E. L. Carey & A. Hart, c.1839. 5 p. l., 17–216 p., 7 pl., 5¾ x 3½. N.Y., L.C., B.P. (823)

—— ——, a Christmas and New Year's present, **1840,** ed. by Miss Leslie. [v. 3.] Philadelphia, Carey & Hart, c. 1839. 3 p. l., 17–216 p., 6 pl., 5¾ x 3¾.
N.Y., L.C., U.W. (824)

—— ——, a Christmas and New Year's gift for 1842. Philadelphia, Carey & Hart, **1842,** c. 1841. 216 p., 8 pl., 5¾ x 3¾. N.Y., L.C., U.W. (825)

—— ——, a Christmas and New Year's gift. New York. **1850.** 6 pl., 16mo. * (826)

—— ——, a Christmas and New Year's gift. New York, George A. Leavitt, **1869.** 2 p. l., 7–250 p., [6 pl.,] 6⅛ x 4. P.M. (827)
Also issued by George A. Leavitt, **n. d.** F. (828)
Also by Leavitt & Allen, **n. d.** F. (829)

**Visitor, The,** a Christmas and New Year's token, ed. by B. Field. Boston, Peirce & Williams, **1829.** vi, 7–144 p., [engr. front., 4 pl.,] 4¾ x 3.
N.Y., B.P., U.W. (830)

**Voice of flowers, The,** by Mrs. L. H. Sigourney. Hartford, H. S. Parsons & Co., **1846,** c. 1845. iv, 5–123, 1 p., 2 l., col. front., 4½ x 2¾. L.C. (831)

**Voices of heart and home,** an offering of love from many hearts. Portland [Me.], F. W. Bailey, **1856.** 1 p.l., 7–128 p., 4 pl., 4½ x 3. L.C. (832)

**Waverley garland, The,** a present for all seasons, ed. by "Ellen Louise." Boston, Moses A. Dow, **1853,** c.1852. viii, 9–400 p., front., 10 x 8¼. H.U. (833)
Made up from the "Waverley magazine" articles.

**Wedding gift, The,** or the duties and pleasures of domestic life. Boston, Gould, Kendall & Lincoln. [**circa 1844**], vi, 7–128, vi, 7–128 p., 4¼ x 2¾.
F. (833*a*)
This is "Marriage ring" and "The family circle" bound together, with new t. and pref. prefixed.

—— ——, to all who are entering the marriage state, ed. by Cotesworth Pinckney. Worcester [Mass.], S. A. Howland, **1849,** c. 1848. 128 p., illum. t., 4¼ x 2⅞.
F. (833*b*)

**Wedding guest, The,** a friend of the bride and bridegroom, ed. by T. S. Arthur. Philadelphia, H. C. Peck & Theo. Bliss, c.**1857.** vi, 7–300 p., 6 pl., 7⅛ x 4¾.
F. (834)

**Wedding-ring, The,** ed. by J. S. A. Boston, J. Buffum, **n. d.** c. n. d. 96 p., 2⅞ x 2⅜. F. (834*a*)

**Western souvenir, The,** a Christmas and New Year's gift for **1829.** Cincinnati, N. & G. Guilford. ix, 10–324 p., 7 pl., 5½ x 3½. N.Y., L.C., B.P., U.W. (835)

**Wheat-sheaf, The,** or gleanings for the wayside and fire-side. Philadelphia, Willis P. Hazard, **1853,** c. 1852. xii, 13–416 p., [5 pl.], 8½ x 5¾. F. (836)
At least 3 vols. issued.

**White veil, The,** a bridal gift, ed. by Mrs. Sarah Josepha Hall, elegently illustrated. Philadelphia, E. H. Butler & Co., **1854,** c. 1853. viii, p., 1 l., 17–324 p., 11 pl., 8¼ x 6¾. F. (836*a*)

**Wide-awake gift,** a know-nothing token for **1855,** ed. by "one of 'em." New York, J. C. Derby, 1855, c. 1854. xii, 13–312 p., [5 pl.,] 7½ x 4¾. L.C., B.P., U.W. 837)

**Wild flower, The,** a gift book for the holydays for **1852,** ed. by Grace Maylove. Philadelphia, J. & J. L Gihon, 1852, c. 1851. 260 p., 8 pl. and illum. t., 8½ x 6¼. F. (838)

**Winter-bloom, The,** ed. by Henry D. Moore. Philadelphia, Hogan & Thompson, **c. 1850.** viii p., 2 l., 13–240 p., 9 col. pl., 9 x 5¾. N.Y., L.C., B.P., U.W. (839)

**Wintergreen, The,** a perennial gift for **1844,** ed. by John Keese. New York, Charles Wells & Co., c. 1843. x, 19–247 p., 16 pl., 6¾ x 4½. N.Y., B.P., U.W. (840)

**Winter wreath, A,** of summer flowers, by S. G. Goodrich. New York, D. Appleton & Co., **1855,** c.1854. 320 p., [8 pl.,] 9 x 5¾. F. (841)
Also reprinted in **1867,** c. 1854. B.A., P.M. (842)

**Winter wreath, The,** ed. by N. Parker Willis. New York, Leavitt & Allen, n. d. [1856 or after], **c. 1853.** 224 p., 12 pl., 9¼ x 6½. F. (843)

**Women of the scriptures,** ed. by H. Hastings Weld. Philadelphia, Lindsay & Blakiston, **c. 1848.** xii, 13–240 p., 12 pl., 9¼ x 5⅞. F. (844)

**Woodbine, The,** a holiday gift, ed. by Caroline May. Philadelphia, Lindsay & Blakiston, **c. 1851.** xp., 1 l., 13–322 p., 8 pl., 7¼ x 4¾. L.C. (845)

**Wreath, The,** a collection of poems from celebrated English authors. New York, W. B. Gilley & H. I. Megarey, **1821.** iv, 3–259 p., front. and engr. t., 4 x 3¼. F. (846)
Also an edition Hartford, **1826.** F. (847)

—— ——, designed as a token for the young. [v. 1.] New York, N. B. Holmes, **1836,** c. 1835. 160 p. eng. front. and eng. t. 5¾ x 4½. F. (847*a*)

—— ——, designed as a token for the young, [v. 2.] **1837.** New York, Doolittle & Vermilge. 238 p., illus. * (848)

**Wreath of beauty, The,** ed. by J. R. G. Hassard. New York, D. Appleton & Co., **1864,** c.1863. 336 p., 16 pl., 10¾ x 7¾. F. (849)

**Wreath of wild flowers, The,** from the literary miscellanies of John Milton Stearns. New York, Edward Walker, **1846,** c.1846. x, 276 p., [front. and engr. t.,] 7¼ x 4½. "The refugee." B.P. (850)
A second ed. was issued N. Y., 1848. F. (851)
This book, by J. M. Stearns, was used without credit by the publishers of annuals, a preliminary poem on an inserted unpaged l., and plates being added, and the original front. and engr. t. omitted, and preface changed. It was reissued thus as "Amaranth," 1851, as "Garland," 1852, as "Keepsake of friendship," Bost., 1853, as "Token of friendship," Boston, Phillips & Sampson [1854], and also without date, Boston, and without date, N. Y., and as "Magnolia" [pref. d. 1853]. Almost all these vary in the first unpaged article, and in plates.

**Young lady's cabinet of gems,** a choice collection of pieces of poetry and prose by Virginia DeForest. Boston, Kelley & Brother, **1854,** c.1854. xii, 13–348 p., [col. front. and col. t.,] 7⅜ x 4¾. F. (852)
Called "Lady's cabinet" on back of cover.

**Young ladies' choice, The,** ed. by Mrs. L. G. Abell. Boston, Higgins, Bradley & Dayton, **1858.** 256 p., [1 pl.,] 6¾ x 4½. F. (853)
Also called "Ladies' choice."

**Young lady's companion,** ed. by Margaret Coxe. Cincinnati. 342 p. [**Pref. 1839.**] * (854)

—— —— and token of affection, in a series of letters by Margaret Coxe. Columbus [O.], Isaac N. Whiting, **1846,** c.1845 2d ed. revised and list of books added [p. 343–48]. [Pref. d. Ag. 1840.] x, 348 p., 8 x 5. C.U. (855)

—— ——. Illum. t. of "Lady's companion" reads thus.

**Young lady's gift,** a common-place book of prose an poetry. Providence, B. Cranston & Co., **1836,** c. 1836. viii, 316 p., 5¾ x 3¾. F. (856)

**Young ladies' oasis,** or gems of prose and poetry, ed. by N. L. Ferguson. Lowell, N. L. Dayton, **1851,** c. 1850. 2d ed., 252 p., front. and illum. pl., 6¾ x 4½. C.U. (857)
Also issued in 1854 with p. 253–72 added, different front., and no illum. pl. * (858)

**Young ladies' offering,** or gems of prose and poetry. Boston, Phillips & Sampson, **1848,** c. 1847. iv, 5–264 p., [4 pl.,] 7½ x 4½. "Kindred hearts." N.Y., C.U. (859)
See 1849, 1851, 1853, 1857, identical ed. except pl. vary and article p. 5–8 is at p. 19–22.

—— ——, or gems of prose and poetry, by Mrs. L. H. Sigourney and others. Boston, Phillips & Sampson, **1849,** c. 1847. iv, 5–264 p. [4 pl.], 7½ x 4¾. "The father." N.Y., C.U., U.W. (860)
This is same as 1848, except front. is different and article p. 5–8 transferred to p. 19–22.

**Young ladies' offering**—(*continued*).
An ed. **1851,** c.1847. Same as 1849. 7½ x 4¾. C.U. (861)
An ed. **1853,** c.1847. Same as 1849. Title reads "Young ladies' offering," but back reads "Young lady's offering." N Y., U.W. (862)
An ed. **1857,** c.1847. Same as 1849. C.U. (863)

**Young lady's Sunday book, The,** a practical manual of the Christian duties of piety, benevolence and self-government. Philadelphia, Key & Biddle, **1833,** c. 1833. viii, 312 p., front. and eng. t., 5 x 3⅛. F. (863*a*)
This is not a true Annual.

**Young maiden's mirror, c. 1853.** * (864)
—— ——, by the author of "The child's keepsake." Boston, C. Stone & Co., **1857.** 3rd ed. enlarged, with music, c. 1853. 274 p., 10 p. of music, front. and presentation pl., 6½ x 4¼. F. (864*a*)
—— ——, by the author of "The child's keepsake." Boston, Cyrus Stone, **1858.** 4th ed. enlarged, with music, c. 1853. 274 p., 10 p. of music, front. and presentation pl., 6½ x 4¼.
Same as 1857. U.W. (865)

**Young man, The,** or guide to knowledge, virtue and happiness, by Frank Ferguson. Boston, G. W Cottrell & Co., c. **1848.** 128 p., illum. t., 4½ x 2¾. F. (865*a*)
Illum. t. reads, "The young man's guide to knowledge and virtue."

**Young man's friend, The,** by Daniel C. Eddy. Lowell, Nathaniel L. Dayton, **1850,** c.1849. 3 p.l., 9–264 p., engr. front., 7⅛ x 4½. F. (866)

**Young man's guide, The.** Boston, Lilly, Wait, Colman & Holden, **1833,** c.1833. xii, 13–320 p., front. and engr. t., 6 x 3¾. U.W. (867)

**Young man's offering,** comprising prose and poetical writing of the most eminent authors. Boston, Phillips & Sampson, **1849.** 1 p.l., vi, 7–316 p., [6 pl.,] 7¼ x 4¾. F. (868)
An edition **1850** is the same. U.W. (869)
An edition **1857** is the same. B.P. (870)

**Young man's own book.** Philadelphia [circa 1832?] *
Not an Annual.

**Youth's annual.** Title on back of "Juvenile scrap book." **n. d.**

**Youth's historical gift,** a Christmas, New-Year and birth day present, ed. by R. M. Evans. New York, D-Appleton, **1844.** 40 pl., ¼ x 6¾. F. (871).

**Youth's keepsake,** or Christmas and New Year's present. New York, Leavitt & Allen, **n. d.** [1853 or after]. 4 p.l., 9–252 p., 6 pl., 6¼ x 4¼. "London and country cousin." B.P. (872)

**Youth's keepsake**—(*continued*).

Another ed., Leavitt & Allen, 379 Broadway, n. d. [1856 or after]. P.M. (873)

Another ed. 1869. F. (874)

This is "American juvenile keepsake," c. 1834, with 3 less pl.

See also "Gift," N. Y., 1847, "Gem," 1849.

—— ——, a Christmas and New Year's gift for young people. [v. 1.] Boston, Carter & Hendee, **1830**, c. 1829. 210 p., 6 pl., 5⅞ x 3½. N.Y., B.A. (875)

—— ——, a Christmas and New Year's gift for young people. [v. 2.] Boston, Carter & Hendee, **1831**, c. 1830. 216 p., 7 pl., 5¾ x 3¾. N.Y., L.C., B.P. (876)

**Youth's keep-sake**, a New Year, Christmas and birthday, present for both sexes, with engravings. New York J. C. Ricker, **1834** (date on vig. t. and back of book only). vi, 7–216 p., 8 pl. 5¼ x 4¼. F. (876*a*)

Eng. t. reads "Youth's Keepsake."

**Youth's keepsake**, a Christmas and New Year's gift for young people. Boston, E. R. Broaders, **1835**, c. 1834 viii, 206 p., 7 pl., 6 x 3¾. N.Y., L.C., B.P. (877)

—— ——, a Christmas and New Year's gift for young people. Boston, John Allen & Co., **1836**, c. 1835. 2 p.l., 7–214 p., 6 pl., 6 x 3½. L.C., B.P. (878)

—— ——, a Christmas and New Year's gift for young people. Boston, Otis, Broaders & Co., **1837**, c.1836. 192 p., [3 pl., and 3 paged illus.,] 6 x 4. B.P. (879)

—— ——, a Christmas and New Year's gift for young people. Boston, T. H. Carter, **1838**. 2 p.l., 9–192 p., [3 pl., and 3 paged illus.]. N.Y., B.P. (880)

—— ——, a Christmas and New Year's gift for young people. Boston, Otis, Broaders & Co., **1839**, c. 1838. 2 p. l., 9–195 p., [1 pl. and 7 paged illus.,] 6 x 4. B.P. (881)

—— ——, a Christmas and New Year's gift for young people. Boston, Otis, Broaders & Co., **1840**. 2 p.l., 9–190 p., 1 l., 4 pl., and illus., 6½ x 4. N.Y., B.P., U.W. (882)

—— ——, a Christmas and New Year's gift for young people. Boston, William Crosby & Co., **1841**. 2 p.l., 9–192 p., 2 pl., and illus., 6¼ x 4⅛. B.P. (883)

—— ——, a Christmas and New Year's gift for young people. Boston, William Crosby & Co., **1842**. 2 p.l., 9–191 p., 1 p., [3 pl., illus.,] 6¼ x 4. B.P. (884)

—— ——, a Christmas and New Year's gift for young people. Boston, **1843**. * (885)

—— —— a Christmas and New Year's gift for young people. Boston, T. H. Carter & Co., [**1844** on cover, and half title,] c.1843. xii, 13–206 p., [9 pl.,] 6½ x 4. F (886)

**Youth's keepsake,** a Christmas and New Year's gift for young people. Boston, T. H. Carter & Co. [**1845** on back and at top of p. 9], [vii]–viii, 9–180 p., [6 pl., and il. in text]. 6¼ x 4. F. (887)

—— ——, a Christmas and New Year's gift for young people. Boston, Benj. B. Mussey, n. d. [**1846** on half title and back]. 2 p.l., 9–180 p., [5 pl.,] 6¼ x 4. N.Y. (888)

—— ——, a Christmas and New Year's present. New York, George A. Leavitt, **1869.** 3 p.l., 9–352 p., 6 pl., 6¾ x 4½. "London and country cousin." N. Y. (889)
Also an ed., Leavitt & Allen, n. d. (890)

This is "American juvenile keepsake," c.1834, with 3 less pl.
See also "Gift," N. Y., 1847, "Gem," 1849.

**Youth's parlor annual,** ed. and pub. by Rev. D. Newell, New York. 432 p., 8¾ x 5½. N.Y., H.U. (891)

This is "Family circle," a magazine, nos. 1–12 of v. 1, and called "Parlor annual [and Christian family magazine]" at head of page 9.
See "Family circle."

**Youth's portfolio.** See **Portfolio for youth.**

**Youth's sketch book, The,** Boston, Lilly, Wait & Co., **1834,** c.1833. viii, 9–224 p., 8 pl., 5¼ x 4 U.M. (892)

—— ——, being a selection of tales for children. Boston, **1849.** 18mo. illus. * (893)
Also an edition, **1850.** * (894)

**Youth's visitor, The,** or selections in prose and verse from the Presbyterian Sabbath-school visitor. Philadelphia, Presbyterian Board of Publication, **c.1853.** viii, 9–240 p., [11 pl.,] 5¾ x 4½. P.M. (895)

---

(Including the books in the above American alphabet, which are numbered as a. b. c., etc., there are 1022 volumes listed.)

# PART II.

## ENGLISH.

**Ackermann's juvenile forget me not** for **1830,** ed. by Frederic Shoberl. [v. 1.] London. T.-B. B.M. (1023)
This series is entirely distinct, and a rival and imitator of "Juvenile forget me not," which see.

—— —— for **1831,** ed. by Frederic Shoberl. [v. 2.] London. T.-B. B.M. (1024)

—— ——, a Christmas, New Year's and birthday present for youth of both sexes, **1832.** Ed. by Frederic Shoberl. [v. 3.] London, R. Ackermann. 3–252 p., 10 pl., $5\frac{5}{8}$ x $3\frac{1}{2}$. F. (1025)
See "Victoria keepsake," its successor.

**Affection's gift.** London, **1830.** T.-B. (1026)

—— ——. London, **1831.** T.-B. (1027)

—— ——. London, **1832.** T.-B. (1028)

—— ——. London, **1833.** T.-B. (1029)

—— —— for **1844.** London [1843]. 12mo. T.-B., B.M. (1030)

**Affection's keepsake.** London, **1836.** T.-B., B.M. (1031)

—— ——. London, **1837.** T.-B., B.M. (1032)

—— ——. London, **1838.** T.-B., B.M. (1033)

—— ——. London, **1840.** T.-B., B.M. (1034)

—— ——. London, **1842.** T.-B., B.M. (1035)

—— ——. London, **1843.** T.-B., B.M. (1036)

—— ——, **1846.** Original poetry by Thomas Albin. London, imprinted for the author. xvi, 17–206 p., 1 l., front., engr. t., $4\frac{1}{4}$ x $2\frac{3}{4}$. U.W. (1037)

**Affection's offering.** [v. 1.] London, **1829.** T.-B., B.M. (1038)

—— ——. [v. 2.] London, **1830.** T.-B., B.M. (1039)

—— ——, a book for all seasons, but especially designed as a Christmas and New Year's gift or birthday present. [v. 3.] London, Charles Tilt, **1831.** vii p., 1 l., 13–180 p., [3 pl.]. U.W (1040)

—— ——, **1832.** T.-B. (1041)

**Album wreath,** and bijou littéraire, ed. by J. Francis, London, De la Rue, **1834.** 4to. embossed pl. T.-B., B.M. (1042)

**Album wreath of music and literature.** London, **1840.** sm. 4to. T.-B. (1043)

**Amaranth, The.** London, Renshaw & Co., **1832.** T.-B. (1044)

—— ——, a literary present for the instruction and entertainment of the young, ed. by Randolph Roscoe, with fine steel engravings. London, Renshaw & Co. n. d. [**1836** on back]. 2 p. l., 320 p., 6 x $4\frac{3}{4}$. "The patriot son-in-law." N.Y. (1045)

**Amaranth, The,** a miscellany of original prose and verse, ed. by T. K. Hervey. London, Baily & Co., **1839.** pl., 4to. T.-B. (1046)

—— ——, a literary and religious offering, embellished with many fine engravings. London, Edward Lacey, 16 St. Paul's Churchyard, **n. d.** [circa. 1832]. vii p., 1 l., 352 p., 8 pl., $5\frac{1}{2}$ x $3\frac{3}{4}$. "The orphans." U.W. (1047)
This was also pub. in two parts, I, "Friendship's gift"; II, "Juvenile wreath."

**Amethyst, The.** [v. 1.] Edinburgh, **1832.** T.-B. (1048)

—— —— or Christian's annual for **1833,** ed. by R. Hine, and R. K. Greville. [v. 2.] Edinburgh, William Oliphant, 1833. xii, 382 p., $6\frac{1}{2}$ x 4. U.W. (1049)

—— —— or Christian's annual for **1834,** ed. by Richard Hine and Robert Kaye Greville. [v. 3.] Edinburgh, W. Oliphant & Son, 1834. xii, 352 p., engr. t., $6\frac{1}{2}$ x 4. F. (1050)

**Amulet, The,** or Christian and literary remembrancer for **1826.** [v. 1.] London, Wm. Baynes & Son, 1826. xii, 396 p., 12 pl., $5\frac{3}{8}$ x $3\frac{3}{8}$. L.C. (1051)
Also issued in large paper.

—— ——, or Christian and literary remembrancer. [v.2.] London, W. Baynes & Son and Wightman & Cramp, **1827.** xii, 414 p., 12 pl., $5\frac{1}{4}$ x $3\frac{1}{2}$. N.Y., L.C., P.M. (1052)

—— ——, or Christian and literary remembrancer. [v. 3.] London, W. Baynes & Son, and Wightman & Cramp, **1828.** 418 p., 14 pl., $5\frac{1}{2}$ x $3\frac{1}{4}$. L.C., B.P., U.W., B.A. (1053)

—— ——, or Christian and literary remembrancer, ed. by S. C. Hall. [v. 4.] London, Frederick Westley & A. H. Davis, and Wightman & Co., **1829.** xiv, 394 p., 1 l., 14 pl., $5\frac{1}{2}$ x $3\frac{1}{2}$. N.Y., B.P., L.C. (1054)

—— ——, a Christian and literary remembrancer, ed. by S. C. Hall. [v. 5.] London, Frederick Westley & A. H Davis, **1830.** xii, 13–392 p., 12 pl., $5\frac{3}{4}$ x $3\frac{1}{2}$. N.Y., B.P., L.C. (1055)

—— ——, a Christian and literary remembrancer, ed. by S. C. Hall. [v. 6.] London, Frederick Westley & A. H. Davis, **1831.** x, 11–360 p., 12 pl., $5\frac{7}{8}$ x $3\frac{3}{4}$. N.Y., L.C., B.A. (1056)

—— ——, a Christian and literary remembrancer, ed. by S. C. Hall. [v. 7.] London, Frederick Westley & A. H. Davis, **1832.** viii, 9–318 p., 12 pl., $5\frac{3}{4}$ x $3\frac{3}{4}$. N.Y., L.C., B.P. (1057)

—— ——, a Christian and literary remembrancer, ed. by S. C. Hall. [v. 8.] London, Frederick Westley & A. H. Davis, **1833.** viii, 9–312 p., 12 pl., $5\frac{3}{4}$ x $3\frac{3}{4}$. L.C., B.A., P.M (1058)

—— ——, a Christian and literary remembrancer, ed. by S. C. Hall. [v. 9.] London, Frederick Westley & A. H. Davis, **1834.** vi, 9–318 p., 11 pl., $5\frac{3}{4}$ x $3\frac{3}{4}$. L.C. (1059)

—— ——, ed. by S. C. Hall. [v. 10.] London, Frederick Westley & A. H. Davis, **1835.** viii, 9–286 p., 10 pl., $6\frac{1}{2}$ x $4\frac{1}{8}$. N.Y., L.C., U.W. (1060)

**Amulet, The,** ed. by S. C. Hall. [v. 11.] London, Frederick Westley & A. H. Davis, **1836.** vi, 7–304 p., 10 pl., 6½ x 4. N.Y., B.P. (1061)

**Andalusian annual, The,** for **1837.** Ed. by M. B. Houan. London, 1836. 4to, col. pls. * (1061a)

**Angler's souvenir, The,** by "P. Fisher, Esq." [A. W. Chatto.] assisted by several eminent piscatory characters. London, Charles Tilt, **1835.** pl., 12mo., pictorial border. T.-B., F. (1062)

—— ——, **1845.** T.-B. (1063)

—— ——, ed. by G. C. Davies. London, **1886.** pl., 4to. T.-B. (1064)

**Anniversary, The,** an elegant literary present, ed. by Horace Harvey. London, R. A. Charlton, **n. d.** vii, 312 p., [10 pl.,] 6¾ x 4½. B.P. (1065)

—— ——, or poetry and prose for **1829,** ed. by Allan Cunningham. [v.1.] London, John Sharpe, 1829. xvi, 320 p., 20 pl., 7¾ x 5. N.Y. (1066)

Also issued in large paper, 9¼ x 5¾.

Some copies vary in sub-title, having "or prose and poetry for 1829, ed. by Allan Cunningham."

—— —— **1830.** T.-B. (1067)

An edition was partly prepared for 1830, the plates being engraved, but not published.

**Annual gift-book, The,** a drawing-room portrait gallery of eminent personages, London. Joint Stock Co., **1859.** iv p., 1 l., 40 pl., each with text, paged separate, 15¾ x 11½. B.P. (1068)

This was title of vol. 1 of "Drawing-room portrait gallery."

**Annual, The, of British landscape scenery.** Ed. by Louisa Anne Twamley. London, W. S. Orr & Co. [1839 on back of cover.] Preface dated 1838. 152 p., 1 l., 20 pl. 8½ x 5¼. F. (1069)

**Annual souvenir** (Catholic). London, ed. and pub. by Booker, **1834,** illus. with aquatints, the only annual so illustrated. T.-B. (1070)

**Annual token,** London. Edward Lacey, **1835** [?]. 6 pl. * (1071)

**Apollo's gift,** or the musical souvenir, a musical annual, ed. by Ed. and M. Clementi and J. B. Cramer. London, Willis & Co., **1830.** 4to, pl. T.-B. (1072)

—— ——, **1831.** T.-B. (1073)

**Aurora borealis, The,** a literary annual, ed. by members of the Society of Friends. Newcastle-upon-Tyne, Tilt, **1833.** xiv p., 1 l., 1–274 p., 1 l., [2 pl.,] 6½x4. F. (1074)

Issued as "Friend's annual," 1834.

**Ayrshire wreath, The, 1843.** A collection of original pieces in prose and verse, chiefly by native authors, on subjects relating to Ayrshire. Kilmarnock, H. Crawford & Son, 1843. xii, 13–214 p., 1 l., front., 6¾ x 4¼. N.Y. (1075)

**Baxter's agricultural and horticultural annual,** ed. by Baxter & Son. London, Simpkin, **1836,** has 2 Baxter prints. T.-B. (1076)

**Bengal annual,** a literary keepsake for **1830.** ed. by David Lester Richardson. Calcutta, Samuel Smith & Co., 1830. viii, 352 p., 7 pl. (etchings; the only annual so illus.) N.Y. (1077)

—— ——, **1831.** T.-B. (1078)

—— ——, **1832.** T.-B. (1079)

—— ——, **1833.** T.-B. (1080)

—— ——, **1834.** T.-B. (1081)

**Biblical annual.** London, **1833.** T.-B. (1082)

—— ——, **1834.** T.-B. (1083)

**Biblical keepsake,** or landscape illustrations of the most remarkable places mentioned in the Holy Scriptures, by Rev. Thomas H. Horne. London, [1st series,] John Murray, **1835.** xxiv, 156 p., 32 pl., 8¼ x 5¼. U. M. (1084)

—— ——, or landscape illustrations of the most remarkable places mentioned in the Scriptures. Text by T. H. Horne. 2d series. London, John Murray, **1836.** xvi, 171 p., 32 pl., 8⅝ x 5¾ U.M. (1085)

—— ——, or landscape illustrations of the most remarkable places mentioned in the Scriptures. 3d series. London, Horne, **1837.** xii, 168 p., 22 pl., 8¼ x 5¼. U.M. (1086)

**Bijou, The,** or annual of literature and the arts. [v. 1.] London, Wm. Pickering, **1828.** xiv, 335 p., 15.pl., 6¼ x 4. L.C., P.M., B.A. (1087)

—— ——, or annual of literature and the arts. [v. 2.] London, Wm. Pickering, **1829.** xii, 288 p., 10 pl. and vig. t., 6¼ x 4. N.Y., L.C., B.A. (1088)

—— ——, an annual of literature and the arts. [v. 3.] London, Wm. Pickering, **1830.** xiii p., 1 p.l., 288 p., 9 pl., 6¼ x 4. N.Y., L.C., B.A. (1089)

**Bijou almanac,** ed. by L. E. L. London, Schloss, **1839.** T.-B. (1090)

—— ——, ed. by S. Lover. London, Schloss, **1840.** T.-B. (1091)

**Biographical keepsake.** Historical and characteristic sketches of the most distinguished persons of the present time. 1st series. London, Edward Lacey, **n. d.** [circa 1830]. x, 324 p. [8 pl.,] 5½ x 3½. N.Y. (1092)

—— ——. 2d series. London, Edward Lacey, **n. d.** [circa 1830]. iv p., 8 l., 324 p., [8 pl.] 5½ x 3½. N.Y. (1093)

These were originally issued in numbers in 1827–, each with a pl., and called "Public characters of the present day."

**Birthday gift, A.** The dial of love, a book for young people, by Mary Howitt. London, **n. d.** (1094)

This is really a magazine, "Dial of love."

**Blossoms at Christmas,** and first flowers of the New Year, for **1825.** [v. 1.] London, J. Poole, Oct. 10, 1824. 2 p. l., 271 p., [3 pl.,] 5¾ x 3¾. U.W (1095)

—— ——, and first flowers of the new year. London, **1826.** [9 pl.] T.-B. (1096)

**Book of beauty, The.** London, **1845.** T.-B. (1097)

—— ——, for the Queen's boudoir, musical annual for **1848.** London, C. Jeffrey's. 117 p., pl. 3½ x 10. F. (1098)

—— ——, or regal gallery, **1848,** ed. by the Countess of Blessington. London, D. Bogue. 2 p. l., 302 p., 12 pl., 9 x 6½. B.P. (1099)
Continuation of "Heath's book of beauty."

—— ——, or regal gallery, **1849,** ed. by the Countess of Blessington. London, David Bogue, 1849. 2 p. l., 316 p., 13 pl., 9 x 6¼. C.U. (1100)

**Book of flowers,** London. Pirated edition of Flora's interpreter, Boston [circa 1832]. T.-B. (1101)

**Book of gems.** The poets and artists of Great Britain, ed. by S. C. Hall. [v. 1.] London, Saunders & Otley, **1836.** xvi, 304 p., 53 illus. in text, 2 l. of autographs, 8¼ x 5¼. F. (1102)

—— ——. The poets and artists of Great Britain, ed. by S. C. Hall. [v. 2.] London, Saunders & Otley, **1837.** xvi, 304 p., 53 illus. in text, 2 l. autographs, 8¼ x 5¼. F. (1103)

—— ——. The modern poets and artists of Great Britain, ed. by S. C. Hall. [v. 3.] London, Whittaker & Co., **1838.** xvi, 304 p., 43 illus. in text, 2 l. autographs, 8¼ x 5¼. F. (1104)

**Book of royalty,** ed. by Mrs. S. C. Hall. London, Ackermann & Co., **1839.** col. pl. T.-B. (1105)

**Botanic annual,** ed. by R. Mudie. London, Cochrane & Co., **1832.** T.-B. (1106)

**Bouquet,** a new annual. London, Lacey, **1832.** T.-B. (1107)

—— ——. London, Lacey, **1833.** T.-B. (1108)

—— ——. London, Lacey, **1834.** T.-B. (1109)

**Bouquet des souvenirs, Le,** a wreath of friendship. The botanical portion by Rev. J. S. Henslow. London, Robert Tyas, **1840.** 216 p., 25 col. pl., 7¾ x 5. F. (1110)

**Bow in the cloud,** ed. by B. Barton. London, Jackson & Co., **1834.** T.-B. (1111)

**Bridal bouquet** culled from the garden of literature by Henry Southgate. London, **1890.** 400 p., 8vo, illus. T.-B. (1112)

**Broken shaft, The.** Annual for **1886.** London, 1886. T.-B. (1113)

**Cabinet album.** London, Hurst & Co., **1830.**, T.-B. (1114)

—— ——. London, **1831.** T.-B. (1115)

—— ——. London, **1832.** T.-B. (1116)

**Cabinet for youth.** London, Whittaker, **1832.** T.-B. (1117)

**Cabinet of curiosities.** London, **1829.** T.-B. (1118)

**Cabinet of literary gems,** ed. by Bernard Bowring, illustrated with fine engravings. London, Renshaw & Co., **n. d.** iv, 320 p., pl., 6⅛ x 4. N.Y., C.U. (1119)

—— ——. London, Manning & Co., **1832.** T.-B. (1120)

**Cabinet of modern art, The,** and literary souvenir, ed. by Alaric A. Watts. 2d series. [v. 1.] London, Whittaker & Co., **1836.** xvi, 224 p., 24 pl., 7½ x 5¼. L.C. (1121)

This is a new series of "Literary souvenir, and cabinet of modern art," which ceased publication with 1835.

—— ——, and literary souvenir, ed. by Alaric A. Watts. 3d series. [v. 2.] London, Whittaker & Co., **1837.** xiv, 224 p., 24 pl., 7½ x 5¼. L.C. (1122)

—— ——, ed. by Alaric A. Watts, with 24 line engravings. [v. 3.] London, Whittaker & Co., **1842.** xiv, 225 p., 24 pl., 7½ x 5¾. N.Y. (1123)

**Cadeau,** a musical annual. London, **1831.** 4to. T.-B. (1124)

—— ——. London, **1832,** 4to. T.-B. (1125)

—— ——. London, **1833,** 4to. T.-B. (1126)

**Cameo.** London, Pickering, **1831.** T.-B. (1127)

**Cameo, The,** a mélange of literature and the arts selected from the Bijou. London, William Pickering. **n. d.** 288 p. [7 pl.] 6¼ x 4. F. (1127a)

**Campbell's scenic annual,** ed. by T. Campbell. London, Virtue, **1838.** 36 engr. dedicated to Duchess of Kent. T.-B. (1128)

**Carcanet, The.** London, **1828.** T.-B. (1129)

—— ——, select passages from the most distinguished writers. London, Pickering, **1830.** T.-B (1130)

**Caricature annual.** See **Looking glass** or caricature annual.

**Casket, The,** a miscellany, consisting of unpublished poems. London, John Murray, **1829.** xxii p., 1 l., 451 p., 8½ x 5½. F. (1131)

**Casquet of literary gems,** ed. by Alex. Whitelaw. Glasgow, Blaikie & Son, **n. d.** [1829]. v. 1. xii, 3–386 p. 7 x 4. T.-B., P.M. (1132)

—— ——, ed. by Alex. Whitelaw. Glasgow, Blaikie & Son, **n. d.** v. 2. x, 3–362 p. 7 x 4. P.M. (1133)

—— ——, ed. by Alex. Whitelaw. Glasgow, Blaikie & Son, **n. d.** v. 3. xii, 3–374 p. 7 x 4. P.M. (1134)

—— ——, ed. by Alex. Whitelaw. Glasgow, Blaikie & Son, **n. d.** v. 4. x, 3–374 p. 7 x 4. P.M. (1135)

**Cattermole's historical annual.** The great civil war of Charles I. and his parliament, by Rev. R. Cattermole. [v. 1.] London, Longman, Orme, Brown, Green & Longmans, **1841.** viii p., 1 l., 288 p., 15 pl., 9 x 6½. N.Y. (1136)

Except last two paragraphs same as Heath's historical annual, 1842.

**Cattermole's historical annual, 1844.** [v. 2.] vi p., 1 l., 311 p., 15 pl. N.Y. (1137)

Same as "Heath's picturesque annual," 1845.

**Caunter's and Daniell's oriental annual, 1839.** Eastern legends by the Rev. Hobart Caunter. London, Whittaker & Co., 1838. vi p., 1 l., 268 p., 22 pl., 7¾ x 5. N.Y. (1138)

See "Oriental annual," 1834–40.

**Chameleon,** a Scottish annual. Robinson, **1831.** T.-B. (1139)

—— ——. Robinson, **1832.** T.-B. (1140)

—— ——. Robinson, **1833.** T.-B. (1141)

**Chaplet.** London, Harwood, **1845,** 4to. T.-B. (1142)

—— ——. London, Harwood, **1846**, 4to. T.-B. (1143)

**Christian forget-me-not. 1829** or 1830. T.-B. (1144)

**Christian keepsake, The,** and missionary annual, **1835,** ed. by the Rev. William Ellis. [v. 1.] London, H. Fisher, R. Fisher & P. Jackson. viiii, 9–306 p., 13 pl., 6½ x 4. B.P., U.W. (1145)

—— ——, and missionary annual, **1836,** ed. by the Rev. William Ellis. [v. 2.] London, Fisher & Son. viii, 9–202 p., 17 pl., 7¾ x 5¼. N.Y., B.P. (1146)

—— ——, and missionary annual, **1837,** ed. by the Rev. William Ellis. [v. 3.] London, Fisher & Son. viii, 9–206 p., 16 pl., 7¾ x 5¼. B.P., P M. (1147)

—— ——, and missionary annual, **1838,** ed. by the Rev. William Ellis. [v. 4.] London, Fisher & Son. 206 p., 16 pl., 7¾ x 5¼. N.Y., B.P., U.W. (1148)

—— ——, **1840.** T.-B. (1149)

—— —— for **1850,** by Mrs. Ellet. Family pictures from the Bible. London. 8vo. B.M. (1150)

**Christian offering and christian keepsake.** London, Holmes, **n. d.,** [circa 1845.] T.-B. (1151)

**Christian souvenir,** a literary and religious offering, with fine steel engravings. London, Thomas Holmes, **n. d.** viii, 312 p., [10 pl.,] 8¼ x 5½. N.Y., U.W. (1152)

Some copies have engr. t. added, reading "Christian souvenir, a literary and religious keepsake."
Also issued with imprint John Reynolds.

—— ——. London, **1830.** T.-B. (1153)

—— ——, ed. by Rev. Charles B. Tayler. The Scripture illustrations by Rev. Thomas Dale. London, Tilt & Bogue, **1842.** xii, 276 p., 12 pl., 7½ x 4¾. P.M. (1154)

**Christmas box, The,** an annual present for children, ed. by T. Crofton Croker. [v. 1.] London, Wm. Harrison Ainsworth, **1828.** xii p., 1 l., 3–233 p., 6⅝ x 4. B.P. (1155)

—— ——, an annual present to young persons, ed. by T. Crofton Croker, Esq. [v. 2.] London, John Ebers & Co., **1829.** iv, 240 p., illus., 6⅛ x 3¾. N.Y. (1156)

—— ——. Title on back of "Marshall's Christmas box," 1832, which see.

**Christmas tales,** historical and domestic, by W. H. Harrison. London, A. K. Newman & Co., **n. d.** [circa 1833]. 3 p. l., 280 p., 6 pl., 6¼ x 4. N.Y. (1157)

**Christmas tales,** a new annual, ed. by W. H. Harrison. London, Jennings, **1833.** T.-B. (1158)

**Comic album.** London, Orr & Co., **1843.** T.-B. (1159)

**Comic almanac, The.** Published annually by Bogue and Charles Tilt. London, **1835-1853,** inclusive, illus. by Cruickshank. 6½ x 4½. T.-B. (1160–1160R)

**Comic annual, The,** by Thomas Hood. pub. **1830-39, 1842,** 11 vols. [no issue in 1840, 1841]. London, Charles Tilt, etc. 6½ x 4. F. (1161–1171)
See "Hood's comic annual."

**Comic miscellany, The for 1845,** by John Poole, Esq. London, Henry Colburn, 1845. 7¾ x 4¾. L.C. (1172)

**Comic offering, The,** or the ladies' melange of literary mirth, ed. by Louisa H. Sheridan. London. Smith, Elder & Co., illus., 6⅛ x 3¾. **1831 [v. 1]-1835 [v. 5].** N.Y. (1173–1177)

**Continental annual, The,** and romantic cabinet for **1832.** with illus. by Samuel Prout, ed. by Wm. Kennedy. [v. 1.] London, Smith, Elder & Co. x, 313 p., 13 pl, 7½ x 4½. B.P. (1178)
Also issued in large paper, proof before letters.

**Continental landscape annual of European scenery,** ed. by Frederick Ferguson, **1835.** [v. 1.] London, H. Riley, 1835. 2 p. l., 1–284 p.,[pl.,] 7¼ x 4¾. F. (1179)
Title on back of cloth case, "Landscape annual."

—— ——, **1837.** T.-B. (1180)

—— ——, **1838.** T.-B. (1181)

**Continental tourist.** London, **1835,** roy. 8vo. T.-B. (1182)

**Coronal, The,** or prose, poetry and art. A book for all seasons, at home and abroad. London, Religious Tract Society, **n.d.** iv, 252 p., [8 col. pl.,] 6¼ x 3¾. "The queen of flowers." P.M. (1183)
"A new edition," also n.d.

—— ——, an annual of literature and the fine arts, London, Edward Lacey, n.d.[**1834** on engr. t.]. viii p., 1 l., 312 p., [7 pl. and engr. t.,] 6⅛ x 3¾. "The town child and the country child." B.P.,U.W. (1184)

—— ——. **1846.** T.-B. (1185)

**Court album,** London, Bogue, **1850-1857,** 4to, pors. of female aristocracy. T.-B. (1186–1193)

**Cynosure, The,** select passages from the most distinguished writers. London, Pickering, **1837.** T.-B. (1194)

**Diadem.** London, **1832.** T.-B. (1195)

—— ——, ed. by L. H. Sheridan. London, **1839.** T.-B. (1196)

**Dial of love,** a magazine for young people issued as "Birthday gift " London, which see.
Also see "Dial of love," Phila.

**Dramatic annual, The,** comprising a playwright's adventures, by Frederick Reynolds. London, Longman, **1831.** 2 p. l., 356 p., illus., 5½ x 3½. U.W. (1197)

**Dramatic souvenir, The,** being literary and graphical illustrations of Shakespeare and other celebrated English dramatists. London, Charles Tilt, **1833.** Nearly 200 engravings on wood. 8vo. T.-B. (1198)

**Drawing room portrait gallery of eminent personages.** London, **1859-60.** Series 2–4. (1199–1200)
Series 1 called "Annual gift book."
These were supplements to "Illustrated news of the world," issued as an annual.

**Drawing room scrap-book.** Title on cover of **Fisher's drawing room scrap-book,** London.

**Easter gift,** ed. by L. E. L. London, Fisher. **1832** and **1836-38.** T.-B. (1201–1204)

**Easter offering,** or Catholic annual. London, Booker, **1832.** T.-B. (1205)

**Ellis's missionary annual.** London, **1833.** T.-B. (1206)

**Elgin annual. 1833.** T.-B. (1207)

**Emanuel,** a religious offering, ed. by Rev. Wm. Shepherd. London, Maunder, **1830.** T.-B. (1208)

**Emerald, The,** an annual keepsake of beauty, art, and literature. London, H. Riley, n. d. [circa **1836**]. 2 p. l., 264 p., [6. pl.,] 7⅜ x 4⅝. H.U. (1209)

—— ——, a literary present for instruction and entertainment, ed. by Randolph Roscoe. London, Renshaw & Kirkman, **n. d.** [circa 183–]. 2 p. l., 320 p., [5 pl.,] 6⅛ x 3¾. "The patriot son-in-law." U.W. (1210)

**English annual, The,** for **1834,** ed. by the Hon. Mrs. Norton. [v. 1.] London, Edward Bull. vi, 380 p., 15 pl., 8¼ x 5⅜. N.Y., B.P., L.C. (1211)

—— ——, for **1835,** ed. by the Hon. Mrs Norton. [v. 2.] London, Bull & Churton. 4 p. l., 384 p., 15 pl., 8 x 5 N.Y., L.C. (1212)
The vols. for 1834, 1835 were circulated in France, Germany and America exclusively.

—— ——, for **1836.** [v. 3.] London, Edward Churton, 1836. vi p., 1 l., 376 p., 16 pl., 8 x 5¼. N.Y., U.W. (1213)

—— ——, for **1837.** [v. 4.] London, Edward Churton, 1837. vi p., 1 l., 359 p., 16 pl., 8 x 5. L.C., B.P. (1214)
"Contents are a reprint from a popular periodical."

—— ——, for **1838.** [v. 5.] London, Edward Churton, 1838. vi p., 1 l., 360 p., 14 pl., 8⅛ x 5¼. B.P. (1215)
Contents a reprint from a popular periodical.

**English helicon,** ed. by T. K. Hervey. London, **1841.** Steel plates by Turner, Cattermole, selections from Coleridge, Wordsworth, Shelley, Byron, Rogers. T.-B. (1216)

**English keepsake. 1831.** T.-B. (1217)

**Evergreen.** London, **1832.** T.-B. (1218)

—— ——. London, **1842.** T.-B. (1219)

**Excitement, The. 1830–45.** T.-B. (1220–1235)

—— ——, or a book to induce young people to read, **1840,** ed. by Robt. Jamieson. Edinburgh, 1840. xii, 13–414 p., 4 pl., 5¾ x 3½. N.Y. (1230)
"11th of the series."

**Exhilaration** (juvenile). London, **1837.** T.-B. (1236)

**[Falstaff's] comic annual,** London. See "New comic annual."

**Father's present to his son, A.** Dublin, Leckie, **1831.** T.-B. (1237)

—— ——. **1833.** * (1238)

**Finden's portraits of female aristocracy.** London, Hogarth, **1840-41.** T.-B. (1239–1240)

**Finden's royal gallery of British art.** London, Ackermann, **1840.** T.-B. (1241)

**Finden's tableaux,** ed. by Miss Mitford and others. London, Hogarth, **1837-44.** folio T.-B. (1242–1249)

**First flowers.** London, Poole, **1825.** T.-B. (1250)

—— ——. London, Poole, **1826.** T.-B. (1251)

—— ——. London, Poole, **1827.** T.-B. (1252)

—— ——. London, Poole, **1828.** T.-B. (1253)

—— ——. London, Poole, **1829.** T.-B. (1254)

**Fisher's drawing room scrap-book,** with poetical illustrations by L. E. L., **1832.** Has, as frontispiece a rare 'Baxter-type' plate. [v. 1.] London, H. Fisher, R. Fisher & P. Jackson, 1832. 36 pl., 11 x 8½. T.-B. (1255)

—— ——, **1833.** [v. 2.] London, Fisher, 1833. 36 pl., 11 x 8½. T.-B. (1256)

—— ——, **1834.** [v. 3.] London, Fisher, 1834. 36 pl., 11 x 8½. T.-B. (1258)

—— ——, **1835.** [v. 4.] London, H. Fisher, R. Fisher, & P. Jackson, 1835. 64 p., 36 pl., 11 x 8½. U.W. (1259)

—— ——, **1836.** [v. 5.] London, Fisher, Son & Co. 58 p., 36 pl., 11 x 8½. U.W. (1260)

—— ——, **1837.** * (1261)

—— ——, **1838.** London, Fisher, Son & Co. 36 pl. * (1262)
There was also an edition with 16 pl.

—— ——, **1839-1846,** in B. M. (1263–1270)

—— ——, for **1847,** by the Hon. Mrs. Norton. London, Fisher, Son & Co. 3d ed. 84 p., 36 pl., 10¾ x 8¾. F. (1271)

—— —— for **1848,** by the Hon. Mrs. Norton. London, Fisher, Son & Co. 68 p., 36 pl., 10¾ x 8¾. F. (1272)

—— ——, **1849.** [?] * (1273)

—— ——, **1850,** by Charles Mackay. London, Peter Jackson, late Fisher, Son & Co. 72 p., 36 pl., 10½ x 8½ B.A. (1274)

—— ——, **1851, 1853, 1854,** in B.M. (1275–1277)

**Fisher's juvenile scrap-book,** by Bernard Barton, **1836.** [v. 1.] London, Fisher & Son. 80 p., 20 pl., 7¾ x 5½. N.Y. (1278)

—— ——, by Agnes Strickland and Bernard Barton. **1837** [v. 2.]. * (1279)

—— ——, by Agnes Strickland and Bernard Barton, **1838.** [v. 3.] London, Fisher, Son & Co. vi, 7–86 p., 16 pl., 7¾ x 5½. C.U. (1280)

"Juvenile scrap-book" on back of book.

—— ——, by Agnes Strickland and B. Barton. [v. 4.] London, **1839.** B. M. (1281)

This series is continued by "Juvenile scrap-book," which see.

**Fisher's national portrait gallery,** ed. by Wm. Jerden. London, **1830-33.** T.B. (1282-1285)

**Fisher's oriental keepsake, 1837-39,** ed. by I. Carner. London, Fisher, Son & Co., pl., 4to. T.-B. (1286-1288)

**Fisher's Waverly forget-me-not,** ed. by G. N. Wright. London, Fisher, Son & Co., **1838,** 4to. T.-B. (1289)

**Floral offering, The,** a series of twelve plates of flowers in colours, with poetry in gold appropriate to the months of the year. London, Paul Jerrard, **n. d.** [circa 1850]. 10½ x 7¼. F. (1290)

**Flora's gems,** or the treasures of the parterre, by Louisa Anne Twamley. London, Charles Tilt, **n. d.** 12 l., 14½ x 10¾ F. (1291)

**Flowers of loveliness,** ed by Lady Blessington, T. H. Bagley, L. E. L., etc. London, Ackermann, **1836-41,** 4 to. T.-B. (1292-1297)

**Forget-me-not, a** Christmas and New Year's present for **1823.** [v. 1.] London, R. Ackermann. viii, 3–392 p., [14 pl.,] 5 x 3. P.M. (1298)

"The first attempt to rival the numerous and elegant publications of the continent." *Pref.*

—— ——, a Christmas and New Year's present for **1824.** [v. 2.] London, R. Ackermann. vi, 390 p., 1 l., 12 p., 12 pl., 5¼ x 3¼. F. (1299)

—— ——, a Christmas and New Year's present for **1825.** [v. 3.] London, R. Ackermann. vi, 393 p., 5 x 3. P.M. (1300)

—— ——, a Christmas and New Year's present for **1826.** [v. 4.] London, R. Ackermann. viii, 386 p., 13 **pl.,** 5½ x 3½. N.Y., U.W. (1301)

—— ——, a Christmas and New Year's present for **1827,** ed. by Frederic Shoberl. [v. 5.] London, R. Ackermann. xii, 416 p., 13 pl. and presentation pl., 5½ x 3½. B.P., P.M., U.W. (1302)

—— ——, a Christmas and New Year's present for **1828,** ed. by Frederic Shoberl. [v. 6.] London, R. Ackermann. x, 418 p., 13 pl., 5¼ x 3¼. N.Y., B.P. (1303)

—— ——, a Christmas and New Year's present for **1829,** ed. by Frederic Shoberl. [v. 7.] London, R. Ackermann. x, 422 p., 14 pl., 5½ x 3½. B.P., U.W. (1304)

**Forget-me-not**, a Christmas, New Year's and birthday present for **1830**, ed. by Frederic Shoberl. [v. 8.] London, R. Ackermann & Co. x, 422 p., 14 pl., 5½ x 3½. F. (1305)

—— ——, a Christmas, New Year's and birthday present for **1831**, ed. by Frederic Shoberl. [v. 9.] London. R. Ackermann. x, 386 p., 15 pl., 5½ x 3½. P.M. (1306)

—— ——, a Christmas, New Year's and birthday present for **1832**, ed. by Frederic Shoberl. [v. 10.] London, Ackermann; and Carey & Lea, Philadelphia. 356 p., 12 pl., 6 x 3¾. N.Y., P.M. (1307)
The first issue of new series.

—— ——, a Christmas, New Year's and birthday present for **1833**, ed. by Frederic Shoberl. [v. 11.] London, R. Ackermann. 356 p., 11 pl., 6 x 3¾. N.Y., P.M. (1308)

—— ——, a Christmas, New Year's and birthday present, **1834**, ed. by Frederick Shoberl. [v. 12.] London, Ackermann & Co. 356 p., 11 pl., 6 x 3¾. P.M. (1309)
Also issued without date. N.Y. (1310)

—— ——, a Christmas, New Year's and birthday present for **1835**, ed. by Frederic Shoberl. [v. 13.] London, Ackermann & Co. 356 p., 10 pl., 6¼ x 4. N.Y., B.P. (1311)

—— ——, a Christmas, New Year's and birthday present for **1836**, ed. by Frederic Shoberl. [v. 14.] London, Ackermann & Co. 356 p., 11 pl., 6¼ x 4. P.M. (1312)
Also issued without date. N.Y. (1313)

—— ——, a Christmas, New Year's and birthday present for **1837**, ed. by Frederic Shoberl. [v. 15.] London, Ackermann & Co. 356 p., 11 pl., 6¼ x 4. N.Y., P.M. (1314)

—— ——, a Christmas, New Year's and birthday present for **1838**, ed. by Frederic Shoberl. [v. 16.] London, Ackermann & Co. 360 p., 11 pl., 6¼ x 4. P.M. (1315)
Also issued without date. N Y. (1316)

—— ——, a Christmas, New Year's and birthday present for **1839**, ed. by Frederic Shoberl. [v. 17.] London, Ackermann & Co. 360 p., 11 pl., 6¼ x 4. N.Y., B.P. (1317)

—— ——, a Christmas, New Year's and birthday present, ed. by Frederic Shoberl. [v 18.] London, Ackermann & Co., **1840**. viii, 9–360 p., 11 p ., 6¼ x 4. N.Y., B.P. (1318)

—— ——, a Christmas, New Year's and birthday present for **1841**, ed. by Frederic Shoberl. [v. 19.] London, Ackermann & Co. 354 p., 11 pl., 6¼ x 4. P.M. (1319)

**Forget-me-not**, a Christmas, New Year's and birthday present for **1842**, ed. by Frederic Shoberl. [v. 20.] London, Ackermann & Co. 354 p., 11 pl., 6¼ x 4. B.P., P.M. (1320)

—— ——, a Christmas, New Year's and birthday present for **1843**, ed. by Frederic Shoberl. [v. 21.] London. 354 p., 11 pl., 6¼ x 4. B.P., P.M. (1321)

—— ——, a Christmas, New Year's and birthday present for **1844**, ed. by Frederic Shoberl. [v. 22.] London, Ackermann & Co., 354 p., 11 pl., 6¼ x 4. N.Y., P.M. (1322)

—— ——, a Christmas, New Year's and birthday present for **1845**, ed. by Frederic Shoberl. [v. 23.] London. 322 p., 10 pl., 6¼ x 4. N.Y. (1323)

—— ——, a Christmas, New Year's and birthday present for **1846**, ed. by Frederic Shoberl. [v. 24.] London, Ackermann & Co. 286 p., 10 pl., 6½ x 4½. N.Y. (1324)

—— ——, a Christmas, New Year's and birthday present for **1847**, ed. by Frederic Shoberl. [v. 25.] London, Ackermann & Co. 286 p., 10 pl., 6¾ x 4⅜. B.P. (1325)

The last issue.

**Forget me not.** London, **1856.** T.-B. (1325a)

—— ——. London, T. Nelson & Sons, **1863.** xi p., 1 l., 13–192 p., front., 5¼ x 3½. U.W. (1326)

**Friends' annual**, or aurora borealis for **1834**, ed. by members of the Society of Friends. Newcastle-upon-Tyne, Charles Empson. xiv p., 1 l., 274 p., [2 pl.,] 6¼ x 4. N.Y., B.P., L.C. U.W. (1327)

Issued in 1833 as "Aurora borealis."

**Friendship's gift**, London. See **"Amaranth,"** London, Ed. Lacey, n. d.

—— ——, London. Reprint, ed. by C. Cecil, London. Holmes, successor to Lacey [circa **1850**]. T.-B. (1327a)

**Friendship's offering**, London, G. Kershaw & Son, **n. d.** viii, 9–256 p., [6 pl.,] 7 x 4½. "To a friend." U.W. (1328)

—— ——, a literary album, ed. by Thomas K. Hervey. [v. 1.] London, Lupton Relfe, **1824.** vi, 222 p., [6 pl.,] 5¼ x 3⅜. B.A. (1329)

—— ——, or annual remembrancer. A Christmas and New Year's gift for **1825.** [v 2.] London, Lupton Relfe. viii p., 1 l., 291, 60 p., 14 pl. [only 13 in reality], 5¼ x 3⅜. B.A. (1330)

—— ——, a literary album, ed. by Thomas K. Hervey. [v. 3.] London, Lupton Relfe, **1826.** xvi, 398 p., 13 pl., 5½ x 3½. B.P., B.A. (1331)

—— ——, a literary album, ed. by Thomas K. Hervey. [v. 4.] London, **1827.** xii, 348 p., 11 pl., 5½ x 3½. B.P., B.A. (1332)

**Friendship's offering**, a literary album and Christmas and New Year's present for **1828.** [v. 5.] London, Smith, Elder & Co., 1828. xii p., 1 l., 385 p., 13 pl., $5\frac{5}{8}$ x $3\frac{3}{8}$. B.A. (1333)

—— ——, a literary album, and Christmas and New Year's present for **1829.** [v. 6.] London, Smith, Elder & Co., 1829. xii, 420 p , 13 pl., $5\frac{1}{2}$ x $3\frac{1}{2}$. N.Y., B.P., B.A. (1334)

—— ——, a literary album, and Christmas and New Year's present for **1830.** [v. 7.] London, Smith, Elder & Co., 1830. xii, 384 p., 13 pl., 6 x $3\frac{3}{4}$. N.Y., B.A. (1335)

—— ——, a literary album, and Christmas and New Year's present for **1831.** [v. 8.] London, Smith, Elder & Co., 1831. xii, 408 p., 13 pl., 6 x $3\frac{3}{4}$. N.Y., B.P., B.A. (1336)

—— ——, a literary album, and Christmas and New Year's present for **1832.** [v. 9.] London, Smith, Elder & Co., 1832. xii, 384 p., 12 pl., $6\frac{1}{8}$ x $3\frac{7}{8}$. N.Y., B.P., B.A. (1337)

—— —— and winter's wreath, a Christmas and New Year's present for **1833.** [v. 10.] London, Smith, Elder & Co., 1833. xii, 384 p., 12 pl., 6 x $3\frac{3}{4}$. N.Y., B.A., P.M. (1338)

With this issue absorbed "The winter's wreath."

—— —— and winter's wreath, a Christmas and New Year's present for **1834.** [v. 11.] London, Smith, Elder & Co., 1834. xii, 384 p., 12 pl., 6 x 4. N.Y., B.P., B.A. (1339)

—— —— and winter's wreath, a Christmas and New Year's present for **1835.** [v. 12.] London, Smith, Elder & Co., 1835. xii, 384 p., 12 pl., $6\frac{1}{8}$ x $3\frac{7}{8}$. N.Y., B.P. B.A., (1340)

—— —— and winter's wreath, a Christmas and New Year's present for **1836.** [v. 13.] London, Smith, Elder & Co., 1836. xii, 382 p., 11 pl., 6 x 4. B.P., B.A., U.W. (1341)

—— —— and winter's wreath, a Christmas and New Year's present for **1837.** [v. 14.] London, Smith, Elder & Co., 1837. xii, 384 p., 11 pl., 6 x 4. N.Y., B.P., B.A., U.W. (1342)

—— —— and winter's wreath, a Christmas and New Year's present for **1838.** [v. 15.] London, Smith, Elder & Co., 1838. xii, 384 p., 11 pl., 6 x 4. N.Y., B.P., B.A. (1343)

—— —— and winter's wreath, a Christmas and New Year's present for **1839.** [v. 16.] London, Smith, Elder & Co., 1839. xii, 384 p., 10 pl., $6\frac{1}{8}$ x $3\frac{7}{8}$. N.Y., B.P., B.A., U.W. (1344)

—— —— and winter's wreath, a Christmas and New Year's present for **1840.** [v. 17.] London, Smith, Elder & Co., 1840. xii, 384 p., 10 pl., 6 x 4. N.Y., B.A., U.W. (1345)

**Friendship's offering** and winter's wreath, a Christmas and New Year's present for **1841**. [v. 18.] London, Smith, Elder & Co., 1841. xii, 384 p., 11 pl., 6⅛ x 3⅞. N.Y., B.P., B.A. (1346)

—— —— and winter's wreath, a Christmas and New Year's present for **1842**. [v. 19.] London, Smith, Elder & Co , 1842. xii, 384 p., 10 pl., 6 x 3⅞. B.P., B.A., C.U. (1347)

—— —— and winter's wreath, a Christmas and New Year's present for **1843**. [v. 20.] London, Smith, Elder & Co., 1843. xii, 384 p., 9 pl. [pl. no. 4 was never issued, see preface], 6 x 4. N.Y., B.A. (1348)

—— —— of sentiment and mirth, **1844**. [v. 21.] London, Smith, Elder & Co., 1844. viii, 240 p., 10 pl., 8½ x 5½. N.Y., L.C., B.A., U.W. (1349)

**Gage d'amitie.** London, Fisher, **1834-41.** T.-B. (1350-1357)

**Garland, The,** London, **1852.** T.-B. (1358)

**Gem, The,** a literary annual, ed. by Thomas Hood. [v. 1.] London, Wm. Marshall, **1829.** 324 p., 16 pl., 6 x 3¾. N.Y. B.P., (1359)

Also issued in large paper, 7¼ x 4½. L.C. (1360)

—— ——, a literary annual, ed. by Thomas Hood. [v. 2.] London, W. Marshall, **1830.** xii, 275 p., 13 pl., 6¼ x 4¼. N.Y., P.M. (1361)

—— ——, a literary annual. [v. 3.] London, W. Marshall, **1831.** xii, 276 p., 12 pl., 6½ x 4¼. F. (1362)

Also issued as "Hibernian keepsake," 1832.

—— ——, a literary annual. [v. 4.] London, Wm. Marshall, **1832.** viii, 276 p., 12 pl., 6½ x 4⅛. N.Y., L.C. (1363)

**Gem of art, The,** one hundred steel plates selected from The keepsake, Heath's annuals, etc. London, folio, **1830, 1834.** 2 vols. T.-B. (1364-1365)

**Gem of loveliness** for **1843,** by H. I. & W. Stevens. 2d ed. London [1843]. 8vo. T.-B. B.M. (1366)

**Gems of art.** A token of remembrance, illustrated by superb line engravings. London, Whittaker & Co. **n. d.** xvi, 224 p., 23 pl., 7¾ x 5¼. B.P., C.U., (1367)

**Gems of beauty** displayed in a series of highly finished engravings after Cattermole, Paris, etc. Text by the Countess of Blessington. London Virtue. royal 4to. **1836–40.** 4 vols. T.-B., B.M. (1368-1371)

**Geographical Annual, The, 1832–6.** Lond. Bull. 8vo. T.-B. (1372-1376)

**Gift, The,** a book of tales and pencillings in poetry and prose, illustrated by great artists. London, T. Nelson & Sons, **1866.** viii, 9–336 p., [17 pl.,] 6⅞ x 4¾. B.A. (1377)

**Gift for all seasons, The,** ed. by William Anderson. London, Smith, Elder & Co.,**1839.** x, 354 p., 1 l., 9 pl. 6¼ x 4. U.W. (1378)

—— ——, ed. by William Anderson. London. 2d edition. John Chidley, **1840.** x, 243 p., [pl.,] 6¼ x 3¾. P.M. (1379)

Same as 1839, except last pages omitted.

**Gift of Love and Friendship, The,** London, Nelson, **1846.** 12mo. T.-B. (1380)

**Golden childhood,** or the child's own annual of pictures, poetry and music. London, Ward, Lock & Tyler, **n. d.** viii, 9–320 p., illus., 7½ x 6. F. (1381)

**Graces, The,** or literary souvenir for **1824.** London, Hurst & Co., 1824. T.-B., B.M. (1382)

**Heath's book of beauty, 1833.** ed. by L. E. L[andon]. [v. 1] London, Longman, Rees, Orme, Brown. Green & Longman. vi p., 1 l., 264 p., 19 pl., 7½ x 4½. N.Y., B.A. (1383)

—— ——, **1834,** ed. by Countess of Blessington. [v. 2.] London, Longman, Rees, Orme, Brown, Green & Longman. vi p., 1 l., 280 p., 19 pl., 7¾ x 4¾. N.Y., P.M. (1384)

—— ——, **1835,** ed. by the Countess of Blessington. [v. 3.] London, Longman, Rees, Orme, Brown, Green & Longman. vi p., 1 l., 264 p., 19 pl., 7½ x 4½. N.Y. (1385)

—— ——, **1836,** ed. by the Countess of Blessington, [v. 4.] London, Longman, Rees, Orme, Brown, Green & Longman. vi p., 1 l., 280 p., 19 pl., 7½ x 4¾. N.Y., B.A., U.W. (1386)

—— ——, **1837,** ed. by the Countess of Blessington. [v. 5.] London, Longman, Rees, Orme, Brown, Green & Longman. vi p., 1 l., 264 p., 19 pl., 7½ x 4¾. B.A., P.M. (1387)

—— ——, **1838,** ed. by the Countess of Blessington. [v. 6.] London, Longman, Orme, Brown, Green & Longmans. vi, 280 p., pl., 9¼ x 6½. P.M. (1388)

—— ——, **1839,** ed. by the Countess of Blessington. [v. 7.] London, Longman, Orme, Brown, Green & Longmans. vi p., 1 l., 280 p., 12 pl., 9 x 6¼. B.P., N.Y. (1389)

—— ——, **1840,** ed. by the Countess of Blessington. [v. 8.] London, Longman, Orme, Brown, Green & Longmans. vi p., 1 l., 280 p., 13 pl., 8¾ x 6. (1390)

—— ——, **1841,** ed. by the Countess of Blessington. [v. 9.] London. vi p., 1 l., 280 p., 16 pl., 9¼ x 6¾. N.Y., B.P., B.A. (1391)

—— ——, **1842,** ed. by the Countess of Blessington. [v. 10.] London, Longman, Brown, Green & Longmans. vi p., 1 l., 278 p., 1 l., 13 pl., 8¾ x 6. C.U. (1392)

—— ——, **1843,** ed. by the Countess of Blessington. [v. 11.] London, Longman, Brown, Green & Longmans. vi p., 1 l., 280 p., 13 pl., 9 x 6½. B.P. (1393)

—— ——, **1844,** ed. by the Countess of Blessington. [v. 12.] London, Longman, Brown, Green & Longmans. vi p., 1 l., 280 p., 13 pl., 9 x 6. C.U. (1394)

—— ——, **1845,** ed. by the Countess of Blessington. [v. 13.] London, Longman, Brown, Green & Longmans. vi p., 1 l., 280 p., 13 pl., 8¾ x 6. C.U., B.A. (1395)

**Heath's book of beauty, 1846,** ed. by the Countess of Blessington. [v. 14.] London. * (1396)

—— ——, **1847,** ed. by the Countess of Blessington. [v. 15.] Longman, Brown, Green, & Longman. vi p., 1 l., 1–280 p., 13 pl., 9 x 6½. (1397)
Continued as "Book of beauty," 1848.

**Heath's gallery of engravings,** 4to, **1836,** ed. by C. Heath. London, Longman. T.-B. (1398)

—— ——, **1837**, ed. by C. Heath, London, Longman. T.-B. (1399)

—— ——, **1838,** ed. by C. Heath, London, Longman. T.-B. (1400)

**Heath's gems of Beauty,** 4to, ed. by Lady Blessington. London, Longman, **1836–40.** See **Gems of beauty.**

**Heath's picturesque annual.** [v. 1.] London, Longman, Rees, Orme, Brown & Green, **1832.** iv p., 2 l., 256 p., 26 pl., 7½ x 4¾. B.P. (1401)
Also pub. in large paper with proof plates. T.-B.

—— ——. [v. 2.] London, Longman, Rees, Orme, Brown, Green & Longman, **1833.** iv p., 2 l., 256 p., 26 pl., 7⅛ x 4⅞. B.P. (1402)
Also pub. in large paper with proof plates. T.-B.

—— ——, for **1834.** [v. 3.] London, Longman, Rees, Orme, Brown, Green & Longman, 1834. 3 p. l., 256 p., 21 pl., 7⅝ x 4⅞. B.P. (1403)
Also pub. in large paper with proof plates. T.-B.

—— ——, for **1835.** [v. 4.] London, Longman, Rees, Orme, Brown, Green & Longman, 1835. iv p., 2 l., 256 p., 21 pl., 7¾ x 4¾. U.W. (1404)
Also pub. in large paper with proof plates. T.-B.

—— ——, for **1836.** [v. 5.] London, Longman, Rees, Orme, Brown, Green & Longman, 1836. iv p., 2 l., 256 p., 7¾ x 4¾. U.W. (1405)
Also pub. in large paper with proof plates. T.-B.

—— ——. [v. 6.] London, Longman, Rees, Orme, Brown & Longman, **1837.** vi p., 1 l., 264 p., 20 pl., 9¼ x 6½. F. (1406)

—— ——. London, Longman, Rees, Orme, Brown Green & Longman, **1838.** vi p., 1 l., 264 p., 19 pl., 9¼ x 6½. F. (1407)

—— ——. London, Longman, Orme, Brown, Green & Longmans, **1839.** vi p., 1 l., 256 p., 20 pl., 9¼ x 6½. F. (1408)

—— ——, for 1840. London, Longman, Orme, Brown, Green & Longmans, **1840.** viii, 274 p., 15 pl., 9½ x 6¼. U.W. (1409)

—— ——, for 1841. London, Longman, Orme, Brown, Green & Longmans, **1841.** viii, 288 p., 16 pl., 9¼ x 6½. B.P., U.W. (1410)

—— ——. London, **1842,** Longman, Brown, Green & Longmans. viii, 268 p., 21 pl., 9½ x 6¼. B.P. (1411)

**Heath's picturesque annual.** London, Longman, Brown, Green & Longmans, **1843.** viii, 256 p., 18 pl., 9½ x 6¼. F. (1412)

—— ——, for **1844.** London, Longman, Brown, Green, & Longmans, 1844. xiv p., 1 l., 246 p., 18 pl., 9¼ x 6½. U.W. (1413)

—— ——, **1845.** Longman, Brown, Green & Longmans, 1845. viii, 311 p., 13 pl., 9 x 6⅝. F. (1414)
This is vol. 2 of "Cattermole's historical annual."

**Hibernian keepsake** for **1832, The.** London, C. Fleming. xii, 276 p., 12 pl., 7¾ x 5. F. (1415)
Same as "Gem," 1831.

**Historical keepsake.** London. T.-B. (1416)

—— ——. 2d series. ed. by John W. Dalby. London, T. Hurst, **1836.** 365 p., 20 pl., 6¼ x 4. N.Y., P.M. (1417)

**Historical souvenir and literary cabinet, The.** London. circa **1840.** 8vo. T.-B. (1418)

**Hive, The,** a Selection of Poetry. London, **1832.** T.-B. (1419)

**Holiday keepsake,** by Mrs. Sherwood. London. illus., post 8vo. n. d. [circa 1840]. * (1420)

**Hommage aux dames.** London, John Setts, Jr., **1825.** iv, 159 p., 4 p. music, many blank p. for notes, 1–15 p., [7 pl.]. N.Y., B.P. (1421)

**[Hood's] comic annual.** See **Comic annual.**

**Hood's comic annual.** London, [v.1–20] **1869–88.** 8⅛ x 6¼. B.P. (1422–1441)

**Humourist, The,** a companion for the Christmas fireside, by W. H. Harrison, with 50 engravings from designs by T. Rowlandson. London, **1831,** R. Ackermann. xiv, 286 p., 50 pl., 7 x 4¼. F. (1442)

—— ——, a companion for the Christmas fireside, by W. H. Harrison, embellished with 80 engravings. London, R. Ackermann, **1832.** xii, 3–288 p., 81 pl., 7 x 4. F. (1443)

**Hunter's annual, The.** London, Baily & Co., **1838.** 12 mo. T.-B. (1444)

—— ——. London, Baily & Co., **1839.** 12 mo. T.-B. (1445)

**Imperial, The,** a Christmas and New-Year's present for **1839.** London, Wm. Tombleson. 2 p.l., 9–195 p., 10 pl., 8 x 5. N.Y., B.P., B.A. (1446)
Also issued "for **1841,** Wm. Tombleson & Co., 1841." B.P. (1447)

**Infants annual, The:** or Nursery Present. London, **1831.** T.-B. (1448)

—— ——. London, **1832.** T.-B. (1449)

—— ——. London, **1833.** T.-B. (1450)

**Iris, The,** a literary and religious offering, ed. by Rev. Thomas Dale. [v. 1.] London, Sampson Low, **1830.** xii, 332 p., 11 pl., 6¼ x 4. N.Y. (1451)
Follows "Offering," 1829.

**Iris, The,** a religious and literary offering, ed. by Rev. Thomas Dale. [v. 2.] London, Sampson Low, **1831.** x p., 1 l., 334 p., 11 pl., 6¼ x 4. N.Y., B.P. (1452)

**Iris of prose, poetry and art,** for **1840,** ed. by Mary Russell Mitford. London, 1839. pl. T.-B. (1453)

**Janus.** Edinburgh, Oliver & Boyd, **1826,** (no illustrations). T.-B. (1454)

**Jennings' landscape annual, 1835, 1836.** See **Landscape annual.**

**Johnson's shooter's annual: 1830, The,** London, Johnson. T.-B. (1455)

**Juvenile Album, The, 1832:** a reprint of the Forget-me-not for **1831.** London, Tarry & Co., T.-B. (1456)

**Juvenile amulet.** London, Edward Lacey, **1835** [?]. 6 pl. T.-B. (1457)

**Juvenile bijou,** ed. by Miss Leslie. London, n. d. circa **1830,** reprinted circa **1844.** T.-B. (1458–1459)

**Juvenile forget me not, The.** See also **"Ackermann's Juvenile forget me not,"** an entirely different publication.

—— ——, **1828.** [v. 1.] T.-B. (1460)

—— ——, a Christmas and New Year's gift, a birthday present for **1829,** ed. by Mrs. S. C. Hall. [v. 2.] London, N. Hailes. x p., 1 l., 239 p., 16 pl., 6⅝ x 4. U.W. (1461)

—— ——, a Christmas and New Year's gift, or birthday present for the year **1830,** ed. by Mrs. S. C. Hall. [v. 3.] London, N. Hailes. viii, 229 p., 12 pl., 6½ x 4. N.Y., B.P. (1462)

"Ackermann's juvenile forget me not," 1830 and following years, is entirely distinct, being a rival and imitator of this series.

—— ——, a Christmas and New Year's gift, or birthday present for the year **1831,** ed. by Mrs. S. C. Hall. [v. 4.] London, Frederick Westley & A. H. Davis. viii, 224 p., 12 pl., 6½ x 4. N.Y. (1463)

—— ——, **1832,** ed. by Mrs. S. C. Hall. [v. 5.] London, Westley & Davis. viii, 9–221 p., 8 pl., 6½ x 4. F. (1464)

**Juvenile forget-me-not,** a Christmas and New Year's gift, or birth-day present, 1833, ed. by Mrs. S. C. Hall. [v. 6.] London, R. Ackermann, **1833.** viii p., 1 l., 11–224 p., 11 pl., 6½ x 4. N.Y. (1465)

—— ——, a Christmas and New Year's gift, or birth-day present, **1834,** ed. by Mrs. S. C. Hall. [v. 7.] London, Ackermann & Co. viii, 9–240 p. [237–40 are ads.]. N.Y., B.P. (1466)

—— ——, **1835.** [v. 8.] T.-B., B.M. (1467)

—— ——, a Christmas and New Year's gift, or birth-day present, **1836,** ed. by Mrs. S. C. Hall. [v. 9.] London, Ackermann & Co. iv p., 1 l., 7–232 p., 10 pl., 6½ x 4. N.Y., P.M. (1468)

**Juvenile forget-me-not,** a Christmas and New-Year's gift, or birth-day present, **1837,** ed. by Mrs. S. C. Hall. [v. 10.] London, Ackermann & Co., 1837. iv p., 1 l., 7–240 p., 10 pl., 6½ x 4. U.W. (1469)

**Juvenile forget-me-not, The,** ed. by Mrs. S. C. Hall. London, R. Ackermann, **n. d.** iv, 7–254 p., [4 pl.,] 6¼ x 3¾. N.Y. (1470)

—— ——. ed. by Mrs. S. C. Hall. London, T. Nelson & Sons, **1862.** viii, 9–224 p., 6½ x 4. P.M. (1471)

**Juvenile keepsake, 1829,** ed. by Thomas Roscoe. London, Hurst, Chance & Co., 1829. xiv, 224 p. [8 pl.,] 6½ x 4. N.Y. (1472)

—— ——, **1830.** T.-B., B.M. (1473)

—— ——. London, Edward Lacey, **1835.** T.-B. (1474)

**Juvenile keepsake, The,** sm. 4to, ed. by P. Carle. London, Darton & Co., **1850.** T.-B. (1475)

**Juvenile landscape annual, The.** London, c. **1830.** T.-B. (1475a)

**Juvenile missionary keepsake.** London, **1846.** 8vo. T.-B., B.M. (1476)

**Juvenile offering, The.** London, Leicester [**1848.**] 16mo. T.-B., B.M. (1477)

**Juvenile scrap-book, The,** by Mrs. Ellis. London, **1840.** [v. 5.] 105 p., 16 pl., 7¾ x 5¼. P.M. (1478)
Continuation of "Fisher's juvenile scrap-book" series.

—— ——, **1841.** T.-B. (1479)

—— ——, **1842,** by Mrs. Ellis. London, Fisher, Son & Co. vi p., 1 l., 92 p., 16 pl., 7½ x 5. B.P. (1480)
Engr. t. reads, "Fisher's juvenile scrap-book."

—— ——, **1843,** by Mrs. Ellis. London, Fisher, Son & Co. 2 p. l., 103 p., 16 pl., 7¾ x 5½. N.Y. (1481)

—— ——, by the author of "The women of England." [S. S. Ellis.] **1844.** London, Fisher, Son & Co. 2 p.l., 100 p., 16 pl. 7¾ x 5½. N.Y. (1482)

—— ——, **1845,** by Mrs. Ellis. T.-B., B.M. (1483)

—— ——, **1846,** by Mrs. Ellis. T.-B., B.M. (1484)

—— ——, by the author of "The women of England," **1847.** Fisher, Son & Co., London. 102 p., 16 pl., 7¾ x 5. F. (1485)
Vig. t. reads "Fisher's juvenile scrap-book."

—— ——, by Mrs. Ellis, **1848.** T.-B., B.M. (1486)

—— ——, by J. Strickland, **1849.** T.-B. (1487)

—— ——, by Mrs. Milner, **1850.** T.-B. (1488)

**Juvenile wreath.** The title of Part 2 of **Amaranth,** n. d., Edward Lacey.

**Keepsake, The,** for **1828.** [v. 1.] London, Hurst, Chance & Co. xii, 312 p., 19 pl., 7½ x 4¾. L.C., B.P., B.A. (1489)

—— ——, for **1829,** ed. by Frederic Mansel Reynolds. [v. 2.] London, Hurst, Chance & Co. viii, 360 p., 19 pl., 7½ x 4¾. L.C., B.P., B.A. (1490)

**Keepsake, The**, for **1830**, ed. by Frederic Mansel Reynolds [v. 3.] London, Hurst, Chance & Co. viii, 352 p., 18 pl., 7½ x 4¾. N.Y., L.C., B.A. (1491)

—— ——, for **1831**, ed. by Frederic Mansel Reynolds. [v. 4.] London, Hurst, Chance & Co. viii, 320 p., 18 pl., 7¼ x 4¾. N.Y., L.C., B.P. (1492)

—— ——, for **1832**, ed. by Frederic Mansel Reynolds. [v. 5.] London, Longman, Rees, Orme, Brown & Green. iv, 320 p., 17 pl., 7¼ x 4¾. N.Y., L.C., B.A. (1493)

—— ——, for **1833**, ed. by Frederic Mansel Reynolds. [v. 6.] London, Longman, Rees, Orme, Brown, Green & Longman. iv, 308 p., 17 pl., 7¼ x 4¾. N.Y., L.C., B.A. (1494)

—— ——, for **1834**, ed. by Frederic Mansel Reynolds. [v. 7.] London, Longman, Rees, Orme, Brown, Green & Longman. vi p., 1 l., 312 p., 17 pl., 7¼ x 4¾. N.Y., L.C., B.P. (1495)

—— ——, for **1835**, ed. by Frederic Mansel Reynolds. [v. 8.] London, Longman, Rees, Orme, Brown, Green & Longman. vi p., 1 l., 296 p., 17 pl., 7½ x 5. N.Y., L.C., B.P. (1496)

—— ——, for **1836**, ed. by the Hon. Mrs. Norton. [v. 9.] London, Longman, Rees, Orme, Brown, Green & Longman. 2 p. l., 324 p., 19 pl., 7¼ x 4¾. N.Y., L.C., B.P. (1497)

—— ——, for **1837**, ed. by Lady Emeline Stuart Wortley. [v. 10.] London, Longman, Orme, Brown, Green & Longman. vi p., 1 l., 328 p., 18 pl., 7¼ x 4¾. L.C., B.A. (1498)

—— ——, for **1838**. [v. 11.] London, Longman, Orme, Brown, Green & Longmans. vi p., 1 l., 272 p., 12 pl., 9¼ x 6½. N.Y., L.C., B.A. (1499)

—— ——, for **1839**, ed. by F. M. Reynolds. [v. 12.] London, Longman, Orme, Brown, Green & Longmans. iv p., 2 l., 272 p., 12 pl., 9¼ x 6½. N.Y., L.C., B.A. (1500)

—— ——, for **1840**, ed. by Lady E. Stuart Wortley. [v. 13.] London, Longman, Orme, Brown, Green & Longmans. vi p., 2 l., 264 p., 12 pl., 9¼ x 6¼. N.Y., L.C., B.A. (1501)

—— ——, for **1841**, ed. by the Countess of Blessington. [v. 14.] London, Longman, Orme, Brown, Green & Longmans. iv p., 2 l., 272 p., 15 pl., 9¼ x 6¼. N.Y., L.C., B.A. (1502)

—— ——, for **1842**, ed. by the Countess of Blessington. [v. 15.] London, Longman, Brown Green & Longmans. iv p., 2 l., 280 p., 13 pl., 9¼ x 6¼. N.Y., L.C., B.P. (1503)

—— ——, for **1843**, ed. by the Countess of Blessington. [v. 16.] London, Longman, Brown, Green & Longmans. iv p., 2 l., 272 p., 13 pl., 9 x 6¼. N.Y., L.C., P.M. (1504)

**Keepsake, The,** for **1844,** ed. by the Countess of Blessington. [v. 17.] London, Longman, Brown, Green & Longmans. iv p., 2 l., 270 p., 13 pl., 9⅛ x 6¼. F. (1505)

—— ——, for **1845,** ed. by the Countess of Blessington. [v. 18.] London, Longman, Brown, Green & Longman, etc. iv p., 2 l, 272 p., 13 pl., 9 x 6. N.Y., L.C. (1506)

—— ——, for **1846,** ed. by the Countess of Blessington. [v. 19.] London, Longman, Brown, Green & Longmans. iv p., 2 l., 278 p., 13 pl., 9 x 6. N.Y., L.C., B.A. (1507)

—— ——, for **1847,** ed. by the Countess of Blessington. [v. 20.] London, Longman, Brown, Green, Longmans. iv p., 2 l., 288 p., 13 pl., 9⅛ x 6¼. N.Y., L.C., B.A. (1508)

—— ——, for **1848,** ed. by the Countess of Blessington. [v. 21.] London, David Bogue. 3 p. l., 280 p., 12 pl., 9¼ x 6½. N.Y, L.C., B.A. (1509)

—— ——. London and Edinburgh, Thomas Nelson, **1848.** 2 p. l., 128 p., 3¾ x 2⅝. F. (1510)

—— ——, **1849,** ed. by the Countess of Blessington. [v. 22.] London, David Bogue, 1849. 3 p. l., 276 p., 12 pl., 9⅜ x 6½. N.Y., L.C., B.A. (1511)

—— ——, **1850,** ed. by the Countess of Blessington. [v. 23.] London, David Bogue, 1850. viii, 272 p., 12 pl., 9¼ x 6½. N.Y., L.C., B.A. (1512)

—— ——, **1851,** ed. by Miss Power. [v. 24.] London, David Bogue, 1851. vi p., 1 l., 272 p., 12 pl., 9¼ x 6½. N Y., L.C., B.A. (1513)

—— ——, **1852,** ed. by Miss Power. [v. 25.] London, David Bogue, 1852. vi p., 1 l., 272 p., 12 pl., 9¼ x 6½. N.Y., L.C., B.A. (1514)

—— ——, **1853,** ed. by Miss Power. [v. 26.] London, David Bogue, 1853. vi p., 1 l., 272 p., 12 pl., 9¼ x 6½. N.Y., L.C., B.A. (1515)

—— ——, **1854,** ed. by Miss Power. [v. 27.] London, David Bogue. vi p., 1 l., 272 p., 12 pl., 9¼ x 6½. N.Y., L.C., B.A. (1516)

—— ——, **1855,** ed. by Miss Power. [v. 28.] London, David Bogue, 1855. vi p., 1 l., 272 p., 12 pl., 9 x 6¼. N.Y., L.C. (1517)

—— ——, **1856,** ed. by Miss Power. [v. 29.] London, David Bogue, 1856. vi p., 1 l., 272 p., 12 pl., 9 x 6¼. N.Y., L.C., P.M. (1518)

—— ——, **1857,** ed. by Miss Power. [v. 30.] London, David Bogue, 1857. vi p., 1 l., 272 p., 12 pl., 9 x 6¼. N.Y., L.C. (1519)

—— ——, **1861.** London, Nelson & Son. T.-B. (1520)
Temporary revival, or imitation.

**Keepsake francais, Le. 1830.** ed. by Mrs. A. A. Watts. London, Whittaker. T.-B. (1521)

—— ——, ou souvenir de litterature contemporaine. **1831,** deuxième année, Paris, Giraldon-Bovinet et cie. London, Whittaker, Treacher & Co. T.-B. (1522)

**Ladies' and gentlemen's** polite assistant and useful remembrancer, **1831.** London, Sutterly. T.-B. (1523)

**Ladies' poetical album, 1831.** London. T.-B. (1524)

**Lady's keepsake** and maternal monitor. London, Edward Lacey, **1835.** 18mo. (1525)
Not a true literary gift-book.

**Ladies keepsake,** London, **1840.** T.-B. (1526)

**Lady's scrap book.** London. quarto. *circa* 1840 T.-B. (1527)

**Landscape album, The,** or Great Britain illustrated in a series of 61 views by W. Westall with descriptions by Thomas Moule. London, Charles Tilt, **1832.** viii, 120 p., [61 pl.,] 7⅝ x 5. N.Y. (1528)

—— ——. 2d series. London, Charles Tilt, **1834.** viii, 118 p., 59 pl., 7⅝ x 5. F. (1529)

**Landscape annual, 1830.** Tourist in Switzerland and Italy, by T. Roscoe. [v. 1.] London. viii, 278 p., 25 pl. and vig. t., 7¾ x 5. N.Y. (1530)
This and the following 9 vols. were issued also in large paper, proof impressions on India paper.

An edition was issued in 1835 with 5 pl., different and not by Prout, same text but reset. 2 pl., 278 p. (1531)

—— ——, **1831.** Tourist in Italy, by Thomas Roscoe. [v. 2.] London, Robt. Jennings,1831. vi p., 1 l., 271 p., 26 pl., 7¾ x 5. N.Y. (1532)

—— ——, **1832.** Tourist in Italy, by Thomas Roscoe. [v. 3.] London, Jennings & Chaplin, 1832. iv, 287 p., 26 pl., 7½ x 4¾. U.W. (1533)

—— ——, **1833,** or tourist in Italy, by Thomas Roscoe. [v. 4.] London, Jennings & Chaplin, 1833. 3 p. l., 271 p., 24 pl., 7½ x 4¾. N.Y. (1534)

—— ——. The tourist in France, by Thomas Roscoe. [v. 5 ] London, Jennings & Chaplin, **1834.** vi p., 1 l., 280 p., 26 pl., 7½ x 4¾. N.Y., U.W. (1535)

—— ——. The tourist in Spain, Grenada, by T. Roscoe. [v. 6.] London, Robt. Jennings & Co., **1835.** xv p., 1 l., 288 p., 21 pl., 7½ x 4¾. U.W. (1536)
There was also an edition in 1835 of the 1830 vol., but with different pl. and text reset. (1537)

—— ——. The tourist in Spain, by T. Roscoe. [v. 7.] London, Robt. Jennings, **1836.** xii, 280 p., 21 pl., 7½ x 4¾ N.Y., U.W. (1538)
Engr. t. reads, "Jennings' landscape annual."

—— ——. The tourist in Spain for **1837.** [v. 8.] London, Robt. Jennings, 1837. vi p., 1 l., 294 p., 21 pl., 7½ x 4¾. N.Y., U.W. (1539)

—— ——, or the tourist in Spain and Morocco, by Thos. Roscoe. [v. 9.] London, Robt. Jennings, **1838.** x p., 1 l., 292 p., 21 pl., 7¾ x 4¾. N.Y., U.W. (1540)

—— ——, or tourist in Portugal, by W. H. Harrison. [v. 10.] London, Robt. Jennings, **1839.** xi p., 1 l., 290 p., 18 pl., 7¾ x 4¾. N.Y., U.W. (1541)

**Landscape souvenir** for **1835,** a second series of 45 views of cities and scenery in Italy, Switzerland and France from drawings by Prout and Harding, with descriptions in English and French by Thos. Roscoe London, Fisher, Son & Co. 4to. 45 pl. T.-B. (1542)

—— ——, **1837.** T.-B. (1543)

—— ——, **1838.** T.-B. (1544)

—— ——, **1839.** T.-B. (1545)

**Landscape wreath.** ed. by T. Campbell. London. Virtue, **n. d.** T.-B. (1546)

**Laurel.** London, Sharpe. **1830.** T.-B. (1547)

**Liliputian annual, The.** London, **1841.** 1½ x 1¼. T.-B. (1548)

**Literary and pictorial souvenir, The,** a museum of entertainment and instruction. London, Thomas Holmes, **n. d.** 2 p. l., 313 p., [7 pl.,] 8½ x 5¼. B.P. (1549)

**Literary and pictorial repository.** London, Berger, **1838.** T.-B. (1550)

**Literary and pictorial souvenir.** London, I. Holme, circa **1845.** T.-B. (1551)

**Literary bluebook, The, 1830.** London, Marsh. T.-B. (1552)

**Literary cabinet, The, 1839.** T.-B. (1553)

**Literary coronal, The,** for **1825-6.** [v. 3.] Glasgow, Richard Griffin & Co., 1825. v p., 1 l., 9–383 p., engr. t., 4¼ x 3. F. (1554)

**Literary gem, The,** for **1830.** London, 1830. 1 p. l., vii–viii, 542 p., 7½ x 4½. U.W. (1555)

**Literary gift book, The.** London, Marshall, **1834.** T.-B. (1556)

—— ——, for fireside, seaside and garden, ed. by Geo. Frederick Pardon. London, James Blackwood, **n. d.** [pref. d. Oct. 1856]. viii, 144 p., 10 pl., 9¼ x 6¾. P.M. (1557)

**Literary keepsake.** London and Glasgow, Griffin & Co., **n. d.** [circa 1850.] T.-B. (1558)

**Literary souvenir,** or cabinet of poetry and romance, ed. by Alaric A. Watts. [v. 1.] London, Hurst, Robinson & Co., **1825.** xii, 394 p., 13 pl., 5½ x 3½. U.W. (1559)

Also in large paper, 7¾ x 4¾. N.Y., L.C.

—— ——, or cabinet of poetry and romance, ed. by Alaric A. Watts. [v. 2.] London, Hurst, Robinson & Co., **1826.** xvi, 410 p., 1 l., 12 pl., 5½ x 3½. * (1560)

Large paper, 7¾ x 4¾. N.Y., L.C.

—— ——, or cabinet of poetry and romance, ed. by Alaric A. Watts. [v. 3.] London, Longman, Rees, Orme, Brown & Green, **1827.** xxiv, 402 p., 12 pl., 5⅛ x 3¼. B.P., (1561)

Also large paper, 7¾ x 4¾. N.Y., L.C.

**Literary souvenir,** or cabinet of poetry and romance, ed. by Alaric A. Watts. [v. 4.] London, Longman, Rees, Orme, Brown & Green, **1828.** xxii, 406 p., 14 pl., 5¼ x 3½. N.Y., B.P. (1562)
Also large paper, 7¾ x 4¾. L. C.

—— ——, ed. by Alaric A. Watts. [v. 5.] London, Longman, Rees, Orme, Brown & Green, **1829.** xviii, 362 p., 12 pl., 5½ x 3½. B.A. (1563)
Also large paper, 7½ x 4¾. N. Y., L. C.

—— ——, ed. by Alaric A. Watts. [v. 6.] London, Longman, Rees, Orme, Brown & Green, **1830.** xviii p., 1 l., 362 p., 1 l., 12 pl., 5⅞ x 3¾. B.P. (1564)
Also large paper, 7¾ x 4¾. L. C.

—— ——, ed. by Alaric A. Watts. [v. 7.] London, Longman, Rees, Orme, Brown & Green, **1831.** xiv, 346 p., 12 pl., 5¾ x 3¾. C.U., B.A. (1565)
Also large paper, 7½ x 4¾. N. Y., L. C.

—— ——, ed. by Alaric A. Watts. [v. 8.] London, Longman, Rees, Orme, Brown & Green, **1832.** xvi, 340 p., 12 pl., 5¾ x 3¾. B.P. (1566)
Also large paper, 7½ x 4¾. N. Y., L. C.

—— ——, ed. by Alaric A. Watts. [v. 9.] London, Longman, Rees, Orme, Brown, Green & Longman, **1833.** xiv, 306 p., 10 pl., 5¾ x 3¾. B.P. (1567)
Also large paper, 7½ x 4¾. N. Y., L. C.

—— ——, ed. by Alaric A. Watts. [v. 10.] London, Longman, Rees, Orme, Brown, Green & Longman, **1834.** xiv, 306 p., 10 pl., 5⅞ x 3⅞. B.P. (1568)
Also large paper, 7½ x 4¾. N. Y., L. C.

—— ——, and cabinet of modern art, ed. by Alaric A. Watts. New series. [v. 11.] London, Whittaker & Co., **1835.** xiv, 222 p., 25 pl., 7¼ x 5¼. N. Y., L.C. (1569)
Followed by "Cabinet of modern art."

**Looking glass, The,** a caricature annual. London, McLean, **1830-35.** v. 1–6, folio. il. by R. Seymour and W. Heath. T.-B. (1570–75)

—— ——, **1836, 1837.** * (1576–77)

**Love gift, A,** for **1842**[**-45**]. 4 v. T.-B. (1578–81)

**Love's offering,** a musical annual, **1831-32.** 2 v. London. T.-B. (1582–83)

**Lyre, The.** London, **1830–31.** T.-B. (1584–85)

**Magnet, The,** ed. by Cecil. London, Renshaw, **1838.** T.-B. (1586)

**Manchester keepsake, The,** ed. by W. Gaskey. Manchester, **1844.** T.-B. (1587)

**Marshall's Christmas box,** a juvenile annual. London, W. Marshall, **1831.** B.M. (1588)

—— ——, a juvenile annual. London, W. Marshall, **1832.** vi p., 1 l., 215 p., 8 pl., 6⅝ x 4¼. N.Y. (1589)
Title on back. "The Christmas box."
This was reissued with date 1835. N.Y. (1590)

**May you like it,** by Chas. B. Taylor. London, 6th ed., **1840.** xii, 404 p., 6½ x 4½. F. (1591)

**Midsummer comic annual, The,** for **1836,** ed. by author of "Lays for light hearts." London, William Marshall. 48 p., 13 pl., 6⅞ x 4. F. (1592)

**Midsummer keepsake, The,** a literary present. London, William Marshall, **1834.** iv p., 1 l., 136 p., [10 pl.,] 5½ x 3¼. B.P. (1593)
**Military annual, The.** London, Colburn, **1844.** 8vo. T.-B. (1594)
**Miniature almanach, The.** London, **1839.** T.-B. (1595)
**Mirror of the graces, The. 1831.** London. T.-B. (1596)
**Missionary annual** for **1833,** ed. by William Ellis. London, Seeley & Sons. 300 p., 17 pl., 6¼ x 4. U. W. (1597)
**Mr. Matthews' comic annual,** ed. by R. Cruickshank, **1831.** T.-B. (1597a)
**Mother's present to her daughter, A.** Dublin, Leckie, **1831.** T.-B. (1598)
**Musical bijou, The.** Quarto, **1830–32,** London. T.-B. (1599–1601)
—— ——, oblong quarto, ed. by W. A. Field. il. by Cruickshank. London, **1836.** T.-B. (1602)
—— ——. London, **1837.** T.-B. (1603)
—— ——, an album of music and poetry, ed. by F. H. Burney. London, D'Almaine. **1845, 1846, 1847.** T.-B. (1604–6)
—— ——, for **1848.** An album of music and poetry, ed. by F. H. Bourney. London, D'Almaine & Co. 2 p. l., 1–100 p., [4 pl.,] 14 x 10. F. (1607)
—— ——, **1849-52.** London. T.-B. (1608–11)
**Musical forget me not, 1830–31.** London, quarto. T.-B. (1612–13)
**Musical gem, 1829–33.** London, quarto. T.-B. (1614–18)
—— ——, for **1835,** ed. by Nicholas More. London, quarto, 4 pors. T.-B. (1619)
—— ——. London, Goulding and D'Almaine, **1845.** T.-B. (1620)
**Musical souvenir, 1830.** London. T.-B. (1621)
**"My own" annual,** ed. by Mark Merrywell. London, Chapman & Hall, **1848.** T.-B. (1622)
**Nautilus, 1829.** London. T.-B. (1623)
**Naval annual, The,** or stories of the sea, by Capt. Marryat. London, Longman, Rees, Orme, Brown, Green & Longman, **1836.** 2 p. l., 315 p., 19 pl., 8¼ x 5¾. F. (1624)
Not a true annual gift.
**New casket, The,** a gift book for all seasons. London, Tract Soc. 12 mo. T.-B. (1625)
**New comic annual, The,** for **1831.** London, Hurst, Chance & Co., xvi, 192 p., 49 pl. and numerous illus., 6½ x 4. F. (1626)
Called Falstaff's Comic Annual on back, and in preface.
There was a New comic annual pub. in 1835.
**New forget me not for parting friends.** London, Simpkin. 48mo. T.-B. (1627)
**New gift book for youth.** London, R. Clarke. 16mo. T.-B. (1628)
**New juvenile keepsake,** by Mrs. Landon. London, **1839,** Colburn. 12mo. T.-B. (1629)

**New musical annual, The.** London, **1831.** T.-B. (1630)

**New Year's gift** and juvenile souvenir, ed. by Mrs. Alaric Watts. [v. 1.] London, Longman, Rees, Orme, Brown & Green, **1829.** xii, 240 p., 12 pl., 5¼ x 3½. B.P. (1631)

—— ——, and juvenile souvenir, ed. by Mrs. Alaric Watts. [v. 2.] London, Longman, Rees, Orme, Brown & Green, **1830.** x, 240 p., 8 pl., 5¾ x 3¾. U.W. (1632)

—— ——, and juvenile souvenir, ed. by Mrs. Alaric Watts. [v. 3.] London, Longman, Rees, Orme, Brown & Green, **1831.** T.-B. (1633)

—— ——, and juvenile souvenir, ed. by Mrs. Alaric Watts. [v. 4.] London, Longman, Rees, Orme, Brown & Green, **1832.** x p., 1 l., 240 p., 8 pl., 5¾ x 3½. N.Y. (1634)

—— ——, and juvenile souvenir, ed. by Mrs. Alaric. Watts. [v. 5.] London, Longman, Rees, Orme, Brown, Green & Longman, **1833.** x p., 1 l., 240 p., 9 pl., 6¼ x 4. B.P. (1635)

—— ——. London, **1834.** * (1636)

—— ——, ed. by Mrs. A. A. Watts. [v. 6.] London, Whittaker, **1835.** T.-B. (1637)

—— ——, ed. by Mrs. A. A. Watts. [v. 7.] London, Whittaker, **1836.** T.-B. (1638)

**New Year's token, 1835.** London, Darton (Juvenile). T.-B. (1639)

**Northern poetical keepsake, 1856.** Newcastle (printed in three colors). T.-B. (1640)

**Nosegay,** a musical annual, **1832.** London. T.-B. (1641)

**Nursery annual.** London, circa **1840.** T.-B. (1642)

**Nursery offering, The,** or children's gift for **1835.** Edinburgh, 1835. 8vo. B.M. (1643)

—— —— for **1836.** Edinburgh, 1836. 8vo. B.M. (1644)

**Offering,** ed. by Rev. Thomas Dale. London, Sampson Low, **1829.** T.-B. (1645)
Followed by Iris.

——, **1833, 1834.** London, Lacey. T.-B. (1646–7)
A new edition consisting of (a) Juvenile keepsake, (b) Annual token.

**Olive branch, 1830–31,** ed. by H. S. Baynes. Edinburgh, Baynes. T.-B. (1648–9)

**Oracle of rural life and spring almanach.** London, **1839.** T.-B. (1650)

**Orient pearl, The,** for **1835,** ed. by W. Kirkpatrick. Calcutta, T. Ostell, 1835. vi p., 1 l., 336 p., 6¼ x 4. U.W. (1651)

**Oriental album, 1846.** London, Crisse. T.-B. (1652)

—— ——. London, Madden, **1848.** * (1653)

—— ——. London, Madden, **1853** (new edition). * (1654)

**Oriental annual,** or scenes in India. [**1834,** v. 1.] London, Edward Bull, 1835. 4 p. l., 254 p., 25 pl., 7½ x 5.
N.Y., B.P. (1655)

—— ——, or scenes in India, **1835.** [v. 2.] London, Bull & Churton. vi p., 1 l., 263 p., 22 pl., 7½ x 5.
N.Y. (1656)

—— ——, or scenes in India, **1836.** [v. 3.] London, Edward Churton, 1836. 4 p. l., 297 p., 22 pl., 7⅝ x 4⅞.
N.Y. (1657)

—— ——. Lives of the Mogul emperors, by Rev. Hobart Caunter [v. 4.] London, Charles Tilt, **1837.** x p., 1 l., 240 p., 22 pl., 7¾ x 5. N.Y. (1658)

—— ——, or scenes in India, by Rev. Hobart Caunter. [v. 5.] London, Charles Tilt, **1838.** 3 p. l., 242 p., 22 pl., 7¾ x 4¾. N.Y., B.P. (1659)
Followed by "Caunter's & Daniels' oriental annual," 1839.

—— ——, containing a series of tales, legends and historical romances, by Thomas Bacon. [v. 6.] London, Charles Tilt, **1839.** x p., 1 l., 250 p., 18 pl., 7¾ x 4¾.
F. (1660)
See "Caunter's and Daniels' oriental annual," 1839.

—— ——, containing a series of tales, legends and historical romances, by Thomas Bacon. [v. 7.] London, Charles Tilt, **1840.** 3 p. l., 244 p., 18 pl., 7¾ x 4¾.
N.Y. (1661)

**Orientalist,** ed. by T. Bacon. London, Arnold, **1841, 1842.** T.-B. (1662–63)
Continuation of "Oriental annual."

**Pearl offering.** London, n. d. See **Pearl offering,** N. Y.

**Perennial.** London, Darten & Co., circa **1845.**
T.-B. (1664)

**Peter Parley's annual** published in London from 1839 for many years was probably really the bound volumes of the "Peter Parley's magazine."

**Phrenological bijou, 1831.** T.-B. (1665)

**Pictorial cabinet, 1846.** London, Harwood.
T.-B. (1666)

**Pledge of affection.** London, Edward Lacey, **1835**[?] 6 pl. T.-B. (1667)

**Pledge of friendship, 1826-1828.** London, Marshall.
T.-B. (1668–70)

—— ——. Dublin, Fleming, **1831.** T.-B. (1671)

**Poetic prism, 1848,** ed. by R. N. Greville, Edinburgh, Maclachlan. T.-B. (1672)

**Poetical album,** ed. by A. A. Watts. London, Hurst & Co., **1825-1829.** * (1673–77)

**Poetical annual,** being selections from the English poets from Spencer to Beattie. London, Scott, Webster & Geary, **1836.** x, 406 p., por., illus., 6¾ x 4¼.
U.W. (1678)

**Poetical forget-me-not.** London, Darton, circa **1842.**
T.-B. (1679)

**Poetical offering, 1831, 1832.** London, Fry.
T.-B. (1680–81)

**Poole's royal sovereign,** a New Year's gift, **1827.** London, J. Poole. 132 p., 1 l., 12 pl., 4½ x 3.
U.W. (1682)

**Portfolio, The.** London, **1832.** T.-B. (1683)

**Portraits of children of the nobility,** ed. by C. Heath. London, C. Heath, **1838-1841.** T.-B. (1684–87)

**Present, The,** a forget me not for the young. Dedicated to L. E. L. and with por. of Queen Adelaide. London, Edward Lacey, **1835.** 6 pl. T.-B. (1688)

**Prism of imagination, 1844,** ed. by Baroness de Calabrella. London, Longmans. T.-B. (1689)

**Protestant annual, The, 1841,** ed. by Charlotte Elizabeth. London, Francis Baisler. xi, 307 p., 10 pl., 7½ x 4¾. B.P., U.W. (1690)
2d ed. called "Protestant Christian keepsake."

**Protestant Christian keepsake.** London, Francis Baisler, **n. d.,** 2d edition [of Protestant annual]. xi, 307 p., 10 pl., 7½ x 4¾. N.Y., B.P. (1691)

**Rainbow,** circa **1840.** London, C. Heath. T.-B. (1692)

**Recordanza,** or friendship's memento, **1832.** London. T.-B. (1693)

**Recreation, The,** a gift-book for young readers, **1841-1847.** Edinburgh. B.M. (1694–99)

—— ——, Edinburgh, John Menzies, **1848.** vi, 346 p., (6 pl.,) 6 x 4. P.M. (1699b)

—— ——, **1849-1850.** * (1700–1)

**Regent,** or royal tablet of memory, **1831-1854.** London, Satterby. T.-B. (1702)

**Relaxation** (Juvenile), **1837.** Edinburgh, Whyte & Co. T.-B. (1703)

—— ——, or a book for Christmas. Longmans, 18mo. * (1704)

**Remember me!** a New Year's gift or Christmas present, **1825.** London, I. Poole. xxiv, 336 p., 8 p. of music, [337–360 p.,] 361–372 p., [9 pl.,] 5¼ x 3¼. B.P. (1705)

—— ——, a token of Christian affection, **1830–1832.** London, Darton & Clark. T.-B. (1706–8)

**Remembrance, The, 1831,** ed. by Thomas Roscoe. London, Jennings & Chaplin. viii, 260 p., 13 pl., 7⅝ x 4⅞. F. (1709)

—— ——, **1838,** new ed. in honor of Queen's accession. T.-B. (1710)

—— ——, **1843.** London, Spalding. 16mo. B.M. (1711)

**Renfrewshire annual** for **1842,** a collection of original pieces in prose and verse chiefly by native authors, ed. by Mrs. Maxwell Paisley. Murray & Stuart and John Neilson, 1842. viii p., 1 l., 320 p., 9 pl., 6½ x 4. U.W. (1712)

**Reynolds dramatic annual, 1831.** See Dramatic annual.

**Rose and holly,** a gift book for all the year. Edinburgh, **1867.** T.-B. (1713)

**Rose of four seasons, 1832.** London. T.-B. (1714)

**Royal repository and picturesque diary, 1831.** London, Satterby. T.-B. (1715)

**Royal sovereign,** a New Year's gift, **1827.** London, ed. and pub. by Toole. T.-B. (1716)

**Royal Victoria keepsake,** circa **1852.** London, Holmes. T.-B. (1717)

**Ruby, The,** a juvenile forget-me-not, and pledge of affection. London, John Reynolds & Son, **n. d.** iv, 7–254 p., [6 pl.,] 6¼ x 3¾. U.W. (1718)

**Sacred annual,** ed. by Rev. R. Montgomery. London, **1834.** T.-B. (1719)

**Sacred harp.** Lond., Leckie, **1831–1832.** T.-B. (1720–21)

**Sacred iris, The,** a literary and religious offering. Liverpool, Henry Lacey, **n. d.** [circa 1831]. vi, 316 p. [2(?) pl.,] 6¼ x 4. F. (1722)
Also issued London, Thomas Holmes, Suc. to Edward Lacey, n. d. P.M. (1723)

**Sacred lyre,** devotional and moral poems, **1832.** London. T.-B. (1724)

**Sacred musical offering, 1833.** London. T.-B. (1725)

**Sacred offering,** ed. by [Mrs.] M. A. J.[evons]. London, Hamilton & Co., **1831-1834.** * (1726–9)
—— ——, **1835, 1838.** B.M. (1730–31)
Selected poems from this series were re-published in America under same title. See "Sacred offering," Boston, 1836, 1838.

**Scenic annual** for **1838,** ed. by Thomas Campbell. London. 36 pl. T.-B. (1732)

**Scottish annual, The,** ed. by William Weir. Glasgow, John Reid & Co., **1836.** viii, 328 p., 12 autograph pl. and 1 vignette, 7½ x 4¼. N.Y., L.C. (1733)
—— ——, (revised), **1859.** Edinb. Black. T.-B. (1734)
—— ——, for **1859,** ed. by O. R. Brown. T.-B. (1735)

**Scottish keepsake, The,** or the songs of the Ayrshire bard [Burns]. Ayrshire, **1857.** 16mo. T.-B. (1736)

**Scrap table, 1831.** T.-B. (1737)

**Shipp's military bijou, 1832.** London. T.-B. (1738)

**Simpson's gentleman's almanack and pocket journal, 1831.** London, Satterby. T.-B. (1739)

**Sister's gift, 1832.** London. T.-B. (1740)

**Souvenir, The,** of art and literature, **1835.** London, Lacey. T.-B. (1741)
—— ——, of literature and art. London, H. Riley, **1834.** 288 p., [4(?)pl.,] 6 x 4. F. (1742)
—— ——, of literature and art, an elegant cabinet miscellany. London, Charles Evelyn Knight, **n. d.** [circa 1846]. ii, 320 p., 6 pl., 6¼ x 4. U.W. (1743)
—— ——, a token of remembrance. Lond., T. Nelson & Sons, **1859.** viii, 280 p., 10 col. pl., 6½ x 4¼. P.M. (1744)

**Souvenir, Le,** or pocket tables, **1831.** London, Satterby & Co. T.-B. (1745)

**Souvenir keepsake** for **1837.** London, Whittaker, Treacher & Arnot, n. d. vi, 312 p., [10 pl.,] 7 x 4½. F. (1746)

**Souvenir keepsake, The,** of literature and art, ed. by Frederick Ferguson. London, H. Riley, n. d. [**1840** on back]. 318 p., [8 pl.,] 8 x 5¼. U.W. (1747)
—— —— of literature and art. Ed. by Frederic Ferguson. London, H. Riley. n. d. [**1842** on back]. iv, 1–316 p., [10 pl.,] 8 x 5½. F. (1747a)

**Souvenir litteraire de France,** ed. by A. A. Watts. Paris and London, **1829.** Longman & Co. T.-B. (1748)

**Spiritual gleaner, 1832.** London. T.-B. (1749)

**Squib annual, The,** of poetry, politics, and personalities for **1836.** London, Chapman & Hall, 1836. viii, 178 p., 12 pl., 5⅞ x 3⅝. F. (1750)

**Talisman, The,** or English keepsake, a bouquet of literature and the fine arts. London, Edward Lacey, **n. d.** vi p., 1 l., 312 p., [10. pl.]. N.Y. (1751)
Imprint on engr. t. is "Whittaker, Treacher & Arnot."

—— ——, a bouquet of literature and the fine arts, ed. by Mrs. A. A. Watts. London, Whittaker, Treacher & Co., **1831.** xiv p., 1 l., 288 p., 18 pl., 7¼ x 4¾. N.Y.S. (1752)

**Times telescope, 1828-1831.** London, Sherwood. T.-B. (1753–6)

**Tit-bits, 1831,** ed. by Heath. London, Akermann. T.-B. (1757)

**Token of friendship,** a parental gift to youthful piety. Watchet, **n. d.** 12mo. T.-B. (1758)

**Tribute, The,** a collection of miscellaneous unpublished poems by various authors, ed. by Lord Northampton. London, John Murray & Harry Lindsell, **1837.** * (1759)

**Troubadour,** a vocal souvenir. London, **1828.** * (1760)

**Turner's annual tour,** ed. by L. Ritchie, il. by J. M. W. Turner. London, Longmans, **1833–1855.** T.-B. (1761–83)

**Victoria,** or the court keepsake, an elegant literary miscellany. London, pub. for the proprietor, **n. d.** iv, 316 p., 20 pl., 9½ x 6½. L.C. (1784)

**Victoria annual.** London, **1844.** quarto. T.-B. (1785)

**Victoria keepsake, The,** for youth of both sexes, formerly Ackermann's Juvenile forget-me-not, ed. by Frederic Shoberl. London, Ackermann & Co., **n. d.** [1836]. xii, 240 p., [10 pl.,] 5⅝ x 3½. B.P. (1786)

**Victoria regia, The,** a volume of original contributions in poetry and prose, ed. by Adelaide A. Proctor. London, Emily Faithfull & Co., **1861.** x p., 1 l., 3–350 p., 9½ x 6¼. P.M. (1787)

**Vocal annual, 1831-1832,** 4to. London. Tegg. T.-B. (1788)

**Waverly album, 1832.** London. T.-B. (1789)

**Waverley keepsake, The,** and Abbotsford album, or beauties of Sir Walter Scott. London, R. A. Charlton, **n. d.** [1837] iv, 308 p., pl., 7½ x 4¾. P.M. (1790)

**Wesleyan juvenile offering.** London, **1847.** [v. 4.] 12mo. * (1791)

**Winter's wreath, The,** a literary album and Chrstmas and New Year's present. London, George Routledge & Co., **n. d.** vi, 316 p., 3 pl., 6¼ x 4. P.M. (1792)

—— ——. Liverpool, Geo. Smith, **1828** [v. 1.] T.-B. (1793)

**Winter's wreath, The,** a collection of original contributions in prose and verse. [v. 2.] London, George B. Whittaker, 1828 [**1829**]. vi p., 3 l., 420 p., 12 pl., 6¼ x 4.
N.Y. (1794)

Engr. t., "The winter's wreath for 1829."
Preface calls it the "Winter's wreath for 1829," and speaks of one of the previous year.

—— ——, for **1830,** a collection of original contributions in prose and verse. [v. 3.] London, Whittaker, Treacher & Co. vi p., 2 l., 384 p., 13 pl., 6⅛ x 3¾.
B.P. (1795)

—— ——, for **1831.** [v. 4.] London, Whittaker, Treacher & Co. vi p., 3 l., 372 p., 13 pl., 6⅛ x 4.
N.Y.S. (1796)

—— ——, for **1832.** [v. 5.]London, Whittaker, Treacher & Co. vi p., 3 l., 372 p., 12 pl., 6½ x 4.
L.C., C.U., P.M. (1797)

Merged in "Friendship's offering," 1833.

**Wreath of friendship, The, 1833.** London, Lacey.
T.-B. (1798)

—— ——, **1834.** London, Lacey. T.-B. (1799)

—— ——, a token of regard, ed. by Charles Cecil. London, Renshaw & Co., n. d. [**1836** on back]. iv, 320 p., [7 pl.,] 6¼ x 4. N.Y. (1800)

**Yorkshire literary annual** for **1832,** ed.by C. F. Edgar. London, Longman, Rees, Orme, Brown & Green, 1832. viii, 358 p., engr. front., 7 x 4½. F. (1801)

**Young gentleman's annual, The,** by Clara Hall. London, Edward Lacey, **1834,** il. by etchings.
T.-B. (1802)

—— ——, by Clara Hall. London, Edward Lacey, n. d. [**1835** on back]. 2 p. l., 248 p., [7 pl.,] 5½ x 3½.
B.P. (1803)

—— ——, circa **1841.** T.-B. (1804)

[1835] and 1841 probably are the same as 1834.

**Young ladies book,** ed. by W. Harvey, **1829.**
T.-B. (1805)

**Young lady's annual, The,** by Clara Hall. London, **n. d.** iv, 248 p., [10 pl.,] 5½ x 3½. C.U. (1806)

**Youth's cabinet, The.** London, Edward Lacey, **1835** [?]. 6 pl. (1807)

**Youth's cornucopia, The.** London, **1832.** 12mo.
T.-B. (1808)

**Youth's keepsake, The.** London, **1831.** 12mo.
T.-B. (1809)

**Zoological keepsake, The.** London, Marsh, **1830.** 12mo. T.-B. (1810)

# ADDENDA AND ERRATA

Where titles already entered are here given again on account of additions or changes, their running number is prefixed in parentheses, ( ), so that quick reference to main entry may be made.

Where new entries are here made a number is prefixed *without* parentheses, and the number chosen is that which will indicate the proper place for the insertion of the new item.

## AMERICAN

(20) **Amaranth, 1850.**
Add to note: Issued as "Keepsake of friendship for 1852."

(27) **American book of beauty, The.**
Add: Same as 27*a* with wider margin, and two less pl.

27*a* **American book of beauty, The,** or token of friendship for **1847,** ed. by a lady. New York, John Levison, 2 p.l., 7–128 p., 9 pl., 9¼ x 6¼. F.
This is the same as (27) with two additional pl., but has smaller margins.
Called "Book of beauty" on side and on back of cover.

29*a* **American historical annual, The,** illustrated with numerous engravings. New York, John S. Taylor, **1853.** vi, 9–388 p., 12 pl., 8⅝ x 5⅝. B. P.

36*a* **American Keepsake, The,** a book for every American. Boston, E. L. Pratt, **1845,** c. 1845. F.
Not a true annual.

40*a* **Amethyst, The,** or poetical gems, a gift book for all seasons, ed. by Mrs. M. P. James. Boston, James French, **1849.** iv, 5–128 p., 4½ x 2¾. F.
Same as 1850 (no.41).

(41) **Amethyst, The**
Add: Same as 1849 (no. 40*a* above).

(53) **Annualette, The.**
The note should be omitted.

53½ **Annualette, The,** a Christmas and New Year's gift, ed. by a lady. Boston, T. H. Carter & Co., **1846.** vii–viii, 9–144 p., [5 pl.], 6 x 3⅝. F.

(55) **Appleton's juvenile annual** for **1869.**
Add note: also issued in 1871.

55*a* **Appleton's juvenile annual** for **1871.** A Christmas and New Year's gift for young people. New York, D. Appleton & Co. 1871, c. 1868. 382 p., 8 pl. and text illus., 7⅜ x 5. F.
Same as 1869 (no. 55).

64*a* **Autographs for freedom,** ed. by Julia Griffiths. Auburn, [N. Y.], Allen Beardsley & Co., **1854,** c. 1854. ix p., 1 l., 11–309 p., [10 pl.], 7½ x 5. F.
Preface says, "This is the second volume."

64*b* **Autumn flowers** and other poems, by Mrs. Southey (late Caroline Bowles). Boston, 3d ed. Saxton & Kelt, **1845.** 128 p., 4¼ x 2¾. F.

64*c* **Autumn leaves,** a collection of miscellaneous poems from various authors. New York, John S. Taylor, **1837,** c. 1836. x p., 1 l., 13–203 p., eng. t., 7 x 4½. F.

66*b* **Beauties of sacred literature,** ed. by Thomas Wyatt. Boston and Cambridge, James Munroe & Co., **c. 1848.** vi p., 1 l., 220 p., 8 pl., 9⅛ x 5¾. F.
Same as 1852 (no. 67).

(67) **Beauties of sacred literature, 1852.**
Add: Also issued with different imprint but other wise same. c. 1848 (no. 66*b* above).

69*a* **Birthday gift;** consisting of original poems and original and selected prose, by Mrs. Harriot S. Arnold. Dedham, H. A. Mann, **1853,** c. 1853. viii, 9–128 p., 4¾ x 3⅛. F.

**Book of beauty.** Title on cover of "American book of beauty," 1847.
See 27*a* above.

82*a* **Bouquet, The,** or spirit of the English annuals for **1835.** Philadelphia, Thomas T. Ash. 224 p., eng. front., 4¼ x 2⅞. F.
Has articles from the following English Annuals: "Keepsake," "English annual," "Oriental annual," "Literary souvenir," "Landscape annual," "Christian annual," "Heath's picturesque annual," "Friendship's offering," "Amulet," "Gem."

82*b* **Bouquet, The,** or token of friendship. Philadelphia, Henry F. Anners, **n. d.** 128 p., eng. front., 4¼ x 2¾. F.

(84) **Bouquet, The, 1845.**
L. should read L. C.
Add to note: Title on back "Bouquet of flowers." Also issued Boston, Benjamin B. Mussey, 1846, c. 1844, and 1851, c. 1844. Also issued as "Bouquet of flowers," 1846.

84[1] **Bouquet, The, 1846.** F.
Same as 1844 except imprint. See note above.

84[2] **Bouquet, The, 1851.** F.
Same as 1846. See above.

84*b* **Bouquet of flowers, The,** containing the poetry and language of flowers, by a lady. Boston, Benjamin B. Mussey, **1846,** c. 1844. 128 p., [2 col. pl.], 4¼ x 2¾. F.
Same as "The Bouquet," 1844.

85*a* **Bridal keepsake, The,** from approved authors. By Mrs. Colman. Rochester, Erastus Darrow, **1852,** c. 1851. viii, 9–126 p., eng. front., 4⅜ x 2⅝. F.

86*a* **Bridal wreath, The,** a wedding souvenir. Boston, **1847,** c. 1845. *
Same as 1848 below.

(87) **Bridal wreath, The,** a wedding souvenir.
Add to complete the record: Ed. by Percy Bryant. Boston, W. J. Reynolds & Co., **1848,** c. 1845. 128 p., col. t., $4\frac{3}{8}$ x $2\frac{3}{4}$. F.
Same as 1847.

89*b* **Broken vase, The,** and other stories for children and youth, compiled by a teacher. Fitchburg, S. & C. Shepley, **1846.** 5–64 p., front., $4\frac{1}{2}$ x $2\frac{3}{4}$. F.
Not a true annual.

97*a* **Casket,** or Youth's pocket library, **1830.** *

101*a* **Casket of Gems, The,** the gift of an uncle and aunt. Boston, Monroe & Francis, **1838.** 288 p., [29 woodcuts paged in], $5\frac{3}{4}$ x $4\frac{1}{2}$. F.
Reissued in 1840 without change. An edition in 1863 had only the first 93 p. and 9 illus. (see no. 102).

101*b* **Casket of gems, The,** the gift of an uncle and aunt. Boston, **1840.** F.
Same as 1838 (see 101*a* above).

(102) **Casket of gems, The, 1863.**
Add: This is the first 93 p. of 1838 with different sub-title, and imprint (see 101*a* above).

**Cecil and Flavel's gift for mourners.**
Title on back, and half-title of "Gift for mourners."

106*a* **Chaplet of roses,** by Park Moody. New York, J. M. Fletcher & Co., n. d., **c. 1851.** iv, 3–284 p., illum. t., and flower pl., $7\frac{3}{4}$ x $4\frac{3}{4}$. F.

110*a* **Children's gift, The,** for the new year, [by Rev. James F. Brown]. Boston, Little Brown & Co., **1854.** $4\frac{5}{8}$ x $3\frac{1}{8}$. F.
Printed for the children of the Sunday-school of the first Congregational society of West Cambridge.

113*a* **Child's companion, The,** and youth's friend. Philadelphia, **1852.** F.
This is a magazine.

$121^1$ **Choice gift, The,** or golden sands from the river of literature, ed. by Sarah C. Carter. Boston, J. Buffum, n. d. c. **1850.** 128 p., col. front., $4\frac{1}{2}$ x $2\frac{3}{4}$. F.
Same as 1851, with p. 103–128 added.

$121^2$ **Choice gift, The,** or golden sands from the river of literature, ed. by Sarah C. Carter. Boston, J. Buffum, **1851,** c. 1850. 102 p., 2 illum. t., $4\frac{1}{2}$ x $2\frac{3}{4}$. F.
This was reissued with added pages (see 121*a* above).

**Christian consolations.** Title on back and on half-title of "Offering of sympathy."

(123) **Christian diadem.**
Add: Also issued in 1854.

133*b* **Christian keepsake,** a gift book for all seasons, ed. by Cuthbert Montgomery. New York, Leavitt & Allen, n. d., **c. 1855.** 5 p. l., 252 p., 6 pl., 7¼ x 5. F.

154*a* **Christmas box, The,** or collection of instruction and amusement. Philadelphia, Thomas T. Ash, **n. d.,** 2 p. l., 9–184 p., eng. front., 6¼ x 3¾. F.

(159) **Christmas tribute, The.**
Add: Also issued for 1852, only date being on back of cover.

$160^{1}$ **Christ's messengers,** or missionary memorial. New York, E. Walker, **1847.** xii, 372 p., [5 pl.], 7½ x 4½. F.
This is same as Christ's Messenger, 1848.

(160*a*) **Christ's messenger, 1848.**
Add: Same as above (no. $160^{1}$).

164*a* **Crocus, The;** a fresh flower for the holidays, ed. by Sarah Josepha Hale. New York, Edward Dunigan & Brother, **c. 1849.** x, 7–277 p., [6 pl. paged in and text illus.], 7 x 4½. F.

167*a* **Daughter's own book,** Boston, **1834.**
Not a true gift-book.

169*a* **Dew-drops,** [New York], American Tract Soc. n. p., **n. d.** 128 p., 2 x 1¼. F.
Has a biblical quotation for each day of year.

177*a* **Diosma, The,** a perennial by Miss H. F. Gould. Boston, Phillips, Sampson & Co., **1851,** c. 1850. 287 p., 7¼ x 4½. F.

(180) **Drops from Flora's cup, c. 1845.**
Add to note: Also issued in 1852.

180*a* **Drops from Flora's cup,** or the poetry of flowers, with a floral vocabulary by Miss Mary M. Griffin. Boston, G. W. Cottrell & Co., **1852,** c. 1845. x, 11–160 p., illum. t., 4⅜ x 2¾. F.
Same as c. 1845 (no. 180), except size is smaller and plate varies.

180*b* **Echoes of infant voices.** Boston, Wm. Crosby & H. P. Nichols, **1849,** c. 1849. 2 p. l., 7–144 p., 7 x 4½. F.

(188*c*) **Family circle** and parlor annual. New York.
Should read: Vols. 1–15, 1843–53., etc.

188*d* **Female prose writers of America,** with portraits; by John S. Hart. Philadelphia, E. H. Butler & Co., **1852.** *

$190^{1}$ **Floral fortune teller.** Boston, **1846,** c. 1846. F.
Same as (190*a*).

(190*a*) **Floral fortune teller. 1848.**
Add: This is the same as 1846.

(190*b*) **Floral gems. 1847.**
Add: Several editions of this were published, the 6th edition being, 1849, and identical with the 3d (no. 190*b*).

190*c* **Floral gems,** 6th ed. Boston, **1849,** c. 1846. F.
Same as 1847 (no. 190*b*).

193*a* **Floral offering, The,** a token of affection and esteem, comprising the language and poetry of flowers, by Henrietta Dumont. Philadelphia, H. C. Peck & Theo. Bliss, **1851,** c. 1851. 300 p., [6 col. pl. of flowers], $7\frac{1}{4}$ x $4\frac{5}{8}$. F.
Also issued in 1853, and 1863 (no. 194).

(194) **Floral offering, The.**
Add: Same as 1851. See no. 193*a* above.

195*a* **Floral wreath, The,** of autumn flowers, by Mrs. Southey. 6th ed. Auburn, N. Y., Alden, Beardsley & Co., **1852.** 128 p., illum. t., $4\frac{3}{8}$ x $2\frac{3}{4}$. F.

196*a* **Flora's album,** containing the language of flowers poetically expressed, ed. by John S. Adams. Boston, Elias Howe, **1847,** c. 1847. 128 p., col. front., $4\frac{1}{4}$ x $2\frac{5}{8}$. F.
Also issued without change, except imprint, 1848 (no. 197).

(197) **Flora's album, 1848.**
Add: Same as 1847, except name of publishers, and place. (See 196*a* above.)

197*a* **Flora's dial,** containing a flower dedicated to each day in the year, and an appropriate sentiment for each flower, by J. Wesley Hanson. Lowell, Jonathan Allen, **1846,** c. 1846. vi, 7–192 p., [col. front. and col. t.], $4\frac{1}{2}$ x $2\frac{3}{4}$. F.
Also issued 1853, and 1856, with changed imprint.

197*b* —— ——. . . . Boston, J. Buffum, **1853,** c. 1846. vi, 7–192 p., col. front., $4\frac{1}{3}$ x $2\frac{3}{8}$. F.
Same as 1846 (see no. 197*a* above).

197*c* —— ——. . . . Boston, G. W. Cottrell **1856,** c., 1846. vi, 7–192 p., col. front., $4\frac{1}{3}$ x $2\frac{3}{8}$. Same as 1846 (see no. 197*a* above). F.

197*d* **Flora's gem,** or the bouquet for all seasons, ed. by Alfred A. Phillips. New York, Nafis & Cornish, **n. d.** (preface dated Aug., 1846). viii, 9–104 p., 10 pl., $9\frac{1}{4}$ x $7\frac{3}{8}$. F.

198*a* **Flora's interpreter,** or the American book of flowers and sentiments, by Mrs. Sarah Josepha Hale. 11th edition improved. Boston, Marsh, Capen, Lyon and Webb, **1842,** c. 1833. x p., 1 l., 13–262 p., 1 l., $7\frac{1}{2}$ x $4\frac{3}{4}$. F.
Same as 14th ed. See no. 199.

(199) **Flora's interpreter.** 14th ed.
Add: 11th edition, dated 1842, was identical.

199*b* **Flora's lexicon,** an interpretation of the language of flowers, with an outline of botany, and a poetical introduction, by Catharine H. Waterman. Philadelphia, **1839,** c. 1839. 252 p., 4 pl., $7\frac{1}{2}$ x $4\frac{3}{4}$. F.
Reissued in Philadelphia, 1842; Boston, 1852, 1855, and 1857. 1839 and 1842 have different pl. and list of pl. 1842 and 1855 have different pl., but an identical list of pl.

199*c* —— ——. . . . Philadelphia, **1842.** Same as 1839, except pl. vary. F.

(200) **Flora's lexicon.** . . . *cont.* Boston, **1852.** F.
Add: Reissued from ed. of 1839, plates vary.

200*a* —— ——. . . . Boston, **1855.** F.
Same as 1839, except pl. vary.

200*b* —— ——. . . . Boston, **1857.** F.
Same as earlier editions.

201*a* **Flower people, The.** A token of friendship, by a lady. Hartford, H. T. Wells, **1846,** c., n.d., 228 p., 12 pl., 6⅜ x 4¾. F.

**Forest flowers.** Title on back of "Love, forest flowers, and sea shells."

**Forget-me-not.** Title on back of "Little girl's forget-me-not."

(210) **Forget-me-not. 1847.**
Add: Also issued with sub.-t. spelled "Philopene," but with "Philipena" on back of cover.

210*b* **Forget-me-not,** or the philipena, by Mrs. Lunt. Manchester, N. H., Fiske & Moore, **1848,** c. 1845, vi, 7–128 p., col. front., 4½ x 2¾. F.
Also issued with imprint. Lowell, Nathaniel L. Dayton, 1848, c. 1845.
Same as 1847 (no. 210).

216*a* **Forget-me-not,** or the philipena, by Mrs. Lunt. Boston, Dayton & Wentworth, **1853,** c. 1845. vi, 7–128 p., front., 4⅜ x 2¾. F.
Has "Philipena" on back of cover.
Same as 1846 (no. 209*a*) with sub.-t. spelled differently.

217*a* **Fountain, The,** for every day in the year. New York, John S. Taylor, **1836,** c. 1835. 208 p., front., 3 x 2½. F.
Not a true annual.

(221) **Friendship.**
Add: Also issued as "Friendship's offering," N. Y., n. d., "Cecelia" (see no. 228*b* below).

221*a* **Friendship flower, The,** a gift of the affections. New York, Leavitt & Co., **1851,** p. 189–308, 4¼ x 2¾. F.

(228) **Friendship's offering.**
Read 7¾ for 3¾.

228*b* **Friendship's offering,** a Christmas, New Year and birthday gift. New York, Leavitt & Allen, **n. d.** [circa 1856], viii, 9–264 p.,6 pl., [2 do not agree with list], 7¼ x 4¾. "Cecelia." F.
Also issued as "Moss rose," N. Y., n. d., "Passion Flower," n. d.; "Friendship," c. 1854.

246*a* **Friendship's token,** or the philipena, a present for all seasons. Worcester, S. A. Howland, **1850,** c. 1846. 126 p., illum. t., 4½ x 3¾. F.
This is really "Philipena," 1848.

(248*a*) **Garland, 1830.**
Add to note 1831 (248*a*): Plates vary from those in 1830.

(254) **Garland, 1851.**
Add: See also "Keepsake of friendship," 1852.

(287) **Gems from American female poets,** with brief biographical notices, **1842.**
Should read: x, 11–192 p., 4½ x 2⅞.
Add note: Also issued with only 160 p. (see 287*a* below).
Also issued in 1844, without change (see 287*b* below).

287*a* **Gems from American female poets,** with brief biographical notices, by Rufus W. Griswold. Philadelphia, H. Hooker, **1842,** c. 1842. x, 11–160 p., front. 4½ x 2⅞.
Same as 1842 (no. 287 above) to p. 159; p. 160 varies, pp. 161–192 omitted, and contents page changed to conform.

287*b* —— ——, with brief biographical notices, by Rufus W. Griswold. Philadelphia, H. Hooker, **1844,** c. 1842. x, 11–192 p., 4¼ x 2¾. F.
Same as 1842 (287 above).

(288) **Gems from the American poets.**
Full entry to be inserted: New York, D. Appleton & Co., **c. 1842.** viii, 9–222 p., eng. front., 4 x 2½. F.

288*a* —— ——, with brief biographical notices, by Rufus W. Griswold. Philadelphia, H. Hooker, **1844.** viii, 9–120 p. *

296*b* **Gems of sacred poetry,** 3d ed. Boston, Saxton & Kelt, **1845.** 128 p., 4¼ x 2¾. F.

(300) **Gift. 1835.**
Change: Work should read works.
Add note: There is also an edition having p. 322, 1 l., 1–50 p., eng. front., 5¼ x 3. F.

311*a* **Gift book, A,** of stories and poems for children, by Caroline Gilman. New York, C. S. Francis & Co., **1850,** c. 1846. x p., 1 l., 9–176 p., 1 l., 9–180 p., front., eng. t., 6¼ x 4¼. F.
Title on back, "Mrs. Gilman's gift book."

314*a* **Gift book of the republic.** Gallery of illustrious Americans, containing portraits and biographical sketches of twenty-four most eminent citizens since the death of Washington, ed. by C. E. Lester. New York, **1850,** large folio. *

316*a* **Gift for mourners,** a friendly visit to the homes of mourning, by Rev. Richard Cecil, London. New York, American tract society, **n. d.** 79 p., front., 4 x 2¾. F.
On back, and half title, "Cecil and Flavel's gift for mourners."

316*b* **Gift for my mother, A.** New York, I. C. & J. N. Stearns, **n. d.**
This is really "Mother's magazine," vol. 22, issued with the above title page prefixed, date about 1850.

344[1] **Gift of love,** a token of affection. New York, Leavitt & Allen, 27 Dey Street., **n. d.** [1853, '54 or '55*]*. xii, 17–266 p., 8 pl., 7¼ x 4⅞. "Poetry of the passions." F.

344*c* **Gift of piety,** or Divine breathings in one hundred meditations. Boston, J. Buffum, **n.d.,** 96 p., 3 x 2. B.P.
Same as 1850.

344*d* ——— ———, or Divine breathings in one hundred meditations. Boston, J. Buffum, **1850.** 96 p., 3 x 1⅞. F.

348*a* **Girl's token, The.** Philadelphia, American Sunday-school union, **c. 1844.** vi, 7–131 p., [8 pl.], 4⅝ x 3¾. F.

349*a* **Golden gems for the Christian,** selected from the . . . writings of Rev. John Flavel, with a memoir by Rev. J. Banvard. Salem, John P. Jewett, **1843,** c. 1843. viii, 1–141 p., 4⅜ x 2¾. F.

(350*c*) **Golden gift.**
Add: Also issued Manchester, N. H., Kimball & Harriman, 1848, c. 1846.

(350*d*) **Golden gift, 1851.**
Add: Also issued, Boston, J. Buffum, n. d., c. 1846.

353*a* **Golden grains** from life's harvest field, by T. S. Arthur. Philadelphia, J. W. Bradley, **1853,** c. 1850. vi, 7–240 p., eng. front. F.

356*h* **Golden vase, The,** a miniature gift. Boston, J. Buffum, c. 1851. 96 p., 2⅞ x 2. F.

357*a* **Good boy's annual,** a Christmas and New Year's gift, by Anne W. Abbott. New York, Allen Bros., **n. d.** 279 p., 6⅝ x 4½. F.

358*a* **Happy New Year, The,** a New Year's present for the child, by William M. Thayer. Boston, Cyrus Stone, c. **1853.** viii, 9–89 p., front., 6⅜ x 4¼. F.

361*b* **Hare-bell, The,** a token of friendship, ed. by Rev. C. W. Everest. Hartford, Henry S. Parsons, 3d. edition, **1845,** c. 1843. viii, 9–192 p., 4⅜ x 2¾. F.
Same as 1844 (no. 360).

(363) **Hawthorn, 1845.**
Add: Has 10 pl.

363*a* **Heart-songs;** a book for the gift-season. Boston, Crosby, Nichols & Co., **1856,** c. 1855. vi p., 1 l., 1–144 p., 7 x 4¼. F.

366*a* **Holiday tales;** a juvenile forget-me-not for all seasons. New York, W. B Gilely, **1829.** 2 p. l., 5–180 p., [illus. in text], 5⅝ x 3½. F.

368*a* **Home book of beauty, The.** New York, Geo. P. Putnam, **1852.** *

368*b* **Home book of the picturesque, The,** or American scenery, art and literature. New York, Geo. P. Putnam, **1852.** *

384*a* **Illustrated book of Christian ballads, The,** and other poems, ed. by Rufus W. Griswold. Philadelphia, Lindsay & Blakiston, **c. 1844.** 164 p., 4 pl., 10 x 7½. F.

(388) **Iris, The, 1844.**
Add: Also issued without date. *

394*a* **Jewel, The,** or token of friendship; a Christmas or New Year's present. Hartford, Silas Andrus & Son, **n. d.** 3–248 p., 2 pl., [5 pl. listed and 1 present not called for on list]. 6 x 3¾. F.
This is 1847 issue with slight changes. See 394*b* below.

394*b* —— ——, or token of friendship, **1837.** New York, Bancroft & Holley, 1837, c. 1836. viii, 9–248 p., 5 pl., 6¼ x 3⅝. F.
Reissued in 1839, 1843, 1844, 1846, 1847, and without date; see note (400) below.

(400) —— ——, **1847.**
Add note: This seems to be a variant of 1844. It omits "Advertisement," and the paging is changed. Article entitled "The young mother" with plate of same title is added, and plate "English Flower" omitted.

401*a* **Judson offering, The.** Intended as a token of Christian sympathy with the living and a memento of Christian affection for the dead, ed. by Rev. John Dowling. New York, Lewis Colby & Co., **1846,** c. 1846. x, 1–288 p., 3 pl., 6 x 4. F.

401*b* —— ——. . . , New York, Lewis Colby & Co., **1850,** c. 1848. x, 1–294 p., 6 x 4. *
Same as 1846 except that pp. 289–94 are added, containing three new poems.

408*a* **Juvenile odd-fellow, The.** New York, Edward Walker. **1848.** 287 p., 7⅛ x 4½. F.

(414) **Keepsake, The, n. d.** Change. "John Morley" to "Henry Morley." F.
Add: Also issued by W. H. Appleton, n. d., 5–304 p., illum. t., 8⅜ x 6¼. *

(425) **Keepsake of friendship, The.** Full entry: A Christmas and New Year's annual for **1852,** ed. by G. S. Munroe [v. 4]. Boston, Phillips, Sampson & Co., 1852, c. 1851. 288 p., 6 pl., 7¼ x 4¾. "The village home." F.
This is "Amaranth" with first article changed.
See also "Garland," 1851, "Magnolia" [1853].

428*e* **Kossuth offering, The,** and family souvenir for **1852.** New York, M. H. Newman & Co. 242 p., 16 pl., 9⅝ x 6¼. *

(429) **Lady's Album,** n. d.
Add: Also issued Cornish, Lamport & Co. [**1851**]. xii, 348 p., 8 pl., 7⅜ x 4¾. F.
Same as the others except no. of plates varies.

(434) **Lady's book, The.**
Add: Also issued 1846, c. 1841; 1847, c. 1841; 1848, c. 1841. p. [3]–275 in all these later editions.

437*a* **Ladies' casket,** a gift for all seasons. Highly embellished. New York, John F. Scovill, 8 Spruce st., **n. d.** [? circa 1850], 9–210, 9–208 p., [7 pl.], 8½ x 5¾. F.
Probably a magazine.

(438) **Ladies' casket, The,** containing a gem, together with its sentiment and a poetical description for each day in the week and each month in the year, by J. Wesley Hanson. Lowell, Merrill & Heywood, **1846,** c. 1846. 160 p., illum. t., iv p., 2 l., 9–160 p., 4¼ x 2⅝. *

439*a* **Ladies' diadem, The,** or starry oracles, by J. Wesley Hanson. Lowell, Milton Bonney, **1847,** c. 1848. 164 p., col. t., 4½ x 2¾. F.

439*b* **Ladies' Garland,** devoted to literature, amusement and instruction. Philadelphia, John Libby, **1838.** viii, 1–320 p., 8⅝ x 5½. *

449*a* **Lady's present, The,** or beauties of female character, by A. I. Cummings, M. D. Nashua, N. H., J. Buffum, **1849,** c. 1849. 188 p., 5½ x 3¼. F.

(454) **Lady's token, 1848.**

Read sub-title: "*Or* gift," etc., by Cotesworth Pinckney.

Add: Also reissued in 1850, 1853. See below.

454*ab* —— ——, or gift of friendship, ed. by Cotesworth Pinckney. Nashua, N. H., J. Buffum, **1850,** c. 1848. 128 p., 2 illum. t., 4½ x 2¾. F.

Same as 1848.

Title on back of cover, "Ladies' token."

454*ac* —— ——, or gift of friendship, ed. by Cotesworth Pinckney. Boston, J. Buffum, **1853,** c. 1848. 128 p., col. front., 4⅝ x 2⅞. F.

Same as 1848.

454*bb* **Ladies' vase of wild flowers, The,** a collection of gems from the best authors, by Miss Colman. Auburn, J. C. Derby & Co., **1848,** c. 1846. viii, 9–126 p., col. front., 4½ x 2⅞. F.

Reissued in 1850. See no. 454*bc* below.

Reissued in 1852. See (454*c*).

This is "Wild flowers," c. 1846. (See no. 838*a*.)

454*bc* —— ——, a collection of gems from the best authors, by Miss Colman. Auburn, James M. Allen, **1850,** c. 1846. viii, 9–126 p., col. front., 4¾ x 2⅞. F.

Same as 1848. See 454*bb* above.

(457*a*) **Ladies' wreath, The.**

Add: Also a N. Y. ed., Leavitt & Allen, n. d., same as Boston, n. d. and 1855 editions except that pp. 5–8 (contents and list of illus.) are omitted. F.

457*b* **Language of gems, The,** with their poetic sentiments, by Miss H. J. Woodman. Boston, A. Tompkins and B. B. Mussey, **1845,** c. 1845. iv, 5–160 p., 4½ x 2¾. F.

Reissued 1848 with col. front. added. F.

465*b* **Lays of the western world,** illuminated in gold colors, by T. W. G. Mapleson. New York, Putnam, **n. d.** 20 heavy leaves, unpaged, 10¾ x 7⅞. F.

(471) **Leaflets of memory,** for **1849.**

Add: Ed. by Reynell Coates.

494*a* **Liberty chimes.** Providence, Ladies' Anti-Slavery, Society, **1845.** 148 p., 6¾ x 4½. F.

(496) **Lily, The, c. 1830.**
Add: Also issued 1838. See 496*a* below.

496*a* —— ——, a holiday present with steel embellishments. New York, E. Sands, **1838,** c. 1830. vi, 7–232 p., [9 pl.], 5¾ x 3¾. F.
Same as c. 1830.

519*a* **Little girls' forget-me-not, The.** Philadelphia, American Sunday-school Union, **c. 1843.** 110 p., [8 pl. paged in], 4⅜ x 3¾. F.
Title "Forget-me-not" on back of paper cover.

519*b* **Little keepsake, The,** original and selected, by Mrs. Colman. Boston, G. Colman, **n. d.** 108 p., 10 pl. and front., 3¾ x 3⅛. "Tame owl." F.

523*a* **Love, forest flowers and sea shells,** by Alonzo Lewis. Boston, Benjamin B. Mussey & Co., **1850,** c. 1845. vi, 7–128 p., eng. presentation pl., 4½ x 2¾. F.
Title on back "Forest flowers."

(524*a*) **Lyric gems, c. 1844.**
Sub-title should read, "A collection of original and select sacred poetry."
Add note: Also issued Boston, 1844, c. 1844. F.
Also issued Boston, 1845, c. 1844. F.

(533) **Magnolia, [1853].**
Add: See also "Keepsake of friendship" for 1852.

(537) **Marriage offering, The, 1848.**
Add: Reissued with imprint date 1854, c. 1848, with eng. front. and eng. t., 11th ed. F.

(553) **Memorial.**
Note should read Also issued as "Laurel leaves," 1854.

562*a* **Milk for babes,** or a text and verse for a hymn for every day in the year. New York, American Tract Society, 128 p., 3 x 2¼. F.

**Mrs. Gilman's gift-book.** Title on back of "Gift book of stories and poems."
See 311*a* above.

(569) **Moss rose, The.**
Add: Also issued as "Friendship's offering." N. Y., n. d., but with variations in the pl.

(570) —— ——.
Completed entry: A parting token, by C. W. Everest. Hartford, Gurdon Robins, Jr., **1840,** c. 1840. viii, 1–184 p., 4⅛ x 2¾. F.
The "Moss-rose," 1843, has many of the verses in this volume, differently arranged, and with others added.

574*a* —— ——, for a friend, ed. by Rev. C. W. Everest. Hartford, Brown and Parsons, **1847,** c. 1842. x, 11–192 p., front., 4⅜ x 2¾. F.
Same as 1843 (571).

577*a* **Moss rose, The,** for **1852,** ed. by Mrs. Emeline P. Howard. New York, Cornish, Lamport & Co., c. 1851. vi p., 1 l., 9–344 p., 7 pl., 7¼ x 4⅞. "Isabel." F.
Same as "Moss Rose," c. 1851 (577).

(588) **My teacher's New Year's present, 1850.**
Add: Back of cover reads, "Teacher's gift," side of cover, "Teacher's present, 1850."

591*a* **Newest keepsake, The,** for eighteen hundred thirty-nine, containing the speeches, circumstances and doings of a recent benevolent convention at the chapel of the Marlboro house, Boston. Boston, printed by order of the convention of **1839.** iv, 5–121 p., 5⅞ x 3⅝. F.

(597) **Oasis, The, 1855.**
Add: Also issued with 272 p.
Same as "Young ladies' oasis," 1851, which ends at p. 252.

(613*a*) **Odd fellow's token, The, 1846.**
Add: Also issued 1850. See 613*b* below.

613*b* —— ——, devoted to friendship, love and truth, ed. by Kate Barclay. Auburn, N. Y., James M. Alden, **1850,** c. 1846. 124 p., illum. t., 4½ x 2¾. F.
Same as 1846.

(615) **Odd volume, The.**
Add: Also issued Nafis & Cornish, n. d., 288 p., eng. front., 5⅞ x 4. F.

617*a* **Offering, The,** ed. by S. C. Carter. Boston, G. W. Cottrell, **c. 1852.** 84 p., 3 x 2. F.
Also published with imprint. J. Buffum, c. 1852.

618*b* **Offering of sympathy, An,** to parents bereaved of their children, with an appendix of selections. Boston. Samuel N. Dickinson, **1830.** xviii, 1–224 p., 5⅞ x 3¾. F.
Title on back of cover and on half-title, "Christian consolations."

619*a* **One pearl of great price,** or the precious gift, by Rev. S. Remington. Lowell, Mass., J. E. Short & Co., **1846,** c. 1845. viii, 9–128 p., 4⅜ x 2¾. F.
Title on back "Precious gift."

631*a* **Parting gift, A,** to a Christian friend. Hartford, Brown & Parsons, **1843,** c. 1838. 192 p., 4 x 2¾. F.

(633) **Passion flower, n. d.**
Add to note: Also issued as "Friendship's offering," New York, n. d.

(642) **Pearl, The, 1836.**
Add the paging: iv, 220 p.

648*a* **Perennial flowers,** Boston, printed by Monroe & Francis, **1843,** c. 1843. x, 11–172 p., 6 x 4. F.

653*a* **Philadelphia souvenir, The,** a collection of fugitive pieces from the Philadelphia Press, . . . by J. E. Hall. Philadelphia, **1826,** c. 1826. 5¾ x 3½. F.

(654*a*) **Philipena, The, 1848.**
Add: Also issued as "Friendship's token," **1850.** See 246*a* above.

(663) **Pictorial family annual, 1849.**
Add: Also published 1852, c. 1848.

663*a* **Poet, The,** a metrical romance of the seventeenth century; a keepsake for **1840.** Philadelphia, Carey & Hart, c. 1839. 216 p., eng. front. and eng. t., 6¼ x 4. F.

663*b* **Poets' offering, The,** for **1850**, ed. by Sarah Josepha Hale. Philadelphia, Grigg, Elliot & Co., 1850. c. 1849. vi, p., 1 l., 7-576 p., 14 pl. and col. t., 9⅜ x 6⅜. B.P.

664*a* **Poetry of flowers, The,** original and selected, ed. by Rufus W. Griswold. New York, Leavitt & Co., **1851.** 287 p., eng. front., 5 x 3⅜. F.

665*a* **Poetry of the heart,** by William B. Tappan. Boston, J. Buffum, **c. 1845.** 128 p., col. front., 3½ x 2¾. F.

665*b* **Poetry of the sentiments, The,** ed. by Rufus W. Griswold. Philadelphia, Uriah Hunt & Son, **1846.** x, 11-320 p., 4¼ x 2¾. F.
Preface states: Based on volume with same title published in England in 1841.

667*a* **Polyanthos, The.** New York, **1851.** *

669*a* **Portland sketch book, The,** ed. by Mrs. Ann S. Stephens. Portland [Me.], Colman & Chisholm, **1836,** c. 1836. viii, 9-289 p., eng. t., 7⅛ x 4½. F.
**Precious gift, The.** Title on back of "One pearl of great price."

672*a* **Premium, The, 1838.** *
Same as 1833.

675*a* **Proverbialist and the poet, The.** Proverbs illustrated by passages from the poets, by James Orton. Philadelphia, E. H. Butler & Co., **1852.** *

692*a* **Religious souvenir** for **1847,** ed. by Mrs. Sigourney. 288 p. Probably another reissue of 1840. *

(702) **Rhode Island book, The.**
Add: Also issued with imprint 1845, and with imprint 1846.

702[1] **Rosary, The.** Boston, J. T. Buckingham, **1834.** 252 p., 5⅞ x 3⅝. F.

(702*a*) **Rosary, The, 1849.**
Add: Also issued with only the copyright date (1848), vi, 13-291 p., 6 pl., 9 x 6½. F.

728*a* **Rose bud, The;** a keepsake for the young, with six colored engravings. Philadelphia, Fisher & Butler, **c. 1853.** 108 p., [6 pl.], 5⅜ x 4¼. F.

728*aa* —— ——; a love gift for young hearts for **1855,** ed. by Mrs. C. A. Soule, Boston, A. Tompkins & B. B. Mussey & Co., 1855, c. 1854, iv p., 1 l., 7-168 p., 4 pl., 6⅛ x 4½. B.P.
Preface speaks of this as the second volume.

728*b* **Rosemary, The,** a collection of sacred and religious poetry from the English and American poets, with elegant illustrations. Philadelphia, Lindsay & Blakiston, **c. 1849.** viii, 9–248 p., 8 pl., 8½ x 5½ F.

This is one of a series of annual publications with different titles each year. Other titles were "American female poets"; "British female poets"; "American gallery of art"; "Mirror of life," 1848; "Scenes in the life of the Saviour," 1847; "Scenes in the lives of the Apostles," c. 1846; "Scenes in the lives of the patriarchs and prophets"; "Women of the Scriptures," c. 1848.

735*a* **Sabbath school annual, The,** for **1846,** ed. by Mrs. M. H. Adams. Boston, James M. Usher, 1846, c. 1845. viii, 9–168 p., 7 pl., 6 x 3¾. F.

736*a* —— ——, ed. by Mrs. M. H. Adams. Boston, James M. Usher, **1849,** c. 1848. x, 1–170 p., [4 pl.], 6⅝ x 4¼. F.

737*aa* **Sacred flora, The,** or flowers from the grave of a child, by Henry Bacon. Boston, A. Tompkins & B. B. Mussey, **1847,** c. 1844. viii, 9–160 p., illum. t., 4½ x 2⅞. F.

This was issued again in 1848. See (737*b*).

746*a* **Scenes in the lives of the patriarchs and prophets,** ed. by H. Hastings Weld. Philadelphia, Lindsay & Blakiston, **c. 1847.** xii, 13–240, 8 pl., 9 x 5¼. F.

One of a series of annual volumes, each with a different title. See "Rosemary," 728*a* above for list.

750*ab* **Seasons, The,** ed. by J. S. A[dams]. Boston, G. W. Cottrell. 96 p., 3 x 2¼. F.

750*ac* **Selections from female poets,** a present for ladies. Boston, Samuel Colman, **1837,** c. 1836. viii, 9–192 p., 5¾ x 3⅝. F.

750*ad* **Snow-drop, The;** a New Year's gift for children, by Frances S. Osgood. Providence, Hiram Fuller, **1843,** c. 1842. viii, 1–88 p., 4½ x 3⅝. F.

(750*b*) **Snow-drop, The,** a gift for a friend, ed. by C. W. Everest. New York, J. S. Redfield, **1845,** c. 1845. 128 p., 4½ x 2¾. F.

Also issued in 1848, c. 1845.

760[1] **Songs for the Sabbath,** by various authors. Boston, Oliver L. Perkins, **1844.** vii p., 1 l., 9–128 p., 4⅜ x 3¾. F.

(760*a*) **Song of the flowers, c. 1855.**

Add: Also published with imprint. New York, J. Q. Preble, c. 1855. F.

760*b* **Songs of the seasons, The,** by Cousin Lill. Boston, G. W. Cottrell, **c. 1855.** iv, 5–96 p., 2⅞ x 2. F.

761*a* **Sons of temperance offering, The,** for all seasons, ed. by T. S. Arthur. New York, Cornish, Lamport & Co., **n. d.** c. (no copyright date given). F.

Same as 1850. Also issued with c. 1850, but no other date.

(765) **Souvenir gallery. 1850.**
Add note: Also issued 1851.

770*a* **Sweet home;** or friendship's golden altar, ed. by Frances E. Percival. Boston, L. P. Crown & Co., **1856,** c. 1855. 272 p., eng. front., 6¾ x 4¾. F.

771*a* **Tales and poetry from the English souvenirs** for **1829**, a Christmas and New Years' present, ed. by a lady. Philadelphia, Carey, Lea & Carey, 1829. 3 p. l., 13–292 p., 5¾ x 3¾. F.

**Teacher's gift.** Title on back of cover of "My teacher's New Year's present."

**Teacher's present.** Title on side of cover of "My teacher's New Year's present."

(780) **Temperance token, The, 1848.**
Add: Also issued Auburn, N. Y., 1850.

(799) **Token, The, 1838.**
Add after 5th line of note: Also an edition "Token or affection's gift." New York, A. Edwards [1845 on back of cover], with 6 pl.

818*b* **Token of the heart, A,** or gems of kindness, by Mrs. Abel and others. Boston, Higgins, Bradley & Dayton, **c. 1857.** 256 p., eng. front., 6¾ x 4½. F.

(820) **Unique, The, 1829.**
Add: 3d ed. was Boston, 1830.

820[1] **Unique, The,** a biography of many distinguished characters, with fine portraits. 3d ed. improved. Boston, Charles H. Peabody, **1830.** 254 p., 13 pl. and eng. t., 4¾ x 3½. F.
In this edition the biographies have been abridged and anecdotes inserted.

820*b* **Vase of flowers,** ed. by Anna Elizabeth. Boston, J. Buffum, **c. 1851.** viii, 9–96 p., 3 x 2. F.

834*b* **Weeping willow, The,** by Mrs. L. H. Sigourney. Hartford, Henry S. Parsons, **1849,** c. 1846. vi, 7–128 p., front., 4⅝ x 2¾. F.

838*a* **Wild flowers,** a collection of gems from the best authors by Miss Colman. Boston, S. Colman, **c. 1846.** viii, 9–126 p., col. front., 4½ x 2⅞. F.
Reissued as "Ladies' vase of wild flowers," Auburn, 1848, and 1852. See no. 454*a* above.

(846) **Wreath, The, 1821.**
Size should be 5 x 3¼.

851*a* **Wreaths of friendship,** a gift for the young, by T. S. Arthur and F. C. Woodworth. New York, Baker & Scribner, **1849,** c. 1848. xii, 13–240 p., front., eng. t., illus. in text., 7¼ x 5¾. F.

(857) **Young ladies' oasis, 1851.**
Add: Same as "The Oasis,' 1855, with 252 p.

863[1] **Young lady's own book.** Philadelphia, **1832.**
Not an annual.

870*a* **Young woman's gift, The,** of literature, science and morality, ed. by Cotesworth Pinckney. Boston, J. Buffum, **1851,** c. 1850. viii, 9–192 p., col. front., 5¼ x 3⅝. F.

870*b* **Youth's annual,** a Christmas and New Year's gift, by C. E. C. Illustrated. New York, Leavitt & Allen, **n. d.** 2 p. l., 5–292 p., [5 pl.], 6⅜ x 4⅜. "Lucy's half crown." F.

## ENGLISH

(1100) **Book of beauty, The, 1849.**
Add: Followed by "Court Album."

(1186) **Court Album, 1850.**
Add: Previous vols. called "Book of beauty."

(1306) **Forget-me-not,** London, **1831.**
Add: Reprinted as "Juvenile album," 1832.

1327*a* **Friendship's forget-me-not.** London, Thomas Nelson, **1849.** xii, 13–256 p., 4⅝ x 3. F.

1366*a* **Gems from American poets,** selected and arranged by the author of the "Sentiment of flowers." 7th ed. London, Thomas Tegg, **1844.** xii, 208 p. *

(1479) **Juvenile scrap book.**
Add: by Mrs. Ellis, **1841,** illus., 8vo. *

1756*a* **Thoughts among flowers.** London, Th~ religious tract society, **1845** 139 p., 4⅜ x 3¾. F.
Not a true annual.

1804*a* **Young gentleman's library, The,** of entertaining and useful knowledge. Intended as a holiday or birthday present, by M. B. Pinnock. London, Longman, Rees, Orme, Brown & Green, **1829.** 35 pl., xviii, 1–354p., 1 l., 5¾ x 3¼. F.

The total number of volumes recorded in this bibliography, including addenda, is 2000.

# CHRONOLOGICAL INDEX.

An index in order of years to all dated titles in this bibliography. The small numerals following many of the entries indicate the number of times such titles have occurred in this list. For example "Forget-me-not[17]" indicates that this annual has already been referred to in sixteen previous years, that is, this is its seventeenth mention. The small figures do not necessarily have any reference to any volume numbers appearing on the title pages of the volumes.

Poetical album[5]; Souvenir litteraire de France; Times telescope[2]; Winter's wreath[2]; Young ladies book.

**1830**

*American.* Atlantic souvenir[5]; Casket, or youth's pocket library; Garland, N. Y.; Lily; Offering of sympathy; Pearl[2]; Talisman[3]; Token[3]; Unique[2]; Youth's keepsake.

*English.* Ackermann's juvenile forget me not; Affection's gift; Affection's offering[2]; Amulet[5]; Anniversary[2]; Apollo's gift; Bengal annual; Bijou[3]; Cabinet album; Carcanet[2]; Christian souvenir; Comic annual; Emanuel; Excitement; Fisher's national portrait gallery; Forget-me-not[8]; Friendship's offering[7]; Gem[2]; Gem of art; Iris; Johnson's shooter's annual; Juvenile forget me not[3]; Juvenile keepsake[2]; Juvenile landscape annual; Keepsake[3]; Keepsake français; Landscape annual; Laurel; Literary bluebook; Literary gem; Literary souvenir[6]; Looking glass; Lyre; Musical bijou; Musical forget-me-not; Musical gem[2]; Musical souvenir; New Year's gift[2]; Olive branch; Remember me; Times telescope[3]; Winter's wreath[3]; Zoölogical keepsake.

**1831**

*American.* Amaranth, Newburyport; American comic annual; Amethyst, Balto.; Atlantic souvenir[6]; Child's annual, Phila.; Hyacinth, N. Y.; Keepsake americaine; Lily[2]; Pearl[3]; Scrap table; Spirit of the annuals; Tablet; Token[4]; Youth's keepsake.[3]

*English.* Ackermann's juvenile forget me not[2]; Affection's gift[2]; Affection's offering[3]; Amulet[6]; Apollo's gift[2]; Bengal annual[2]; Cabinet album[2]; Cadeau; Cameo; Chameleon; Comic annual[2]; Comic offering; Dramatic annual; English keepsake; Excitement[2]; Father's present to his son; Fisher's national portrait gallery[2]; Forget-me-not[9]; Friendship's offering[8]; Gem[3]; Humorist; Infant's annual; Iris[2]; Juvenile forget me not[4]; Keepsake[4]; Keepsake français[2]; Ladies' and gentlemen's polite assistant and useful remembrancer; Ladies' poetical album; Landscape annual[2]; Literary souvenir[7]; Looking glass[2]; Love's offering; Lyre[2]; Marshall's Christmas box; Mirror of the graces; Mr. Matthews' comic annual; Mother's present to her daughter; Musical bijou[2]; Musical forget me not[2]; Musical gem[3]; New comic annual; New musical annual; New Year's gift[3]; Olive branch[2]; Phrenological bijou; Pledge of friendship[4]; Poetical offering; Regent; Remember me[2]; Remembrance; Royal repository and picturesque diary; Sacred harp; Sacred offering; Scrap table; Simpson's gentleman's almanack; Souvenir, Le; Talisman; Times telescope[4]; Tit-bits; Vocal annual; Winter's wreath[4]; Youth's keepsake.

**1832**

*American.* Affection's gift, N. Y.; Annual; Atlantic souvenir[7]; Christian offering; Compliment for the season; Keepsake americaine[2]; Lady's cabinet album; Lily[3]; Odd volume; Pearl[4]; Token[5]; Young lady's own book.

*English.* Ackermann's juvenile forget me not[3]; Affection's gift[3]; Affection's offering[4]; Amaranth; Amethyst; Amulet[7]; Bengal annual[3]; Botanic annual; Bouquet; Cabinet album[3]; Cabinet for youth; Cabinet of literary gems; Cadeau[2]; Chameleon[2]; Comic annual[3]; Comic offering[2]; Continental annual; Diadem; Easter gift; Easter offering; Evergreen; Excitement[3]; Fisher's drawing room scrap-book; Fisher's national portrait gallery[3]; Forget-me-not[10]; Friendship's offering[9]; Gem[4]; Geographical annual; Heath's picturesque annual; Hibernian keepsake; Hive; Humourist[2]; Infant's annual[2]; Juvenile album; Juvenile forget me not[5]; Keepsake[5]; Landscape album; Landscape annual[3]; Literary souvenir[8]; Looking glass[3]; Love's offering[2]; Marshall's Christmas box[2]; Musical bijou[3]; Musical gem[4]; New Year's gift[4]; Nosegay; Poetical offering[2]; Portfolio; Recordanza; Regent[2]; Remember me[3]; Rose of four seasons; Sacred harp[2]; Sacred lyre; Sacred offering[2]; Shipp's military bijou; Sister's gift; Spiritual gleaner; Vocal annual[2]; Waverley album; Winter's wreath[5]; Yorkshire literary annual; Youth's cornucopia.

**1833**

*American.* Annual[2]; Child's gem; Miscellanies; Odd volume[2]; Pearl[5]; Premium; Religious souvenir; Token[6]; Young lady's Sunday book; Young man's guide.

*English.* Affection's gift[4]; Amethyst[2]; Amulet[8]; Aurora borealis; Bengal annual[4]; Biblical annual; Bouquet[2]; Cadeau[3]; Chameleon[3]; Christmas tales; Comic annual[4]; Comic offering[3]; Dramatic souvenir; Ellis's missionary annual; Elgin annual; Excitement[4]; Father's present to his son[2]; Fisher's drawing room scrap-book[2]; Fisher's national portrait gallery[4]; Forget-me-not[11]; Friendship's offering[10]; Geographical annual[2]; Heath's book of beauty; Heath's picturesque annual[2]; Infant's annual[3]; Juvenile forget-me-not[6]; Keepsake[6]; Landscape annual[4]; Literary souvenir[9]; Looking glass[4]; Missionary annual; Musical gem[5]; New Year's gift[5]; Offering[2]; Regent[3]; Sacred musical offering; Sacred offering[3]; Turner's annual tour; Wreath of friendship.

**1834**

*American.* American juvenile keepsake; Annual[3]; Casket, or or youth's pocket library[2]; Child's annual, Bost.; Daughter's own book; Ladies' and gentlemen's pocket annual; Lady's cabinet album[2]; Lily[4]; Oasis[2]; Offering[2]; Pearl[6]; Religious souvenir[2]; Rosary; Token[7]; Unique[3]; Youth's keep-sake; Youth's sketch book.

*English.* Album wreath; Amethyst[3]; Amulet[9]; Annual souvenir; Bengal annual[5]; Biblical annual[2]; Bouquet[3]; Bow in the cloud; Comic annual[5]; Comic offering[4]; Coronal; English annual; Excitement[5]; Fisher's drawing room scrap-book[3]; Forget-me-not[12]; Friends' annual; Friendship's offering[11]; Gage d'amitié; Gem of art[2]; Geographical annual[3]; Heath's book of beauty[2]; Heath's picturesque annual[3]; Juvenile forget me not[7]; Keepsake[7]; Landscape album[2]; Landscape annual[5]; Literary gift book; Literary souvenir[10]; Looking glass[5]; Midsummer keepsake; New Year's gift[6]; Offering[3]; Oriental annual; Regent[4]; Sacred annual; Sacred offering[4]; Souvenir; Turner's annual tour[2]; Wreath of friendship[2]; Young gentleman's annual.

**1835**

*American.* American juvenile keepsake[2]; Annual[4]; Beauties of the English annuals; Bouquet, Phila.; Gift, Concord; Lady's cabinet album[3]; Lily[5]; Odd volume[3]; Parent's present; Portfolio for youth; Premium[2]; Religious souvenir[3]; Token[8]; Youth's keepsake.[3]

*English.* Amulet[10]; Angler's souvenir; Annual token; Biblical keepsake; Christian keepsake; Comic almanac; Comic annual[6]; Comic offering[5]; Continental landscape annual of European scenery; Continental tourist; English annual[2]; Excitement[6]; Finden's tableaux; Fisher's drawing room scrap-book[4]; Forget-me-not[13]; Friendship's offering[12]; Gage d'amitié[2]; Geographical annual[4]; Heath's book of beauty[3]; Heath's picturesque annual[4]; Juvenile amulet; Juvenile forget-me-not[8]; Juvenile keepsake[3]; Keepsake[8]; Lady's keepsake and maternal monitor; Landscape annual[6]; Landscape souvenir; Literary souvenir[11]; Looking glass[6]; Marshall's Christmas box[3]; Musical gem[6]; New Year's gift[7]; New Year's token; Nursery offering; Orient pearl; Oriental annual[2]; Pledge of affection; Present; Regent[5]; Sacred offering[5]; Souvenir[2]; Turner's annual tour[3]; Youth's cabinet.

## 1836

*American.* American juvenile keepsake[3]; Boston book; Flora and Thalia; Fountain; Gift; Laurel; Magnolia; Parlour scrap book; Pearl[7]; Philadelphia book; Portland sketch book; Premium[3]; Religious souvenir[4]; Sacred offering; Stranger's gift; Token[9]; Wreath, Young lady's gift; Youth's keepsake[4].

*English.* Affection's keepsake; Amaranth[2]; Amulet[11]; Baxter's agricultural and horticultural annual; Biblical keepsake[2]; Book of gems; Cabinet of modern art; Christian keepsake[2]; Comic almanac[2]; Comic annual[7]; Easter gift[2]; Emerald; English annual[3]; Excitement[7]; Finden's tableaux[2]; Fisher's drawing room scrap-book[5]; Fisher's juvenile scrap-book; Flowers of loveliness; Forget-me-not[14]; Friendship's offering[13]; Gage d'amitié[3]; Gems of beauty; Geographical annual[5]; Heath's book of beauty[4]; Heath's gallery of engravings; Heath's picturesque annual[5]; Historical keepsake; Juvenile forget me not[9]; Keepsake[9]; Landscape annual[7]; Looking glass[7]; Midsummer comic annual; Musical bijou[4]; Naval annual; New Year's gift[8]; Nursery offering[2]; Oriental annual[3]; Poetical annual; Regent[6]; Scottish annual; Squib annual; Turner's annual tour[4].

## 1837

*American.* American juvenile keepsake[4]; Autumn leaves; Boston book[2]; Child's annual, Bost.[2]; Christian offering[2]; Evergreen, Phila.; Gift[2]; Jewel; Lady's cabinet album[4]; Ladies' wreath; Laurel[2]; Magnolia[2]; Pearl[8]; Religious souvenir[5]; Selections from female poets; Token[10]; Union annual; Violet; Wreath[2]; Youth's keepsake[5].

*English.* Affection's keepsake[2]; Andalusian annual; Biblical keepsake[3]; Book of gems[2]; Cabinet of modern art[2]; Christian keepsake[3]; Comic almanac[3]; Comic annual[7]; Continental landscape annual of European scenery[2]; Cynosure; Easter gift[3]; English annual[4]; Excitement[8]; Exhilaration; Finden's tableaux[3]; Fisher's drawing room scrap-book[6]; Fisher's juvenile scrap-book[2]; Fisher's oriental keepsake; Flowers of loveliness[2]; Forget-me-not[15]; Friendship's offering[14]; Gage d'amitié[4]; Gems of beauty[2]; Heath's book of beauty[5]; Heath's gallery of engravings[2]; Heath's picturesque annual[6]; Juvênile forget me not[10]; Keepsake[10]; Landscape annual[8]; Landscape souvenir[2]; Looking glass[5]; Musical bijou[5]; Oriental annual[4]; Regent[7]; Relaxation; Souvenir keepsake; Tribute; Turner's annual tour.[5]

## 1838

*American.* Baltimore book; Casket of gems; Child's gem[2]; Christian keepsake; Gift from fairyland; Ladies' garland; Lily[2]; Literary souvenir; Parlour book; Premium[4]; Token[11]; Youth's keepsake[6].

*English.* Affection's keepsake[3]; Book of gems[3]; Campbell's scenic annual; Christian keepsake[4]; Comic almanac[4]; Comic annual[9]; Continental landscape annual of European scenery[3]; Easter gift[4]; English annual[5]; Excitement[9]; Finden's tableaux[4]; Fisher's drawing room scrap-book[7]; Fisher's juvenile scrap-book[3]; Fisher's oriental keepsake[2]; Fisher's Waverly forget-me-not; Flowers of loveliness[3]; Forget-me-not[16]; Friendship's offering[15]; Gage d'amitié[5]; Gems of beauty[3]; Heath's book of beauty[6]; Heath's gallery of engravings[3]; Heath's picturesque annual[7]; Hunter's annual; Keepsake[11]; Landscape annual[9]; Landscape souvenir[3]; Literary and pictorial repository; Magnet; Oriental annual[5]; Portraits of children of the nobility; Regent[8]; Remembrance[2]; Sacred offering[6]; Scenic annual; Turner's annual tour[6].

### 1839

*American.* Boys' scrap book; Christian keepsake[2]; Christian offering, N. Y.; Flora's lexicon; Garland, Bost.; Gift[3]; Girls' scrap book; Infant's annual; Jewel[2]; Juvenile forget me not; Ladies' wreath[2]; Liberty bell; Lily[6]; Magnolia[3]; Newest keepsake, Bost.; Peter Parley's gift; Religious offering; Religious souvenir[6]; Sacred offering[2]; Sacred wreath; Token[12]; Violet[2]; Young lady's companion; Youth's keepsake.[7]

*English.* Amaranth[3]; Annual of British landscape scenery; Bijou almanac; Book of royalty; Caunter's and Daniell's oriental annual; Comic almanac[5]; Comic annual[10]; Diadem[2]; Excitement[10]; Finden's tableaux[5]; Fisher's drawing room scrap-book[8]; Fisher's juvenile scrap-book[4]; Fisher's oriental keepsake[3]; Flowers of loveliness[4]; Forget-me-not[17]; Friendship's offering[16]; Gage d'amitié[6]; Gems of beauty[4]; Gift for all seasons; Heath's book of beauty[7]; Heath's picturesque annual[8]; Hunter's annual[2]; Imperial; Keepsake[12]; Landscape annual[10]; Landscape souvenir[4]; Literary cabinet; Miniature almanach; New juvenile keepsake; Oracle of rural life and spring almanach; Oriental annual[6]; Portraits of children of the nobility[2]; Regent[9]; Turner's annual tour[7].

### 1840

*American.* American juvenile keepsake[5]; Annualette; Casket of gems[2]; Christian keepsake[3]; Flower garden; Freedom's gift; Garland, Bost.[2]; Gem; Gift[4]; Literary amaranth; Literary souvenir[2]; Merry's annual for all seasons; Moss-rose, Hartford; Newest keepsake, Norwich; North star; Pearl[9]; Poet; Poetic wreath; Religious offering[2]; Religious souvenir[7]; Rose of Sharon; Token[13]; Violet[3]; Youth's keepsake[8].

*English.* Affection's keepsake[4]; Album wreath of music and literature; Bijou almanac[2]; Bouquet des souvenirs; Christian keepsake[5]; Comic almanac[6]; Excitement[11]; Excitement, Edin.; Finden's portraits of female aristocracy; Finden's royal gallery of British art; Finden's tableaux[6]; Fisher's drawing room scrap-book[9]; Flowers of loveliness[5]; Forget-me-not[18]; Friendship's offering[17]; Gage d'amitié[7]; Gems of beauty[5]; Gift for all seasons[2]; Heath's book of beauty[8]; Heath's picturesque annual[9]; Historical souvenir and literary cabinet; Iris of prose, poetry and art; Juvenile scrap-book; Keepsake[13]; Ladies' keepsake; May you like it; Nursery annual; Oriental annual[7]; Portraits of children of the nobility[3]; Rainbow; Regent[10]; Souvenir keepsake; Turner's annual tour[8].

### 1841

*American.* Amaranth, Phila.; Annualette[2]; Biographical annual; Boston book[3]; Friendship's offering; Juvenile forget me not[2]; Liberty bell[2]; Magnolia[4]; Mourner's gift; Remembrancer; Rhode Island book; Rose of Sharon[2]; Token[14]; Youth's keepsake[9].

*English.* Cattermole's historical annual; Comic almanac[7]; English helicon; Excitement[12]; Finden's portraits of female aristocracy[2];

Finden's tableaux[7]; Fisher's drawing room scrap-book[10]; Flowers of loveliness[6]; Forget-me-not[19]; Friendship's offering[18]; Gage d'amitié[8]; Heath's book of beauty[9]; Heath's picturesque annual[10]; Imperial[2]; Juvenile scrap-book[2]; Keepsake[14]; Liliputian annual; Orientalist; Portraits of children of the nobility[4]; Protestant annual; Recreation; Regent[11]; Turner's annual tour[9].

**1842**

*American.* Amaranth, Phila.[2]; Annualette[3]; Child's gem[3]; Child's token; Christian year; Dahlia; Flora's interpreter; Flora's lexicon[2]; Friendship's offering[2]; Gem[2]; Gems from American female poets; Gems from the American poets; Gift[5]; Lady's book; Liberty bell[3]; Magnolia[5]; Marriage ring; Mignonette; New Hampshire book; Poetry of the seasons; Rose; Rose of Sharon[3]; Sunday-school gift; Token[15]; Token, N. Y.; Violet[4]; Youth's keepsake[10].

*English.* Affection's keepsake[5]; Cabinet of modern art[3]; Christian souvenir[2]; Comic almanac[8]; Comic annual[11]; Evergreen[2]; Excitement[13]; Finden's tableaux[8]; Fisher's drawing room scrap-book[11]; Forget-me-not[20]; Friendship's offering[19]; Heath's book of beauty[10]; Heath's picturesque annual[11]; Juvenile scrap-book[3]; Keepsake[15]; Love gift; Orientalist[2]; Poetical forget-me-not; Recreation[2]; Regent[12]; Renfrewshire annual; Souvenir keepsake; Turner's annual tour[10].

**1843**

*American.* Annualette[4]; Casket of entertaining and useful reading; Christian family annual; Christian souvenir, Bost.; Drawing-room annual; Family circle; Fireside poetical readings; Friendship's offering[3]; Gift[6]; Golden gems for the Christian; Holiday gem for girls; Jewel[3]; Lady's book[2]; Liberty bell[4]; Little girl's forget-me-not; Little keepsake; Magnolia[6]; Moss-rose, Hartford[2]; Odd-fellows offering; Parting gift; Perennial flowers; Rose[2]; Rose of Sharon[4]; Saint Nicholas annual; Snow-drop, Prov.; Youth's keepsake[11].

*English.* Affection's keepsake[6]; Ayrshire wreath; Comic album; Comic almanac[9]; Excitement[14]; Finden's tableaux[9]; Fisher's drawing room scrap-book[12]; Forget-me-not[21]; Friendship's offering[20]; Gem of loveliness; Heath's book of beauty[11]; Heath's picturesque annual[12]; Juvenile scrap-book[4]; Keepsake[16]; Love gift[2]; Recreation[3]; Regent[13]; Remembrance[3]; Turner's annual tour[11].

**1844**

*American.* Annualette[5]; Bouquet, Bost.; Child's gem[4]; Christian family annual[2]; Christian offering[3]; Evergreen, New Haven; Fables of Flora; Family circle[2]; Flower vase; Friendship's offering[4]; Gem[3]; Gems from American female poets[2]; Gems from the American poets[2]; Gift[7]; Gift for all seasons, Phila.; Girl's token; Golden vase; Hare-bell, N. Y.; Hare-bell, Hartford; Housekeepers' annual; Illustrated book of Christian ballads; Iris, N. Y.; Jewel[4]; Jewel, a holiday gift; Liberty bell[5]; Literary souvenir[3]; Little gift; Little keepsake[2]; Lyric gems; Magnolia[7]; Mourner's chaplet; New Hampshire book[2]; Odd-fellows offering[2]; Opal; Philopœna; Rose[3]; Rose of Sharon[5]; Saint Nicholas gift; Songs for the Sabbath; Token, N. Y.[2]; Wintergreen; Youth's historical gift; Youth's keepsake[12].

*English.* Affection's gift[5]; Cattermole's historical annual[2]; Comic almanac[10]; Excitement[15]; Finden's tableaux[10]; Fisher's drawing room scrap-book[13]; Forget-me-not[22]; Friendship's offering[21]; Heath's book of beauty[12]; Heath's picturesque annual[13]; Juvenile bijou; Juvenile scrap-book[5]; Keepsake[17]; Love gift[3]; Manchester keepsake; Military annual; Prism of imagination; Recreation[4]; Regent[14]; Turner's annual tour[12]; Victoria annual.

**1845**

*American.* American keepsake; Annualette[6]; Autumn flowers; Bouquet, Bost.[2]; Bouquet of flowers; Casket, N. Y.; Catholic keepsake; Charleston book; Child's gem[5]; Christian family annual[3]; Diadem; Drops from Flora's cup; Family circle[3]; Friendship's offering[5]; Gems of sacred poetry; Gift[8]; Hare-bell, Hartford[2]; Hawthorn; Housekeepers' annual[2]; Hyacinth; Juvenile scrap-book; Keepsake; Ladies' scrap-book; Language of gems; Laurel wreath; Leaflets of memory; Liberty bell[6]; Liberty chimes; Literary amaranth[2]; Literary souvenir[4]; Little keepsake[3]; Love gift; Moss rose; Odd fellows gem; Odd-fellows offering[3]; Opal[2]; Poetry of the heart; Poet's gift; Religious souvenir[8]; Rhode Island book[2]; Rose[4]; Rose of Sharon[6]; Saint Nicholas gift[2]; Snow drop, N. Y.; Youth's keepsake[13].

*English.* Angler's souvenir[2]; Book of beauty; Chaplet; Comic almanac[11]; Comic miscellany; Excitement[16]; Fisher's drawing room scrap-book[14]; Forget-me-not[23]; Heath's book of beauty[13]; Heath's picturesque annual[14]; Juvenile scrap-book[6]; Keepsake[18]; Literary and pictorial souvenir; Love gift[4]; Musical bijou[6]; Musical gem[7]; Perennial; Recreation[5]; Regent[15]; Turner's annual tour[13].

**1846**

*American.* Amulet; Annualette[7]; Boudoir annual; Bouquet, Bost.[3]; Bouquet of flowers[2]; Bridal token; Broken vase; Christian's annual; Dew-drops of the nineteenth century; Diadem[2]; Family circle[4]; Floral fortune teller; Flower dial; Flower people; Forget-me-not; Forget-me-not, Lowell; Friendship's offering[6]; Gathered leaves; Gem of the season; Golden gift; Hyacinth[2]; Jewel[5]; Judson offering; Juvenile gem; Lady's book[3]; Ladies' casket; Laurel wreath[2]; Leaflets of memory[2]; Liberty bell[7]; Mayflower; Missionary memorial; Moss rose[2]; Odd fellows gem[2]; Odd-fellows offering[4]; Odd-fellows token; One pearl of great price; Opal[3]; Parlor annual; Poetry of the sentiments; Religious keepsake; Religious souvenir[9]; Rhode Island book[3]; Rose[5]; Rose of Sharon[7]; Rosette; Sabbath school annual; Scenes in the lives of the Apostles; Scenes in the life of the Saviour; Snow flake; Token, Hartford; Voice of flowers; Wild flowers; Wreath of wild flowers; Young lady's companion; Youth's keepsake[14].

*English.* Chaplet[2]; Comic almanac[12]; Coronal[2]; Fisher's drawing room scrap book[15]; Forget-me-not[24]; Gift of love and friendship; Heath's book of beauty[14]; Juvenile missionary keepsake; Juvenile scrap-book[7]; Keepsake[19]; Musical bijou[7]; Oriental album; Pictorial cabinet; Recreation[6]; Regent[16]; Turner's annual tour[14].

**1847**

*American.* Amaranth; American book of beauty; Annualette[7]; Bridal wreath; Christian keepsake[4]; Christian souvenir, Phila.; Christian wreath; Christmas blossoms; Christ's messengers; Diadem[3]; Evergreen, Phila.; Family circle[5]; Floral gems; Floral offering; Floral year; Flora's album; Flora's interpreter; Flower vase[2]; Forget-me-not, Lowell[2]; Fountain, Phila.; Friendship's gift of moral and entertaining literature; Friendship's offering[7]; Gift[9]; Gift of friendship; Golden gift[2]; Hyacinth[3]; Jewel[6]; Lady's book[4]; Ladies' diadem, Lowell; Ladies' vase; Ladies' wreath, N. Y.; Laurel wreath[3]; Leaflets of memory[3]; Liberty bell[8]; Little gem; Magnolia Bost.; Mayflower[2]; Memento; Moss rose[3]; Moss-rose,

Hartford[3]; Mother's present; My teacher's new year's present; Odd-fellows offering[5]; Opal[4]; Pastor's gift; Philipena, Lowell; Philopœna[2]; Rainbow; Religious souvenir[10]; Rose[6]; Rose of Sharon[8]; Sabbath school annual[2]; Sacred flora; Scenes in the lives of the patriarchs and prophets; Token, Hartford[2].

*English.* Affection's keepsake[7]; Comic almanac[13]; Fisher's drawing room scrap-book[16]; Forget-me-not[25]; Heath's book of beauty[15]; Juvenile scrap-book[8]; Keepsake[20]; Musical bijou[8]; Recreation[7]; Regent[17]; Turner's annual tour[15]; Wesleyan juvenile offering.

**1848**

*American.* Amaranth[2]; Apples of gold; Beauties of sacred literature; Bridal wreath[2]; Child's first gift; Christian keepsake[5]; Christmas blossoms[2]; Christmas roses[2]; Christ's messenger; Family circle[6]; Floral fortune teller[2]; Floral wreath, N. Y.; Flora's album[2]; Flora's gem; Flora's interpreter[2]; Flower vase[3]; Forget-me-not[2]; Forget-me-not, Lowell[3]; Friendship's gift, Bost.; Friendship's offering[8]: Garland; Gem, N. Y.; Gem of the season[2]; Gift of friendship[2]; Gift of friendship, N. Y.; Golden gift[3]; Golden leaflets; Golden present; Honeysuckle; Hyacinth[4]; Juvenile odd-fellow; Keepsake[2]; Lady's book[5]; Ladies' diadem, N. Y.; Lady's token; Ladies' vase of wild flowers; Leaflets of memory[4]; Liberty bell[9]; Little republic; Marriage offering; Mayflower[3]; Memento[2]; Mirror of life; My teacher's new year's present[2]; Odd-fellows offering[6]; Offering of beauty; Opal[5]; Our day; Philipena, Worcester; Poetry of love; Primrose; Rainbow[2]; Rose[7]; Rose of Sharon[9]; Rough and ready annual; Sacred flora[2]; Sacred tableaux; Scripture gift book; Snow drop, N. Y.[2]; Temperance token; Women of the scriptures; Wreath of wild flowers[2]; Young ladies' offering; Young man.

*English.* Book of beauty[2]; Book of beauty, or regal gallery; Comic almanac[14]; Fisher's drawing room scrap-book[17]; Juvenile offering; Juvenile scrap-book[9]; Keepsake[21]; Keepsake, Lond. and Edin.; Musical bijou[9]; "My own" annual; Oriental album[2]; Poetic prism; Recreation[8]; Regent[18]; Turner's annual tour[16].

**1849**

*American.* Amaranth[2]; Amethyst; Book of pearls; Christian keepsake[6]; Christmas blossoms[3]; Christmas roses; Crocus; Echoes of infant voices; Excelsior; Family circle[7]; Floral gems[2]; Forget-me-not[3]; Friendship's offering[9]; Gallery of mezzotints; Garland[2]; Gem, N. Y.[2]; Gem of the season[3]; Gems of beauty; Gift leaves of American poetry; Gift of friendship[3]; Golden present[2]; Hare-bell, Hartford[3]; Holiday gift; Hyacinth[5]; Juvenile scrap book, N. Y.; Keepsake of friendship; Lady's annual; Ladies' gems; Ladies gift; Lady's present; Leaflets of memory[5]; Liberty bell[10]; Maple leaf; Marriage offering[2]; Memento[3]; Odd-fellows offering[7]; Offering to beauty, Phila.; Opal[6]; Pastor's gift[2]; Pearl, a Christmas, new year and birthday present; Pictorial family annual; Rosary[2]; Rose of Sharon[10]; Rose of Sharon, Auburn; Rosemary; Ruby; Sabbath school annual[3]; Snow flake[2]; Wedding gift; Weeping willow; Wreaths of friendship; Young ladies' offering[2]; Young man's offering; Youth's sketch book[2].

*English.* Book of beauty, or regal gallery[2]; Comic almanac[15]; Juvenile scrap-book[10]; Keepsake[22]; Musical bijou[10]; Recreation[9]; Regent[19]; Turner's annual tour[17].

**1850**

*American.* Amaranth[4]; Amethyst, Bost.; Boston book[4]; Brilliant; Buds and blossoms; Choice gift; Christian keepsake, Nashua;

Christmas blossoms[4]; Drawing room scrap-book; Evergreen, N. Y.; Family circle[8]; Floral keepsake; Flower vase[4]; Flowers of literature; Forget-me-not[4]; Friendship's offering[10]; Friendship's token; Garland[3]; Gem of the season[4]; Gems for you; Gems of beauty[2]; Gift book; Gift book of the republic; Gift of friendship[4]; Gift of piety; Golden gift[4]; Golden gift, a wreath of gems; Golden present[3]; Home recreation; Hyacinth[6]; Judson offering[2]; Keepsake of friendship[2]; Ladies' gift[2]; Ladies' scrap-book[2]; Lady's token[2]; Ladies' vase of wild flowers[2]; Leaflets of memory[6]; Love, forest flowers and sea shells; Memento[4]; Moss rose[4]; My teacher's new year's present[3]; National temperance offering; Odd-fellows keepsake; Odd-fellows offering[8]; Odd-fellows token; Poet's offering; Primrose[2]; Rose of Sharon[11]; Ruby[2]; Sacred annual; Snow flake[3]; Sons of temperance offering; Souvenir gallery; Temperance token[2]; Token, Hartford[3]; Violet, N. Y.; Winter-bloom; Young man's friend; Young man's offering[2]; Youth's sketch book[3].

*English.* Christian keepsake[6]; Comic almanac[16]; Court album; Fisher's drawing room scrap-book[18]; Juvenile keepsake, The; Juvenile scrap-book[11]; Keepsake[23]; Musical bijou[11]; Recreation[10]; Regent[20]; Turner's annual tour[18].

### 1851

*American.* Amaranth[5]; American keepsake; Bouquet, Bost.[4]; Chaplet of roses; Choice gift; Christian diadem; Christian parlor book; Christian souvenir, Auburn; Christmas blossoms[5]; Christmas tribute; Diosma; Family circle[9]; Floral offering[2]; Floral wreath, Bost.; Forget-me-not[5]; Forget-me-not, N. Y.; Friendship flower; Friendship's jewel; Friendship's offering[11]; Garland[4]; Gem of the season[5]; Gem of the western world; Gems from the sacred mine; Gems of beauty[3]; Gift[10]; Gift of friendship[5]; Golden gift[5]; Golden present[4]; Golden vase[3]; Holiday gift[2]; Hyacinth[7]; Iris; Irving offering; Juvenile keepsake; Keepsake[3]; Keepsake of friendship[3]; Ladies' companion; Ladies' gift[3]; Leaflets of memory[7]; Liberty bell[11]; Lily of the valley; Marriage offering[3]; Memento of friendship; Memorial, N. Y.; Memory and hope; Moss rose[5]; New Orleans book; Odd-fellows offering[9]; Our gift; Philopœna[3]; Poetry of flowers; Polyanthus; Remember me; Rose of Sharon[12]; Sacred annual[2]; Sacred gift; Snow flake[4]; Sons of temperance offering[2]; Souvenir gallery[2]; Temperance offering; Token of friendship; Vase of flowers; Woodbine; Young ladies' oasis; Young ladies' offering[3]; Young woman's gift.

*English.* Comic almanac[17]; Court album[2]; Fisher's drawing room scrap-book[19]; Keepsake[24]; Musical bijou[12]; Regent[21]; Turner's annual tour[19].

### 1852

*American.* Amaranth[6]; Annual souvenir gallery; Beauties of sacred literature[2]; Bridal keepsake; Cabinet of modern art; Child's companion; Christian parlor book[2]; Christmas blossoms[6]; Christmas tribute[2]; Dew drop; Drops from Flora's cup[2]; Family circle[10]; Female prose writers of America; Floral wreath, Auburn; Flora's lexicon[3]; Flowers of loveliness; Forget-me-not, Lowell[4]; Friendship's gift, Lynn; Friendship's offering[12]; Garland[5]; Gem[4]; Gem of the season[6]; Gems of beauty[4]; Gift of affection; Gift of friendship[6]; Golden leaflets[2]; Hare-bell, Hartford[4]; Home book of beauty; Home book of the picturesque; Hyacinth[8]; Illustrated ladies' keepsake; Illustrated souvenir; Iris[2]; Irving offering[2]; Juvenile annual; Keepsake[4]; Keepsake of friendship[4]; Kossuth offering; Ladies' illustrated keepsake; Ladies' parlor companion; Ladies' vase of

**1853**



**1854**



**1855**

Lily of the valley[5]; Magnolia, Bost.[4]; Mayflower[5]; Oasis[4]; Peter Parley's annual; Portfolio of entertainment and instruction; Remember me[5]; Rose bud, Bost.; Rose of Sharon[16]; Snow flake[6]; Snow flake, N. Y.; Songs of the flowers; Songs of the seasons; Thought-blossom[2]; Wide-awake gift; Winter wreath of summer flowers.

*English.* Court album[6]; Keepsake[28]; Turner's annual tour[23].

**1856**

*American.* American gift book; Book of gems[2]; Flora's dial[3]; Gem of the season[9]; Gift book for young ladies, Bangor; Heart-songs; Leaflets of memory[11]; Liberty bell[14]; Lily of the valley[6]; Mayflower[6]; Mignonette[2]; Mignonette, Bost.; Oasis[5]; Rose of Sharon[17]; Sweet home; Token, a gift for all seasons; Voices of heart and home.

*English.* Court album[7]; Forget me not; Keepsake[29]; Northern poetical keepsake.

**1857**

*American.* Christian's gift; Dial of love; Flora's lexicon[5]; Gift for you, Bost.; Lily of the valley[7]; May-flower, Lynn; Rose of Sharon[18]; Souvenir of friendship; String of diamonds; Token, a gift for all seasons[2]; Token of the heart; Wedding guest; Young ladies' offering[5]; Young maiden's mirror[2]; Young man's offering[3].

*English.* Court album[8]; Keepsake[30]; Scottish keepsake.

**1858**

*American.* Christian souvenir, N. Y.; Liberty bell[15]; Lily of the valley[8]; Young ladies' choice; Young maiden's mirror[3].

**1859**

*American.* Affection's gift for the loving; Atlantic souvenir, N. Y.; Eclectic gift-book; Gift of genius; Josephine gallery; Lily of the valley[9]; Marriage offering[6].

*English.* Annual gift-book; Drawing room portrait gallery of eminent personages; Scottish annual[2]; Souvenir, a token of remembrance.

**1860**

*American.* Centre table; Memories of home; Oasis[6].

*English.* Drawing room portrait gallery of eminent personages[2].

**1861**

*English.* Keepsake[31]; Victoria regia.

**1862**

*American.* Liberty bell, N. Y.

*English.* Juvenile forget-me-not[11].

**1863**

*American.* Casket of gems[3]; Children's garland; Floral offering[4]; Snow flakes.

**1864**

*American.* Cloud crystals; Wreath of beauty.

**1865**

*American.* Gift for you, Albany.

**1866**

*American.* Emerald.

*English.* Gift.

**1867**

*American.* Sapphire; Winter wreath of summer flowers[2].
*English.* Rose and holly.

**1869**

*American.* Amaranth, N. Y.; Appleton's juvenile annual; Garland, N. Y.; Gift of affection[3]; Humming bird; Juvenile forget me not, N. Y.; Keepsake of friendship[8]; Memory's gift; Violet, N. Y.[2]; Youth's keepsake, N. Y.
*English.* Hood's comic annual, 1869–88.

**1871**

*American.* Appleton's juvenile annual[2].

**1873**

*American.* Sabbath bells.

**1876**

*American.* Laurel leaves, Bost.

**1878**

*American.* Christmastide; Masonic token.

**1886**

*English.* Angler's souvenir[3]; Broken shaft.

**1890**

*English.* Bridal bouquet.

**1896**

*American.* Book of beauty.

**1901**

*American.* Christmas garland.

**1902**

*American.* Book of beauty[2].